THE MIGHTY EIGHTH

OSPREY
PUBLISHING

THE MIGHTY EIGHTH

MASTERS OF THE AIR OVER EUROPE 1942–45

DONALD NIJBOER

OSPREY PUBLISHING
Bloomsbury Publishing Plc
Kemp House, Chawley Park, Cumnor Hill,
Oxford OX2 9PH, UK
29 Earlsfort Terrace, Dublin 2, Ireland
1385 Broadway, 5th Floor, New York, NY 10018, USA
E-mail: info@ospreypublishing.com
www.ospreypublishing.com

OSPREY is a trademark of Osprey Publishing Ltd

First published in Great Britain in 2022

A catalog record for this book is available from the British Library.

ISBNs: HB 9781472854216; eBook 9781472854223;
ePDF 9781472854247; XML 9781472854230

22 23 24 25 26   10 9 8 7 6 5 4 3 2 1

For legal purposes the Acknowledgments on p. 309 constitute an
extension of this copyright page.

Maps by Bounford.com
Index by Alison Worthington
Cover, page design and layout by Stewart Larking
Typeset by PDQ Digital Media Solutions, Bungay, UK
Printed and bound in India by Replika Press Private Ltd.

Osprey Publishing supports the
Woodland Trust, the UK's leading
woodland conservation charity.

To find out more about our authors and books visit
www.ospreypublishing.com. Here you will find extracts, author
interviews, details of forthcoming events and the option to sign
up for our newsletter.

Title page (top image): This fully armed B-17F *Thunderbird* was
designated war-weary in late 1943. Many worn-out airframes
were quickly used as VIP transports or whiskey haulers. With
their stretched control cables and tired engines, pilots often found
them a challenge to fly. (Author's collection)

Title page (bottom image): Minus its drop tanks, this 360th
Fighter Group P-51D serial no. 44-15056 has just completed
another long-range escort mission in April 1945. The group
consisted of the 359th, 360th, and 361st Fighter squadrons. Even
with the bubble canopy, this Mustang still has a rear-view mirror
attached on the top of the forward canopy bow. (Author's
collection)

Contents

INTRODUCTION

When the United States entered World War II on December 7, 1941, it had a small air force with approximately 1,100 aircraft, which included 700 bombers of all types. The Eighth Air Force, which was to control bombing and fighter missions over Europe, did not yet exist. As a result of an agreement between President Franklin D. Roosevelt and Prime Minister Winston Churchill, reached nine months before the United States even entered the war, priority was to be given to the defeat of Germany, and hence the majority of American assets were designated for service in Europe. Those assets would soon form the Eighth Air Force. In the months that followed it became one of the most effective fighting forces the world had ever seen and master of the air war over Europe.

GENESIS

During the Great Depression of the early 1930s, less than ten years before America entered the war against Germany, a sense of ultimate faith, fostered by a clique of officers at the US Army Air Corps Tactical School (ACTS) at Maxwell Field, Alabama, slowly but surely formed around the apparent invincibility and capabilities of the heavy bomber as a weapon of strategic offense. This faith eventually emerged as doctrine.

The root of this doctrine, and the cause of so much faith in the heavy bomber, has been attributed to a great extent to the hypothesis espoused by the (at the time) little-known Italian air power theorist, Giulio Douhet. He prophesied the brilliant and conquering future of the aerial bomber, derived from his personal experiences during Italy's war against the Turks in 1911.

Translated into English by 1921, Douhet's controversial theories were to transform military aviation doctrines around the globe, and many came to believe slavishly in the coming age of air power,

Boeing's Model 299 flew for the first time from Seattle on July 28, 1935, carrying the civilian registration X-13372, since it was a company-owned aircraft. This photograph clearly shows its sleek and modern design and the small nose-mounted turret. (Author's collection)

envisaging fleets of high-flying bombers so well-armed that they would fend off—and even destroy—an enemy's disorganized and outnumbered fighter forces.

American writers opined that bombers would be used in mass over urban centers, their vast numbers darkening the sky as they went about destroying factories with such pinpoint accuracy that terrorized citizens of major cities would be left all too ready to surrender under a rain of falling bombs. Indeed, artists painted scenes of an enemy's sky dotted with US Army Air Corps (USAAC) bombers dropping endless sticks of bombs upon defenseless factories. Enemy fighters were depicted firing harmlessly from out of range, or spinning down in flames as victims of the bombers' "fortress-like" armament. It was of course total fantasy, but this view was not without its advocates. Even across the Atlantic, the British Conservative politician Stanley Baldwin stated in late 1932 that "No power on earth can protect the man in the street from being bombed. Whatever people may tell him, the bomber will always get through."

Certainly, the advocates at the ACTS espoused the virtues of bomber technology over the further development of "pursuit" or fighter interceptor aviation. In 1934, for example, captains Harold L. George and Robert M. Webster of the ACTS carried out an in-depth analysis of the vulnerability of New York City to daylight precision bombing. Both officers came to the conclusion that if bombs could be used to accurately strike essential services—i.e. water, electricity and transportation—the effect would be to make the city "unliveable."

Model 299

The faith of George and Webster and many other officers in the heavy bomber was strengthened drastically when, in July 1935, Boeing produced its four-engined, highly streamlined, all-metal Model 299 to conform to an ambitious USAAC requirement for a long-range maritime patrol bomber to protect the extensive US coastline. Powered by four 750hp Pratt & Whitney R-1690-E Hornet nine-cylinder air-cooled radial engines, it featured four blister-type positions for moveable machine guns, each of which could accommodate a 30-cal. or 50-cal. machine gun. An additional station for a nose machine gun was incorporated, and a bomb load of up to eight 600lb bombs could be carried internally.

It had been Brigadier-General William M. "Billy" Mitchell, one-time Assistant Chief of the Air Service, who had warned that the development of the long-range military aircraft fundamentally changed the defensive position of the United States. "Aircraft will project the spearpoint of the nation's offensive and defensive power

A formation of Y1B-17s of the 2nd Bomb Group fly over New York City en route to Buenos Aires, in Argentina, on a much-publicized long-distance test flight in February 1938. The aircraft had flown up from Miami, in Florida, and would return to their home field at Langley, Virginia. This was Douhet's vision upheld. (Author's collection)

against the vital centers of the opposing country," he forecast. "The result of warfare by air will be to bring about quick decisions. Superior air power will cause such havoc, or the threat of such havoc, in the opposing country that a long-drawn-out campaign will be impossible. Woe be to the nation that is weak in the air."

The aircraft's ability to travel much farther and faster than previous means of transportation removed the isolation the USA had previously counted on as part of its security.

It is popularly believed that upon observing the aircraft on its maiden flight at Seattle on July 28, 1935, one impressed newspaper reporter from the *Seattle Daily Times* commented that it had the appearance of a "flying fortress." Equally, the officers at the ACTS were convinced about the impregnability of what eventually became the B-17 Flying Fortress.

However, by the late 1930s any euphoria over the fledgling B-17 ignored the fact that the advent of radar technology and high-performance fighters wholly undermined Douhet's theory that bombers would always "get through." Furthermore, allegiance to the Douhet doctrine ignored the possibility that an enemy's defenses would be developed at all. Indeed, the destruction of the Luftwaffe did not become the main priority of the Anglo-American strategic bombing campaign until the launch of Operation *Pointblank* in 1943.

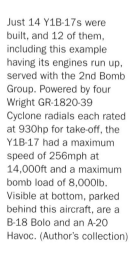

Just 14 Y1B-17s were built, and 12 of them, including this example having its engines run up, served with the 2nd Bomb Group. Powered by four Wright GR-1820-39 Cyclone radials each rated at 930hp for take-off, the Y1B-17 had a maximum speed of 256mph at 14,000ft and a maximum bomb load of 8,000lb. Visible at bottom, parked behind this aircraft, are a B-18 Bolo and an A-20 Havoc. (Author's collection)

Before that, however, from the time the United States Army Air Force (USAAF—as the USAAC was renamed on June 20, 1941) despatched its B-17s to England in mid-1942 to equip the heavy bomber groups of the Eighth Air Force, their crews quickly began to learn the hard way.)

During the early stages of World War II, fighter aircraft from both the Luftwaffe and the RAF were unable to escort and protect bomber formations due to their inadequacies in range. When they were able to engage enemy fighters, they left their charges with no defense other than their own speed and armament, which, at the time, was limited by the bomber's design requirements and poorly performing engines. Ultimately, the unescorted bomber's inability to ward off enemy fighters led to both combatants limiting the scope of their daylight bombing and opting for less effective nocturnal raids instead.

FM 1-10, Tactics and Techniques of Air Attack, November 20, 1940 espoused the doctrine which affected the American strategic bombing campaign. While it favored daylight bombing attacks, it also signified that escort support should be provided, when possible, wherever strong opposition was expected. Nonetheless, even after the failure of the early war daylight bombing campaigns of the Luftwaffe and the RAF, the USAAC continued to believe in the invincibility of the bomber, maintaining its belief that B-17 Flying Fortress and Consolidated B-24 Liberator bombers had enough firepower to complete unescorted missions without sustaining heavy losses.

Eventually equipped with modern, powered turrets that greatly increased the bomber's defensive capability, B-17F/Gs and later model B-24s were acknowledged as being the most heavily armed bombers of the period. Furthermore, the prewar USAAC mantra that "the bomber will always get through" initially made it seem that there would be no need for a fighter escort, as heavy bombers in close formations would create a deadly crossfire of multiple 50-cal. machine guns that would successfully fend off enemy interceptors.

Considered one of the war's premier heavy bombers when the B-17E commenced operations over Europe with Eighth Air Force's Bomber Command in August 1942, the B-17's first encounters with Luftwaffe fighters showed that it did not live up to the "flying fortress" moniker created by the US media prewar.

As the Americans saw it (often forgetting that their British friends had been fighting for more than two years before they began), they were going to use the British Isles as a stepping-stone for a war that would eventually lead to an invasion of occupied Europe and the defeat of Germany. Although poorly prepared for war, and slow in spinning up the capabilities of their enormous industrial heartland, America had "big bombers" and big ideas. From the beginning, some of the top officers of the US Army Air Forces (USAAF) must have sensed that the Eighth Air Force would become as vast as their dreams.

One veteran described the Eighth Air Force's humble beginnings this way: "Men of vision could see putting a thousand bombers in the sky over Europe. But when Brigadier-General Ira C. Eaker went to England, he had five guys with him, and that was what we started with." With a handful of men creating what was to become history's greatest air armada, Eighth Air Force evolved into an organization with four principal components: Air Service Command, Ground-Air Support Command, Fighter Command, and Bomber Command.

For the inexperienced bomber crews who arrived in England in 1942, the battlefield they were about to encounter would be a terrifying and unforgiving hellscape.

Ten thousand American bombers fell in battle during World War II. A large chunk of that total consisted of B-17s and B-24s of the Eighth Air Force. In looking back to those days when the sky was pungent with exhaust fumes, black with exploding shellfire, and swarming with Messerschmitt and Focke-Wulf fighters, some men wondered simply how they had done it. Those who survived were destined to share a bond never experienced by those untested in battle, but their memories differed.

A YB-17 waist gunner manning his M2 Browning 50-cal. machine gun. B-17s had two waist gunners located directly opposite one another toward the rear of the fuselage, which sometimes made maneuvering difficult for them. (Author's collection)

Perhaps no one, themselves included, ever understood how they mustered the stuff for the job they faced. Apart from the terrible cold, the noise, and the constant shaking, it was simply gruesome up there at a typical bombing altitude of 25,500ft, unable to dodge shells or debris after crossing the IP (initial point), flying in formation with aircraft ahead and above exploding in the air, with oxygen masks and body parts tumbling past the window, the swift black clouds of Flak ever closer, the persistent Luftwaffe fighters on a collision course from dead ahead.

There was an insanity to it. Sometimes a bomber came back with its insides smeared with vomit and blood. After a mission, those who did not need to be scraped out of their B-17 or B-24 or rushed to the burn unit were given grapefruit juice, hard candy, and rations of whiskey.

The Americans came to England prepared to use B-17s and the B-24 Liberators, to bomb German-occupied Europe by daylight. At first, they intended to do this with minimal or even no fighter escort. The Royal Air Force, whose Lancaster and Halifax crews had already garnered considerable experience pounding the Continent during the nocturnal hours, scoffed at daylight bombing.

Across the English Channel and with nearly three years' experience of fighting the Polish, French, Dutch, Belgian, British, and Soviet air forces, the Luftwaffe had honed a sophisticated air defense network in occupied Western Europe. By mid-June 1942, the Jagdwaffe fielded a force of nearly 160 Messerschmitt Bf 109F fighters in the West.

But even more formidable and ominous was the appearance in late 1941 of a new German fighter in the skies over France—the pugnacious, radial-engined Focke-Wulf Fw 190.

The Luftwaffe High Command was under no illusions. It knew that the American heavy bombers were coming. Two of the Luftwaffe's most experienced Jagdgeschwader units, Jagdgeschwader 2 and Jagdgeschwader 26, had long been stationed in Northwest Europe as the first line of defense against daylight incursions by RAF fighters and light bombers. So important was their role deemed to be that, by the summer of 1942, both these units had been almost entirely equipped with the most advanced fighter in the Luftwaffe's armory, the Focke-Wulf Fw 190.

This came as a shock to the Allies, and it provided a new dimension to air combat on the Western Front—as did the appearance in strength of the USAAF heavy bombers. The encounters which would follow between the Eighth Air Force's heavy bombers and the fighters of the Jagdwaffe over the next three years would form some of the most titanic and bitter contests of the air war in Western Europe.

VIII FIGHTER COMMAND

Although the United States did not enter World War II until December 1941, by then a significant number of American citizens had seen action in the British cause as fighter pilots serving with the Royal Air Force.

When Britain again went to war with Germany in September 1939, a number of adventurous young Americans—some of them experienced pilots—volunteered their services, often traveling to the UK via Canada, while others were recruited in the USA. Some saw action over France and England in the spring of 1940, while the first American pilots to fly the Spitfire began their training with No. 7 Operational Training Unit in early July, just as the Battle of Britain started. During 1940–41 thousands more would follow, enlisting in the Royal Canadian Air Force (RCAF). By the end of the war 8,864

One of the iconic images of the air war over Germany was taken during Mission 104 to Emden on September 27, 1943. In the center is B-17F *Skippy* of the 570th Squadron, 390th Bomb Group, which was later lost on a mission over France on February 5, 1944. Overhead are the contrails of P-47 fighters conducting their usual weaving maneuver to keep pace with the bombers. (NARA)

**Spitfire Mk IIA of W. R. Dunn,
No. 71 Eagle Squadron, August 1941**

Pilot Officer Bill Dunn was the first American ace of World War II.
(Artwork by Chris Davey © Osprey Publishing)

US citizens had served part of, or all of, their air force careers in the RCAF. Shortly after the Japanese attack on Pearl Harbor on December 7, 1941, negotiations between the two neighbours began to voluntarily repatriate those Americans serving in the RCAF. In the end some 3,797 transferred to the USAAF, with the remaining 5,067 serving their tours of duty with the RCAF.

In the autumn of 1940, the RAF, for a variety of reasons, decided to group the volunteer American pilots into their own distinctive squadrons along the lines of the *Escadrille Lafayette*. So, on September 19, No. 71 Squadron was formed as the first "Eagle" squadron. The unit became operational in February 1941, and two further "Eagle" squadrons—nos. 121 and 133—were formed with Hurricanes.

In mid-1942, the newly created Eighth Air Force began establishing itself in England, with its 31st Fighter Group, comprising the 307th, 308th, and 309th Fighter squadrons, arriving at Atcham and High Ercall, in Shropshire, in late June. There, the group received Spitfires under a reverse lend-lease arrangement.

The 52nd Fighter Group, comprising the 2nd, 4th, and 5th Fighter squadrons, also sailed for Britain at around this time too, and upon its arrival at Eglinton, in Northern Ireland, these units also received Spitfires, much to the delight of their pilots. The 52nd's Executive Officer (XO), Major James Coward, commented at the time: "The Spit is an easy aeroplane to fly, but the braking system and distribution of weight in the nose has caused us a little trouble. The British are to be commended for the excellent job they did of training both air and ground personnel."

Spitfire VB BL722 of 2nd Lieutenant James Goodson, 336th Fighter Squadron, October 1942

Goodson conducted the first flight of an American-marked fighter over the Continent. His plane features white stars painted over the British roundels. (Artwork by Chris Davey © Osprey Publishing)

Gradually, by early August, all the squadrons from both USAAF groups were declared operational and available for combat operations, initially for defensive patrols and some convoy escorts. Later, they participated as escorts for US bombing raids on targets in northern France.

For the hard-pressed RAF, the arrival of six more fighter squadrons was also no doubt welcome. Both the American groups were to fly the British fighter with distinction, with a large number of pilots achieving ace status in the Spitfire.

With the increasing build-up of the Eighth Air Force in Britain, the RAF and USAAF came to the decision that all three "Eagle" squadrons would transfer to their national command at the end of September 1942, forming the 4th Fighter Group with the 334th, 335th, and 336th Fighter squadrons.

Whilst the Eighth Air Force had gained the 4th Fighter Group, it was in the process of losing the 31st and 52nd Fighter groups as, having worked up to an operational pitch, both groups had been earmarked for Operation *Torch*—the Anglo-American invasion of French North Africa. They were therefore taken off operations to prepare, under great secrecy, for this new venture. Both were transferred to Twelfth Air Force control and shipped to Gibraltar, the 31st sailing on October 21 and the 52nd two days later.

As the only operational USAAF fighter unit in Europe, the 4th Fighter Group was subject to great attention by the voracious American press, who naturally wanted to describe every action. They

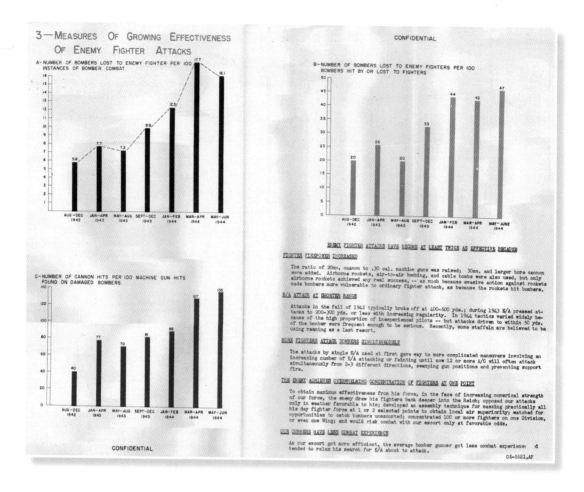

Eighth Air Force bomber crews paid a heavy price during the war. These graphics clearly show how effective Luftwaffe fighter tactics and weapons were during 1943 and early 1944. (Author's collection)

particularly wanted to report success whilst flying American aircraft, and so the 4th Fighter Group was earmarked to become an early recipient of the massive Republic P-47 Thunderbolt. Training on the new fighter began in mid-January.

Like the 31st and 52nd Fighter groups, the first P-38 Lightning groups (1st and 14th) to arrive in England were soon transferred to the Twelfth Air Force for Operation *Torch*. When the P-38 returned to combat in England in mid-1943, it was the American fighter of the period—the Thunderbolt still had range, reliability, and "combatability" problems, the Warhawk had proven unsuitable for the European Theater of Operations (ETO) and the Merlin Mustang was at least six months away from front-line service. Every USAAF fighter group commander wanted the type for his squadrons, but the Lightning was being produced in smaller numbers than any other American fighter.

By the early spring of 1943, three USAAF fighter groups—the 4th, 56th, and 78th—were flying the P-47 Thunderbolt from bases in England. Having American rather than British fighters (the 4th had flown Spitfires from September 1942) in the hands of Army Air Force units undoubtedly gave the planners of the Eighth Air Force's bomber offensive a little more confidence. The P-47 was capable of escorting heavy bombers further than was previously possible with Spitfires, although the operational doctrine of using fighters in this role had hardly been addressed. How best fighters could protect the B-17 and B-24 formations on their daylight heavy bombing missions would remain a matter for discussion throughout much of 1943.

The situation vis-a-vis the P-47 was not helped by a vague operational plan outlined by Eighth Fighter Command that failed to appreciate the important role to be played by the escort fighter in the American daylight bomber offensive. At this stage in the war some bomber commanders still reckoned that they could cope without fighter help by adopting tight, self-defensive formations. Eighth Fighter Command leader, General Frank O'Dell Hunter (who had little fighter experience himself), could hardly counter this school of thought at the time for his early model P-47Cs could not fly much further than Paris on escort duty. It was a combat radius of about 230 miles. It was consequently left to the group commanders, and their flight leaders, to more or less develop their own tactics and deploy their forces to the best advantage.

The YB-40 was not successful because it had poor flying characteristics and most of its armament was not useful in the front quarter, from where the Germans mostly attacked. (Author's collection)

The first attempt to field a deep escort was the YB-40 destroyer escort aircraft, sometimes also called a heavy cruiser. This was a B-17 reinforced with additional machine-gun turrets as well as added armor plating. The first YB-40s arrived in Britain in May 1943 and were assigned to the 92nd Bomb Group. Operational use of these aircraft in the summer of 1943 was very discouraging, as they did not add enough firepower to the combat box while at the same time the extra armor made them sluggish and they could not keep up with the other B-17s after they had dropped their bombs. The abrupt failure of the YB-40 led to its cancellation.

In the meantime, the USAAF had been engaged in a development program to extend fighter range, prompted also by the long-range requirements of the Pacific theater and intercontinental ferrying operations. Two methods were under study: increasing the internal fuel capacity of existing fighters such as the P-38 and P-47, and developing external drop tanks. Of the two approaches, drop tanks presented the greatest engineering challenge since the USAAF sought a design that was bulletproof, lightweight, and sturdy enough that it could be pressurized so that the host fighter didn't require additional fuel pumps. Furthermore, since the tanks were disposable, the USAAF wanted them made from a non-strategic material at low cost. The Firestone 75-gallon tank passed firing trials in June 1942, and an enlarged 105-gallon type was developed. The Eighth Air Force first sought drop tanks in January 1943, and efforts began to have them fabricated by local industry in Britain. As a stopgap measure, in July 1943 Eighth Fighter Command began distributing 200-gallon ferry tanks, which were not ideal for combat use but were useful in defining the requirement. The 75-gallon belly tank became available by July 1943, which extended the P-47's operating radius to 340 miles (550km), providing it with sufficient fuel to reach northwestern Germany. They were first used on the mission that struck Kassel and Oschersleben on July 28, 1943, and won the overwhelming praise of the bomber crews involved. By August 1943, the enlarged 108-gallon belly tank was arriving, which extended the range to 375 miles; by February 1944 the P-47 could be equipped with a 150-gallon belly tank (giving a 425-mile radius) or twin 108-gallon wing tanks (giving a 475-mile radius).

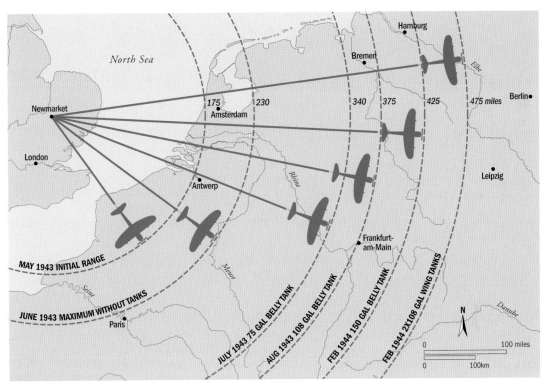

Range Map of P-47

This map reveals how the range of the P-47 was progressively extended through the introduction of ever-larger external fuel tanks. Yet even when fitted with two underwing 108-gallon tanks, the P-47D still only possessed half the endurance of a similarly equipped P-51D.

Lt Cameron Hart's 63rd Fighter Squadron P-47D serial no. 42-26299 UN-B warming prior to take-off in late 1944. P-47s equipped with two 100-gallon drop tanks, such as this one, had a combat radius of 475 miles. (littlefriends.co.uk)

Because of pressure from the Eighth Air Force after the disastrous Schweinfurt raids in 1943, Eighth Fighter Command began to receive the first P-38 group in October and a second in December 1943, as well as the new P-47D. On November 3, P-38s of the 55th Fighter Group performed their first long-range bomber escort mission. As the Luftwaffe sent up a mixed force of Fw 190As and Bf 109Gs to intercept the Americans over Holland, they received a rude surprise. According to Luftwaffe records, the P-38 pilots managed to ambush a formation of its fighters and break it up completely. Thirteen German fighters were reported lost. P-47 pilots of the 56th, 78th, and 4th Fighter groups accounted for six of them, and the 55th the rest.

In the event, the P-38 proved to be a disappointment in the escort role as it had engine-reliability issues when operating at high altitudes, and its combat performance against typical German fighters was mediocre.

The most satisfactory solution to the escort problem was the new North American P-51. The baseline P-51B already had an impressive combat radius of 475 miles (765km), which was further extended by additional internal storage as well as drop tanks. Hunter had preferred the P-47 for the escort-fighter mission, and as a result the P-51B had been allotted to the tactical fighter squadrons of the incoming Ninth Air Force. With the autumn 1943 command changes and the new emphasis on the deep-escort mission, Major-General William Kepner, commander of Eighth Fighter Command, received the support of Major-General Henry "Hap" Arnold, Commanding General, USAAF, to switch the P-51B squadrons to Eighth Air Force control. The first P-51B squadrons arrived in September 1943 and became operational on December 5, 1943.

Republic P-47D-28-RE, serial no. 44-20230, 53rd Fighter Squadron, 36th Fighter Group, RAF Mount Farm (located 3 miles north of Dorchester, Oxfordshire), summer 1944. The late-model P-47D, equipped with three 110-gallon drop tanks, was capable of flying to Berlin and back. (Author's collection)

One of the barracks of the 355th Fighter Group at Steeple Morden, Cambridgeshire, England. Crowded and with little privacy, these barracks could accommodate up to 12 men. (NARA)

CHAPTER 1

THE FRIENDLY INVASION

"Overpaid, Oversexed, and Over Here!"

Well before the first aircrew and aircraft from the Eighth Air Force arrived in the UK, plans for their arrival were already in motion. RAF bases and airfields were being prepared. In 1942, the British Air Ministry made available 77 bases, but this was just the beginning. In the coming weeks and months, airfield construction kicked into high gear on a massive scale. Initially, the bases first occupied by Eighth units were purpose-built prewar RAF bases. Most were comfortable and well-liked by the new air and ground crews. In 1941, members of the Special Observer Group in England examined areas deemed well suited for new airfields and maintenance depots.

In June 1942, the outlines for a comprehensive plan for the location of USAAF installation in the UK was sent to the US War Department. With British approval, the bulk of the new bases were to be located south of the line from the Wash to Leicester and north and northeast of London. The first bomber units would be located near Cambridge, and those arriving later found themselves in East Anglia. Eighth Fighter Command fighter groups were also based in

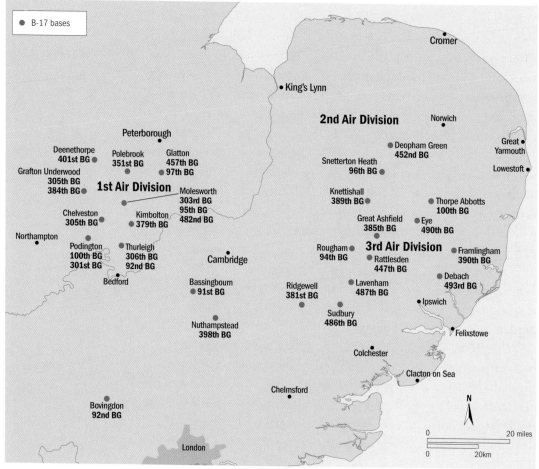

B-17 Bases

The US Eighth Air Force's infrastructure of nearly 30 B-17 bases sprawled across much of the English northern Home Counties and East Anglia, with the three air divisions managing tactical and logistical control. More than 30 B-17 groups equipped the Eighth, in addition to B-24, fighter and support squadrons, and groups.

East Anglia so as to be as close to targets in occupied Europe as possible. Most of the fighter bases were built from scratch. The construction plan that proceeded would become one of the largest civil engineering programs ever undertaken in the United Kingdom. By June 1, 1943, Britain's Air Ministry had 54 bomber bases under construction for the Eighth Air Force.

Original plans called for the construction of 115 airfields, of which 90 would be suitable for bombers. In the end, the Eighth Air

Force utilized 67 airfields: 42 for heavy bombers, 15 for fighters and four reconnaissance. Each airfield would consist of three concrete runways (the main one being a mile and a quarter long), a perimeter track, and concrete hard stands for 50 bombers. Temporary buildings comprised two or three large hangars, workshops, and accommodation for 2,500 personnel, plus vital utilities including fuel storage, electrical generation, and water supply and sewage. To build a new base required 500,000 sq yards of concrete, 400,000 cu yards of excavated soil, and the removal of eight miles of hedgerow and 1,500 trees. In addition to the runways and hardstands, airfields required control towers. Made of concrete and brick these two-story structures featured a balcony for clear views across the airfield. Crew quarters consisted of large Nissen huts made of corrugated iron atop a concrete slab.

The key to victory for the Allies and the Eighth Air Force in World War II was logistics. It wasn't just ground crew that kept the fighters and bombers flying—it was also every imaginable spare part and item needed for uptempo operations. Everything from spare parts, rubber tires, clothing, lubricants, ammunition, bombs, medical supplies, engines to shoelaces had to be shipped from the US and processed through the docks in Liverpool. From there they would flow into the Service Supply Depots. Burtonwood in Warrington developed into the single-largest US supply, storage, and maintenance installation of the war. Over 35,000 men were under the direct control of Burtonwood.

STRATEGIC AIR DEPOTS

As the number of combat airfields expanded, so did the entire depot system. New transit depots were formed and designated Strategic Air Depots (SAD). These depots were staffed and trained to service Air Force Combat Units, and were responsible for third- and fourth-echelon maintenance. On August 1, 1943, there were four SADs in the UK. Combat crew replacement centers were also established to handle the huge influx of aircrew. In all, seven centers were established in Northern Ireland.

The build-up of Eighth Air Force aircraft and personnel in the UK was phenomenal and unprecedented, but despite these achievements,

A T2 hangar under construction. Each base usually had two hangars. Each T2 spanned 115–120ft, was 240ft long and 39ft high. (Author's collection)

injury and death were everywhere on an active air base. During the war, 12,371 B-17s were built with roughly 9,000 flying from the UK. Of that number, 8,300 were destroyed or damaged beyond repair by enemy action or accidents. In the first year of operations, bombers flew with limited fighter escort. The short range of the RAF Spitfire and P-47 meant they had to turn for home long before the bombers reached their targets. Crews who survived their first 25 missions had served their tour of duty and could go home. Unfortunately, only 27 percent of flight crews survived. It was a grim statistic but on average crews completed just eight missions before being shot down. Over time, these numbers improved as the P-47s extended the escort range along with the P-38 and, later, the P-51.

DAILY LIFE AND CONDITIONS OF SERVICE

A great deal is known about the lives and experiences of the men who flew in these machines, not least because they were generally more literate than their compatriots in the Army and Navy, but more importantly because they often had a respite between combat missions on the safety of an air base far from the enemy, where they could log their thoughts and experiences in a diary or journal, or write home. Foot soldiers had nothing more than a tent in which to sleep and could only carry with them what was absolutely essential. Only when withdrawn from the front line might they have the time to jot down some thoughts, but even then there was nowhere to leave such a journal, and they were in any event discouraged from doing so to avoid its capture by the enemy, who could obtain valuable intelligence from its contents. Airmen, on the other hand, could write down what they pleased and leave it safely in their quarters. Even if captured or killed, their journals and letters remained safely back at their base.

Americans found themselves known as "Yanks" in Britain, where a certain degree of jealousy prevailed between American airmen and those in the RAF, since the former received considerably more pay than the latter. Nevertheless, money was seldom of much concern to flyers, and often when on leave crews would combine their pay to create a sizable pot to be spent together. Sometimes men saved a considerable part of their pay, which they sent home every month if they managed not to gamble it away. Their tenuous existence simply rendered money an irrelevance.

The vast majority of American bomber crewmen in Britain maintained positive impressions of their time there: Sam Wilson, who served in a ground crew, wrote home in October 1942:

> England is really beautiful—everything is so neat and orderly. The trains are just like in the movies ... The streets are cobblestone and run in every damned direction! The lower-class English rather resent us; however, the middle class and upper bend over backwards being nice to us ... The Scotch people we have met are really swell, more like Yanks ... We have to watch our slang. Have already had a few misunderstandings that way ... The British version of toilet tissue is equivalent to the rotogravure section of the Sears Roebuck catalogue. There are no oranges. We will soon be eating American food, though I like English food. They have tried to cook our dishes and have flopped so far. But their hospitality extended that far!

Wilson found the blackouts so comprehensive that he bumped into lampposts, only to reply with, "Beg your pardon."

Generally speaking, relations between Britons and Americans were amicable. Lalli Coppinger, a Red Cross Club volunteer, recalled her experiences thus:

> Getting to know the Americans was a memorable highlight of the war. They provided excitement and brought fun back into our lives at the time we most needed it, when we were suffering greatly from the deprivations of the years of war. They livened up our dreary towns and introduced a new world to us. We learned to understand each other's cultural differences, but were also surprised to find out how much alike we were in many ways. When we opened up our homes and hospitality to them, they responded wholeheartedly and gradually became a very large part of our lives. Many were in England for as long as three years, plenty of time to form a special bonding and lasting friendships. The GIs had a great liking for children, who needed no encouragement to make their acquaintance. Their faces would light up when their American friends dug down into their pockets and brought out never-ending supplies of candy and chewing gum. No one will ever forget the catchphrase, "Any gum, chum?"

EASILY REPLACED

OPPOSITE This bucolic image is in sharp contrast to the horrors of air combat high above Germany. A farmer's wife herds a flock of ducks while Master Sergeant J. F. Hallmaker and ground personnel of the 91st Bomb Group clean the guns on a B-17 Flying Fortress nicknamed *Mary Lou*. (NARA)

Once assigned to a base, airmen sometimes found that they were among thousands of other men working in the same capacity and that their status was not as special as before. "We were 'fresh meat,'" Ben Smith recalled, "replacements, soon to be gobbled up by the voracious appetite of the air war like all those who had gone before." Indeed, the casualty rate was so high that crewmen often established strong bonds between them, with distinctions sometimes becoming blurred between officers and non-commissioned officers. Whole crews sometimes went on leave together, and even on the base saluting and military formality was often eschewed except when decorations were awarded or dignitaries visited.

Americans on leave were free to travel, though as John Ramsey, a B-17 navigator, discovered, train schedules were not always published, for security reasons, and making a journey such as from Norfolk to

Prefab buildings and Nissen huts made up the majority of buildings on a typical Eighth Air Force base. They were drafty and hard to heat in winter. (NARA)

Leeds was not easy, requiring frequent transfers and requests for information at numerous stations along the way. He had trouble understanding Yorkshire accents and was surprised by advice given by someone in Leeds to "knock someone up"—a perfect example of what is meant by a people "separated by a common language." Ramsey was quite naturally "momentarily taken aback by this statement, as in American slang it means making someone pregnant. This was the first time I had heard this expression from a Britisher but quickly realized that the woman was telling me to go bang on the door."

John Regan also remembered the British people with fondness:

The British treated us wonderfully. When we had time off, we'd jump into our jeeps, tear off into the countryside firing flares, feeling no pain, having a big time, probably go to the town of Luton, fairly close to our base. We'd go to the same pub and people would see us, really greet us, cheer, sing songs. We got to know everybody there. We enjoyed it so much that one time I got all my men together and we called the fellow that owned the place up in front. I presented him with stripes and made him an honorary sergeant in our squadron.

Red Komarek, another airman, remembered how:

> We were told by the brass that a formal introduction would be necessary
> in order to meet English girls and that the English were more strait-laced
> than us broad-minded Yanks. We found both to be untrue. Whoever
> researched this information must have seen a lot of old British movies. It
> was obvious from our first visit to town (Huntingdon [sic], in Cambridge)
> that boy-meets-girl routines were not very different from those back home.

LOVE, LONDON, AND LONGING

The big cities provided some form of recreation and enjoyment for
many. Tommy Hayes would take himself off to London:

> My trips, the so-called forty-eight-hour pass, was a break from the war
> and the opportunity to relax, to again be an officer and gentleman. For
> me that meant a comfortable hotel, a nice dining room, sleeping on
> sheets that might have been silk and a bath in a tub, the length of which
> exceeded my height. It happened often enough that you remained a
> member of the human race, although always eager to get back and fight.

The men need not travel far, however, for female company. Earl Pate
recalled that:

> About every six weeks the whole group would stand down and there would
> be a party/dance that started about dark and lasted until the next morning.
> The entire nursing staff from a general military hospital up the road would
> be invited. To supplement them, about four in the afternoon of the party,
> GI trucks would go to the several villages in the area and all the English
> girls would be invited. Crowds would gather at the base HQ as the trucks
> returned. If none of the ladies accepted your offer to be her escort for the
> evening, you simply waited a few minutes until the next truck arrived.

The eagerness of the men to escape from base as soon as an opportunity
arose is scarcely surprising, for they were generally dismal,
uncomfortable places. Bases were completely functional and

unattractive, scattered across the English countryside, especially in Norfolk and Cambridgeshire, which were naturally useful areas from which to launch air attacks on Germany and occupied Europe. Apart from the runways, a base contained a control tower, one or more aircraft hangars, and a series of buildings including mess halls, operations rooms, barracks, repair facilities, and other structures, often of prefabricated construction. At Kimbolton, in East Anglia, for instance, the men lived in huts with potbelly stoves for warmth and outdoor toilets. George Hoyt recalled the appearance of his barracks, meant for enlisted men, thus:

Some squadrons had steel Nissan huts, but most of our barracks were long, low, drab-looking wooden buildings with crude doors that had antique hinges and hardware. Inside we were assigned beds which had RAF "biscuit" mattresses that came in three separate pieces. You needed a blanket under you as well as over you to keep the cold air from coming in between the "biscuits." For heat we had two pot-bellied stoves with a four-day ration of coal per week. Out the back door of our barracks stood the latrine in a separate building, and to the left was the "bomb shelter," a dugout with a mound of sod-covered dirt rising to about 6ft.

There was no privacy in this form of accommodation, for it was simply one open space with a single room at the end for the barracks chief.

TENTS AND CASTLES

Some air bases provided separate accommodation for officers and enlisted men, but in many cases crews were so close-knit that such notions were discarded altogether. Archie Old, of the 96th Bomb Group, remembered that: "We kept the crew integrated, the whole damn 10-man crew sleeps and lives in the same quarters." Maintaining high morale also depended on proper supply. "If you feed them better, pay them better, clothe them better, house them better, transport them, this sort of stuff, the better this part is, the more relaxed they are ... We lived as good or better over there than we did at home." In reality, accommodation could vary enormously, from country houses with proper beds and sheets, baths and indoor toilets, to tent cities where the men slept on cots under scores of blankets and trudged through the cold, rain, and mud to the latrines and showers.

Wayne Gatlin, 18, from Duluth, Minnesota, could not believe his good fortune: "We live in a nice old castle—yup, there's a moat filled with water around it and all ... We have our mess right in the castle and a lounge and all. I've a nice sack, a big bed and sheets." Earl Pate lived on simpler, yet perfectly comfortable terms: a permanent RAF installation without Quonset huts, coal stoves, mud, or walks to the latrine. All the quarters were of brick, two stories, with tiled baths and paved roads, all in Georgian style with officers sharing two to a room. Wherever they happened to live, the men often had pin-ups of Betty Grable, Rita Hayworth, or other women on the wall behind or beside their bunks. Movie stars such as Ginger Rogers sometimes sent autographed photographs of themselves in response to requests from the front.

Ben Smith recalled how, on his base:

We seldom wore uniforms. Our dress was flight overalls and leather A-2 jackets. We clomped around a lot in our flight boots, always when we went to the latrine or some short distance, because they were warm. We either went bareheaded or wore the leather fleece-lined gunner's caps. I can recall wearing my flight overalls for days at a time without taking them off. I would sleep in them too ...

If we wanted to take a shower, we had to go a considerable distance to the showers. There was never any hot water. It was just too much trouble and a very punishing experience, so nobody bothered. Sponge baths had to do. After a time we couldn't smell ourselves; or we thought we smelled all right, because everybody else smelled that way.

To pass the time between missions, the men were fond of listening to the radio, either the BBC or the Armed Forces Network (AFN), which played jazz and other contemporary music. Poker and other card games were popular. Some were fond of reading; others took afternoon tea at the local Red Cross club.

Ground personnel get down and dirty digging a drainage ditch. During the fall, winter, and spring wet weather often meant mud. It stuck to everything, making life miserable on base. Proper drainage was important but it never solved the problem. (NARA)

"CONSIDER YOURSELVES ALREADY DEAD"

The reality of death around the corner meant that everything was shared. There was no sense in hoarding food when you might not survive to eat it, though men did tend to look after their whiskey. Flight crews generally shared items sent to them from home with local people, including chewing gum, chocolates, silk stockings, and cigarettes. Ben Smith recalled that, "A few boorish fellows attempted to use these goodies to bargain for the favors of English girls, but only the most insensitive ones responded to such degrading behavior."

To cope with the real prospect of death, some men turned to prayer and attended regular church services, like Philip Ardery:

Part of my reaction to my luck and general combat experience was a ... resurgence of religion. Fellows who hadn't attended services in years found themselves going to Sunday services. My religion didn't take me to these services with regularity, but I went occasionally, not only for myself but to let the men in my squadron know I didn't consider attendance a sign of weakness. I felt if they saw me there it might help some of them to go who wanted to but were kept from going out of embarrassment.

In my case, religion made me say short prayers before going to sleep at night and sometimes during a fleeting instant at the height of combat. I think this undoubtedly made me a better combat officer. It comforted me so that I could sleep before missions, even though I had been briefed for the next mission and knew the assignment of the morning might be my last. It helped me to say to myself with complete calm: "You can't live forever. You have had a great deal in your life span already, much more than many people ever have. You would not shirk the duty tomorrow if you could. Go into it calmly; don't try too hard to live. Don't ever give up hope; never let the fear of death strike panic in your mind and paralyze your reason. Death will find you sometime, if not tomorrow. Give yourself a chance."

Both the air and ground crews of the Eighth Air Force lived unique lives on the ground. Access to entertainment, and the charms of London, pubs, and female companionships, seemed other-worldly, in sharp contrast to the horrors of air combat over Germany. One day they might be coming home drunk from the pub, and the next morning they could be woken up at 0300hrs for another mission. It was a far cry from what the ground forces would experience.

Engine run-up on a B-17E. The first B-17Es assigned to the Eighth Air Force arrived in England in July 1942, these aircraft being armed with eight 0.50-in. machines guns and a single 30-cal weapon in the nose. (Author's collection)

CHAPTER 2

THE LIGHT OF DAY

The USAAF Strategic Bombing of Germany 1942–45

On January 2, 1942, the order activating the Eighth Air Force was signed by Major-General Henry "Hap" Arnold, Commanding General, USAAF. Six days later, the US Army announced that Eighth Bomber Command was to be established in England, and Arnold instructed Brigadier-General Ira C. Eaker to assist in the formation of a headquarters for the American air forces in Great Britain. Eaker was designated as commanding general of Eighth Bomber Command, and one of his first duties was to help prepare the airfields and installations deemed necessary for its groups to operate from. He was also tasked with studying the methods of the Royal Air Force's Bomber Command.

On February 3, 1942, the 97th, 301st, and 303rd Bomb groups were formally activated. These B-17E groups, the 92nd Bomb Group (activated on March 1, 1942), and two Liberator groups, the 44th and 93rd Bomb groups, would form the nucleus of the US heavy bombardment force in England.

In early February 1942, Eaker and his "advanced detachment" of just six men left for England. Initially, he would set up his HQ at RAF Bomber Command headquarters at High Wycombe in Buckinghamshire. Just a matter of days later, on February 22,

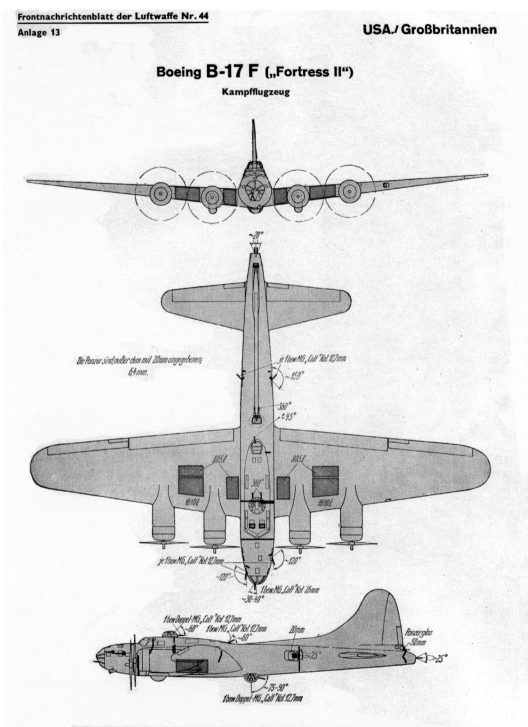

Boeing **B-17 F** („Fortress II")

Kampfflugzeug

Die Panzer sind außer dem mit 20mm angegebenen,
6,4 mm.

je 1 bew MG, Colt "Kal. 12,7mm

~15,0°

360°
±45°

805 L

805 L

360°

1610 L

1610 L

je 1 bew MG, Colt "Kal. 12,7mm

~120°

~120°

1 bew MG, Colt "Kal. 7,6mm

~30-40°

1 bew Doppel-MG, Colt "Kal. 12,7mm

~60°

1 bew MG, Colt "Kal. 12,7mm

~60°

20mm

Panzerglas
~50mm

~25°

~25°

~75-90°

1 bew Doppel-MG, Colt "Kal. 12,7mm

*Die Bewaffnung besteht aus 11 × 12,7 mm-MG. und 1 × 7,6 mm-MG. Mit Ausnahme der beiden kraft-
gesteuerten Drehtürme auf Rumpfoberseite und Rumpfunterseite werden alle Waffen durch Hand betätigt*

Eighth Bomber Command was formally activated. Between March 31 and April 3, Eaker and his staff officers made a more detailed reconnaissance of the Huntingdon area, which had originally been considered by the RAF for the location of a new Bomber Command formation, before it turned its attention to creating additional stations in Lincolnshire and South Yorkshire. The airfield construction program in Huntingdon had continued, however, and these bases would soon house B-17 Flying Fortresses of the 1st Bombardment Wing.

The Americans were firm believers in daylight precision bombing, and they were to lose as little time as possible in putting those beliefs into practice. The first aircrews of the embryonic Eighth Air Force arrived in the United Kingdom on May 11, 1942, five months to the day since Hitler's declaration of war. They immediately began training with an RAF squadron that was equipped with Douglas Boston light bombers.

Other AAF personnel soon began to arrive in the UK. Some made the journey across the Atlantic Ocean aboard the ocean liner *Queen Elizabeth*, which dropped anchor in the Firth of Clyde on the morning of June 9. Amongst the several thousand troops that disembarked were men from the 97th Bomb Group. Like all heavy bomb groups assigned to the ETO, this outfit consisted of four squadrons—the 340th, 341st, 342nd, and 414th Bomb squadrons. Men of the 340th and 341st traveled to their new base at Polebrook (Station 110), in Northamptonshire, whilst personnel from the 342nd and 414th were sent a little further west to Grafton Underwood (Station 106), again in Northamptonshire.

Their B-17s, meanwhile, were not scheduled to fly in from Dow Field, Maine, and Grenier Field, New Hampshire, via the Northern Ferry Route, until mid-June. However, the bombers were delayed by the Japanese threat in the Aleutians (the 97th Bomb Group was temporarily placed on detached duty with Western Defence Command). By June 23, the enemy offensive had been halted, and the 97th returned to Presque Isle, Maine, for the flight to England. Their route would be via Goose Bay, in Labrador, Bluie West 1, in Greenland, the Icelandic capital of Reykjavik and Prestwick, in Scotland.

OPPOSITE Taken from a Luftwaffe aircraft identification manual, this three-view drawing of a B-17F clearly shows the location of armor plating, self-sealing fuel tanks (in red), and defensive armament. American heavy bombers were well armed and armored, which in turn meant that they were able to remain airworthy despite often sustaining extensive damage from Flak and fighters. (Author's collection)

On June 26, the first 15 B-17Es to attempt the crossing set off, but after departing Goose Bay on the second leg of the trip, they encountered bad weather in Greenland and were forced to turn back. Eleven of the B-17s returned to Labrador after having been in the air for over 14 hours, whilst three other crews crash-landed in Greenland after flying into a snowstorm. None of the crewmembers were hurt, however, and they were quickly rescued. Astonishingly, the final B-17 actually managed to land in Greenland, at Bluie West 8 landing-ground, some 400 miles further east of its original destination.

On July 1, 1942, B-17E *Jarring Jenny* became the first Flying Fortress assigned to Eighth Bomber Command to actually land in the UK when she flew into Prestwick. Three days later, the following entry was made at High Wycombe—"Arrival of aircraft: 1 B-17E. Total 1."

1942: FIRST MISSIONS

Symbolically, the Eighth Air Force's first operation was flown on American Independence Day, July 4, 1942. It was a combined Anglo-American mission with 12 RAF Bostons—six crewed by Americans—being despatched to bomb Luftwaffe airfields in Holland. Three of the Bostons failed to return. One, flown by an RAF crew, fell victim to a Luftwaffe fighter, while the other two, crewed by the USAAF,

B-17s over the English Channel on their way to targets in Germany. This serene and beautiful image was one of the benefits of flying. For many Eighth Air Force crews it was their first experience of flight. Sadly, this majestic battlefield was just as deadly and sometimes more so than the experience of a typical infantryman fighting on the ground. (Author's collection)

were both shot down by Flak. They were to be the American squadron's only combat losses as part of the Eighth Air Force. After two more operations flown under their own colors (albeit in ex-RAF machines), the 15th Bomb Squadron (Light) was transferred to the Mediterranean theater in September to join the USAAF's Twelfth Air Force.

In August, the 97th Bomb Group was joined by the 92nd Bomb Group at Bovingdon (Station 112), in Hertfordshire, and the 301st Bomb Group at Chelveston (Station 105) and Podington (Station 109), both in Northamptonshire. All three groups had been hastily formed in the turbulent weeks following Pearl Harbor, and their training was incomplete. Some of the air gunners had actually received little or no training in aerial gunnery, whilst the radio operators were in no better shape, being unable to send or receive morse signals. Finally, many of the pilots sent to the ETO had no experience of high altitude or formation flying.

Many crews, untrained as they were, had only just become familiar with their equipment and each other, when they were pitched headlong into an air war senior AAF officers naively thought they could successfully wage in daylight, without fighter escorts. But the pressure was on Eighth Bomber Command to show the British just what the Eighth Air Force could do.

At the end of July, Colonel Frank A. Armstrong, a "West Pointer," and one of Eaker's original six staff officers at Eighth Bomber Command HQ that had accompanied him to England in February, took over command of the 97th Bomb Group, which was under-performing, from Colonel Cornelius W. Cousland. A tough, no-nonsense North Carolinian, erect in bearing and with a wind-tanned face (he had spent 14 of his 39 years in the cockpits of military aircraft), Armstrong commanded respect.

He turned the 97th around in short order, effectively taking the group apart and putting it back together again in just over two weeks. By mid-August, he was able to report to Eighth Bomber Command HQ that 24 crews were available for daylight combat missions. The group's Executive Officer, Major Paul W. Tibbets (who later commanded the B-29 that dropped the atomic bomb on Hiroshima in August 1945), was to play a crucial part in this reorganization and training. He later recalled:

B-24 of 93rd Bomb Group, October 9, 1942
(previous pages)

On October 9, 1942, 24 B-24Ds from the 93rd Bomb Group made the group's combat debut over the European continent. It was also the first time the Eighth Air Force had despatched more than 100 bombers (24 B-24s and 108 B-17s) on a mission. The five-group raid targeted the steel and engineering works and locomotive and freight car plant in the French city of Lille. Flying Fortresses from the 92nd, 97th, and 301st Bomb groups led the way, with the Liberators falling in behind. Over the target, the B-24s were optically targeted by the Flak defenses and hit by accurate fire. B-24D 41-23722 *Bomergang* of the 93rd Bomb Group's 328th Bomb Squadron received the most attention, with the bomber being nursed back to its Alconbury, Cambridgeshire, base by 1st Lieutenant John Stewart. Once the aircraft was back on the ground, crew chief Master Sergeant Charles A. Chambers could not believe the condition "his bomber" was in—more than 200 holes were counted in the fuselage and wings. However, it was repaired and returned to flying status and became the first B-24 to complete 50 missions in the ETO. (Artwork by Gareth Hector © Osprey Publishing)

The seven weeks of training between our arrival in England and our first raid paid off handsomely. I shudder to think of the results had it not been for the intensive practice afforded during this period. In the States, we had learned to fly the B-17, and that was about it. The bombardiers and gunners arrived in England with insufficient training. The RAF people recognized this too and were helpful in getting us ready for combat. Their fighters were sent up day after day so that we could practice rendezvous procedures with escort aircraft. The RAF even got some planes into the air to act as targets so that our gunners could develop the skills required to fire their weapons and operate turrets in combat.

For all their help, however, we soon learned that it would have made more sense to provide this training over the broad expanse of Texas, and other western states, instead of trying to cram our learning experience into the limited airspace over England. Crews arriving in Europe later in the war would be better trained before leaving the US.

Two groups of B-24D Liberators arrived in England in 1942 and a third in June 1943, but about half of the B-24s were sent to North

Africa between mid-December 1942 and late February 1943, to support Operation *Torch* (the Allied invasion of French North Africa) and several times the whole force was in North Africa. These deployed forces provided three of the five bomb groups used for the disastrous raid on the oil fields of Ploesti, Romania, Operation *Tidal Wave*, on August 1, 1943. Eighth Air Force B-24s were also a part of the very successful raid on August 13, 1943 against the Bf 109 factory at Wiener Neustadt, one of the most heavily defended targets in Europe.

Unfortunately for Liberator crews, they would live forever in the shadow of what they mockingly called "TOB," or "the other bomber." Studies show that the B-17 Flying Fortress is one of the "most recognized" names in aviation where the public is concerned. In contrast, the B-24—despite its numbers, its performance, and its contribution—has been pushed aside by the press coverage during the war and the torrent of postwar books, films, and documentaries centered on the B-17.

The Eighth Air Force in 1943 suffered a frequent dilution of strength because of frequent transfer of its bomber squadrons to the Mediterranean theater to support operations in North Africa, Sicily, and Italy. *Jerk's Natural*, a B-24D-1 of the 93rd Bomb Group, is seen here in England in 1943 after having returned from Mediterranean missions. It was lost over Austria on October 1, 1943. (NARA)

The B-24 had a larger bomb capacity than the B-17 and a longer range, but many crews felt that the B-17 was a more durable aircraft. Both aircraft were just as rugged and the B-24 was the more versatile of the two. In the Eighth Air Force, 1st and 3rd Bombardment divisions operated the B-17 and the 2nd Bombardment Division operated the B-24.

The B-24 had the same problem with head-on attacks as the B-17, but the B-24 had a very narrow nose so it could only carry a single 50-cal. center nose gun mounted to fire only in the horizontal plane. This armament left a blind spot which the upper turret could not cover. The B-24 was also unstable above 20,000ft and could not fly the close formations needed to counter Luftwaffe attacks. There were attempts to fly them in the same attacks with B-17s, but because of their different characteristics, especially speed, this proved impossible, and soon General Eaker began assigning the B-24s to tasks other than daylight bombing. The B-24s were also shuttled back and forth between Africa and England, and it was not until early September 1943 that the Eighth's three B-24 groups were back in England. A new group also arrived, bringing B-24 strength to four groups, while B-17 strength had increased to 16 combat groups, but the B-24s still made relatively little contribution to the Combined Bomber Offensive (CBO) in 1943.

On October 9, 1942, Eighth Bomber Command flew its first truly large-scale mission to Lille in France with 108 heavy bombers, including two dozen Consolidated B-24 Liberators on their first mission. The Luftwaffe made its first real effort against the American bombers, easily slipped past the large escort of British and American fighters, and shot down three B-17 and one B-24, as well as damaging many more. On this mission a problem arose that was to haunt Eighth Bomber Command right through to the end of 1943. The bombers' gunners claimed 56 German fighters destroyed and 26 probables, an impossible score since it would have accounted for 15 percent of the estimated Luftwaffe fighter strength in Western Europe. However, since Eighth Air Force's primary campaign objective was to destroy the Luftwaffe's day fighter arm, these claims went unchallenged. In fact, the Germans lost one fighter that day.

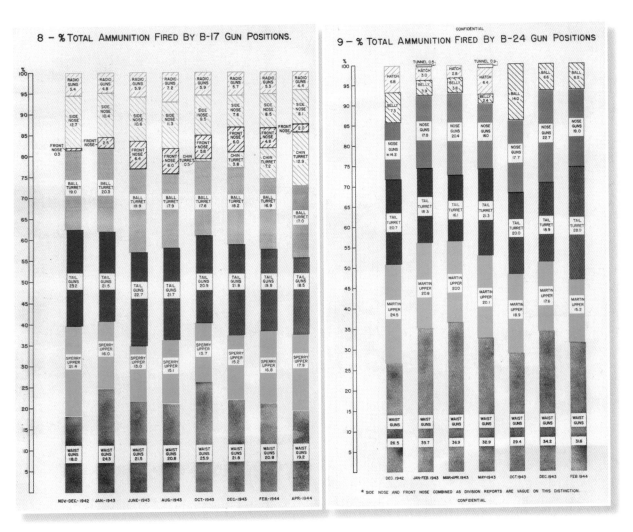

8 – % TOTAL AMMUNITION FIRED BY B-17 GUN POSITIONS.

9 – % TOTAL AMMUNITION FIRED BY B-24 GUN POSITIONS

The scale of American bomber attacks in 1942 was small and experimental until the force could be built up enough to confront more stiffly defended targets deeper into Europe. Through the end of 1942 its operational strength averaged only about 100 bombers, and it was assigned only a single US fighter group for escort. Its build-up was slowed by the need to divert aircraft and personnel to the Twelfth Air Force to conduct combat operations in North Africa and Italy. The focus of the bomber attacks in early 1943 was the German submarine force, including submarine bases at Lorient and St Nazaire as well as submarine yards on Germany's North Sea coast such as at Bremen and Wilhelmshaven.

These two graphics show the percentage of rounds fired from each gun position in the B-17 and B-24 from December 1942 until February 1944. Taken from *An Evaluation of Defensive Measures Taken to Protect Heavy Bombers from Loss and Damage: Operational Analysis Section, November 1944.* (Author's collection)

cron

1943: A DECISIVE YEAR

The short-range bomber missions from the autumn of 1942 through the spring of 1943 could be only partly protected by USAAF and RAF fighter escorts, which lacked the range of the heavy bombers. Missions into Germany could be escorted part of the way to the target area, and then during the return leg of the trip. Although losses during this initial period were sometimes costly, they were not heavy enough to cause US commanders to doubt the core idea of USAAF tactical doctrine: the viability of the self-defending bomber in daytime precision bombing. Losses in 1942 averaged 4.5 percent per mission, climbing to 7.1 percent in the first quarter of 1943 and 7.6 percent in the second quarter. Grossly exaggerated kill claims by the bombers' gunners led to the mistaken belief that the attacks were causing severe losses to the German fighter force.

By April 1943, the Eighth Air Force had only 264 heavy bombers and 172 escort fighters in England. The first mission against a German aircraft factory was conducted on April 5, 1943, against the Erla plant in Antwerp in Belgium, and the first mission against an aircraft factory in Germany itself was conducted on April 17, 1943, against the Fw 190 plant in Bremen.

Operation *Pointblank*

Operation *Pointblank* was among the most decisive air campaigns of World War II. Initiated in the summer of 1943, it aimed to cripple the German fighter force in advance of Operation *Overlord*—the amphibious invasion of Normandy in 1944. Although the campaign ostensibly was part of the Combined Bomber Offensive by both the RAF and the USAAF, in practice, the mission was undertaken primarily by the USAAF.

This fully armed B-17F *Thunderbird* was designated war-weary in late 1943. Many worn-out airframes were quickly used as VIP transports or whiskey haulers. With their stretched control cables and tired engines, pilots often found them a challenge to fly. (Author's collection)

Origins of *Pointblank*

When Roosevelt, Churchill, and other Allied leaders met at the Casablanca Conference in January 1943, one of the things they agreed to do was to attack Germany with bombers until a land invasion was possible. The RAF Bomber Command argued for the RAF's plan for night area bombing of German cities, but American generals George C. Marshall (US Army Chief of Staff), Henry "Hap" Arnold (Army Air Force Chief of Staff), and Eaker vigorously promoted the American plan for daylight precision strategic bombing. Eaker presented a briefing to Churchill, "The Case for Day Bombing," which he defined as round-the-clock bombing of Germany. Churchill liked this and accepted the idea.

There was an important subtext to this. All of the Army Air Force leadership wanted their command to become independent of the Army after the war, and they saw the daylight bombing campaign as a way to a postwar independent Air Force.

On May 18, 1943, the Combined Chiefs of Staff (CCS) approved the formal "Plan for the Combined Bomber Offensive from the United Kingdom," and in June 1943 the Combined Bomber Offensive (CBO) officially began. Eighth Bomber Command was to begin its role in the CBO under the name of Operation *Pointblank*, but the CCS had made it clear to the USAAF and the Eighth Air Force leadership that *Pointblank*'s objective was the defeat or destruction of the German day fighter force. *Pointblank* was only expected to prepare for an invasion, not to "win the war." While the RAF was included in *Pointblank*, at this point it simply could not hit German aircraft factories or airfields with any accuracy, so the destruction of the German day fighter force would be the responsibility of Eighth Air Force, as would most of the other targets that required precision bombing—the remainder of the German aircraft industry, ball-bearing plants, and oil.

As the pace of USAAF daytime attacks began to expand, the Luftwaffe responded by increasing the size of its day fighter force. Much of the defense against the early USAAF bomber strikes came from forward-deployed fighter units of Luftflotte 3 (Air Fleet 3) in France and fighter units based in the Netherlands. The Luftwaffe's heavy combat losses in the spring and summer of 1943 on the Russian

OPPOSITE The business end of a Bf 109G-6. Armed with two 13mm machine guns mounted on the top cowling and one 20mm cannon shooting through the propeller spinner, the G6's armament was too light and ineffective against the B-17 and B-24s of the Eighth Air Force. (Author's collection)

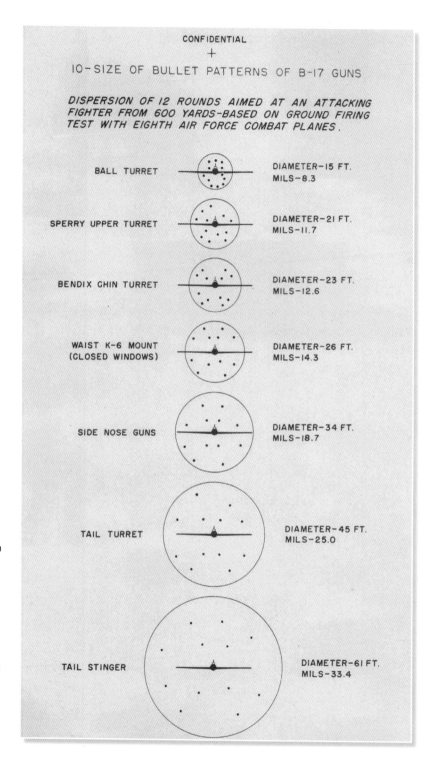

Bullet patterns of B-17 guns. These test results clearly showed that the turret-mounted guns had a tighter dispersion of rounds when firing at an enemy fighter. It must be remembered these test results were done on the ground and when stationary, and do not represent combat conditions. Hitting a small target like an attacking Bf 109 or Fw 190 from a moving B-17 was an extremely difficult task. (Author's collection)

and Mediterranean fronts made it difficult to form enough new fighter units, and much of the increase in Luftwaffe fighter strength in Germany came at the expense of the other theaters, with fighter units being drawn back into the Reich to deal with the American threat. The Luftwaffe day fighter force for Reich defense continued to grow through 1943, though there was a spirited debate over whether day fighters, night fighters, or Flak should receive priority.

By the summer of 1943, the USAAF had become confident enough to begin missions into central Germany, even without fighter escort on the main leg of the mission. The prime targets were aircraft-assembly plants and the ball-bearing industry around Schweinfurt. Ball bearings had been selected for special attention since they were widely used in many military weapons, including aircraft engines, and the German industry was geographically concentrated. Since the USAAF bomber force was still small, there was a special interest in finding these bottlenecks in German industry, an approach that Harris derided as "panacea targets."

During the summer, Eighth Bomber Command expanded in size to 16 groups of B-17s and four of B-24s, and now there were 580 B-17s, of which approximately 400 could be counted on to be airworthy for any one mission.

Schweinfurt and Regensburg, August 17, 1943

On August 17, 1943, the Eighth Air Force staged its largest and deepest-penetrating mission so far, a combined attack against the ball-bearing plants at Schweinfurt and the Bf 109 plant at Regensburg using 367 B-17 bombers.

One hundred and forty-seven B-17s of the 4th Wing, which had the long-range Fortresses with internally mounted, self-sealing "Tokyo" tanks, would strike the Regensburg Messerschmitt factory and then turn south and fly on over the Alps to Allied bases in Algeria. This move was expected to confuse the enemy defenses, who would be expecting the force to return to the United Kingdom.

The second raid by the 1st Wing would follow the Regensburg force by ten minutes on a parallel track, then turn slightly to strike the ball-bearing factories in the Schweinfurt area, and finally return

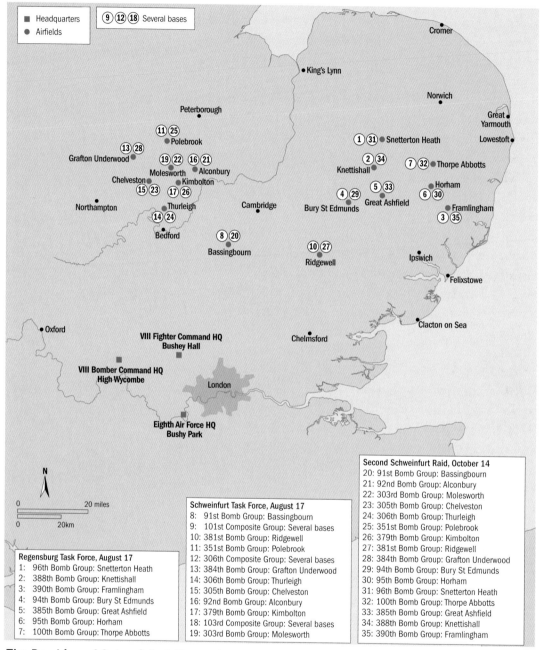

Regensburg Task Force, August 17
1: 96th Bomb Group: Snetterton Heath
2: 388th Bomb Group: Knettishall
3: 390th Bomb Group: Framlingham
4: 94th Bomb Group: Bury St Edmunds
5: 385th Bomb Group: Great Ashfield
6: 95th Bomb Group: Horham
7: 100th Bomb Group: Thorpe Abbotts

Schweinfurt Task Force, August 17
8: 91st Bomb Group: Bassingbourn
9: 101st Composite Group: Several bases
10: 381st Bomb Group: Ridgewell
11: 351st Bomb Group: Polebrook
12: 306th Composite Group: Several bases
13: 384th Bomb Group: Grafton Underwood
14: 306th Bomb Group: Thurleigh
15: 305th Bomb Group: Chelveston
16: 92nd Bomb Group: Alconbury
17: 379th Bomb Group: Kimbolton
18: 103rd Composite Group: Several bases
19: 303rd Bomb Group: Molesworth

Second Schweinfurt Raid, October 14
20: 91st Bomb Group: Bassingbourn
21: 92nd Bomb Group: Alconbury
22: 303rd Bomb Group: Molesworth
23: 305th Bomb Group: Chelveston
24: 306th Bomb Group: Thurleigh
25: 351st Bomb Group: Polebrook
26: 379th Bomb Group: Kimbolton
27: 381st Bomb Group: Ridgewell
28: 384th Bomb Group: Grafton Underwood
29: 94th Bomb Group: Bury St Edmunds
30: 95th Bomb Group: Horham
31: 96th Bomb Group: Snetterton Heath
32: 100th Bomb Group: Thorpe Abbotts
33: 385th Bomb Group: Great Ashfield
34: 388th Bomb Group: Knettishall
35: 390th Bomb Group: Framlingham

The Bombing of Schweinfurt–Regensburg

This mission, carried out by Boeing B-17 Flying Fortress heavy bombers on August 17, 1943, was an ambitious plan to cripple the German aircraft industry, and formed part of Operation *Pointblank*.

to the English bases over the reciprocal of its route to the target. Because of the distances, neither force would have enough fuel to vary its course.

It was expected that the raids would cause a large-scale air battle, so the escort would consist of all four operational P-47 groups—18 squadrons of Thunderbolts, most equipped with paper belly tanks (lightweight auxiliary drop tanks made out of glue-impregnated paper, for one-time use only)—and 16 squadrons of Spitfires.

The two forces' take-off was scheduled for dawn, but morning fog at all the bases forced a delay. The fog at the bases of the 4th Wing destined for Regensburg broke early and, since the Regensburg portion could not be delayed for more than an hour so that the bombers could land at the African bases before dusk, Eighth Bomber Command launched the 4th Wing immediately. The fog remained over 1st Division bases destined for Schweinfurt, so the chance for the two forces to go out together to split and confuse enemy defenses by a two-pronged thrust was lost.

Regensburg

The German controllers, warned of the raids by radio intercepts, were ready and waiting for the Regensburg raid. The Luftwaffe fighters began their head-on attacks on the third wing, mainly directed at the lowest group, and especially the low squadron of the low group, which suffered the heaviest losses. While the third combat wing was being battered, the Thunderbolts escorting the first two groups ran out of fuel and turned back, to see, to their dismay, B-17s going down from the third combat wing. The P-47 pilots, out of fuel, could only watch helplessly as the German pilots repeatedly pressed their attacks.

Once the escorts had left, the German fighters had a relatively easy time. The fighters usually ran out of fuel or ammunition after 30 minutes of combat, but there were so many bases along the route that the American force was attacked during virtually the entire run-in.

Of the 139 B-17s which had crossed the Dutch coast, 14 had been shot down, 13 from the last combat wing; two more had left their formations, released their bombs, and were flying south, hoping to cut a corner and catch up later; and one of the planes still with the

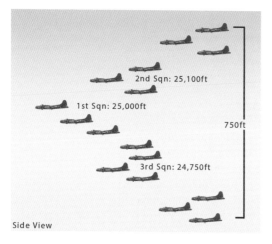

2nd Sqn: 25,100ft

1st Sqn: 25,000ft

750ft

3rd Sqn: 24,750ft

Side View

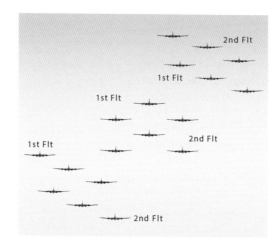

2nd Flt

1st Flt

1st Flt

2nd Flt

1st Flt

2nd Flt

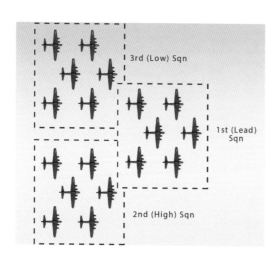

3rd (Low) Sqn

1st (Lead) Sqn

2nd (High) Sqn

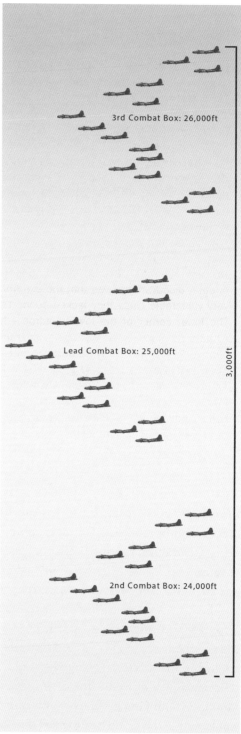

3rd Combat Box: 26,000ft

Lead Combat Box: 25,000ft

3,000ft

2nd Combat Box: 24,000ft

B-17 Formations, 1943 (opposite)

From late 1942, when the Luftwaffe began to aggressively attack, the primary concern of Eighth Bomber Command's formations was defensive. The first step was to have the bombers bomb in formation and drop when a "lead crew" dropped, rather than each bomber dropping on its own. For formations, Eighth Bomber Command first tried 18-aircraft formations in column in early 1943, but it soon became obvious that they would have to concentrate their formations to provide more firepower. To this end, rather than sending bombers in columns, Eighth Bomber Command decided in late April 1943 to stack the wing's groups, one 18-ship formation above and one below the lead group, and the other combat wings would follow three miles behind.

The large formations had many disadvantages—the major one being that they were very hard to maneuver with course changes—but they were still the most effective formation in terms of defensive firepower. Another disadvantage was that the extremities of the formations were very vulnerable since they lacked support from the rest of the group. The lower corner of the low squadron—the easiest for the German fighters to reach—was the most vulnerable, and was referred to as "Purple Heart Corner." A third disadvantage was that the high group often lost sight of the lead group if the lead group turned, and the formation spread out—a sure invitation for a German attack. The formations were constantly "tweaked" to try to improve their defensive capabilities, but there really was no perfect formation developed. In any of these formations, if a bomber was hit and dropped out of formation, it was usually quickly set upon and shot down.

formation had been forced to jettison its bomb load. This left 122 planes with bombs. The German fighters halted their attacks as the Fortresses reached the antiaircraft defenses over the target. Two of the groups in the leading combat wing had not been under serious attack and had so far suffered no casualties.

The Regensburg force lost 24 aircraft. Fourteen were shot down, two force-landed in Switzerland—the first battle-damaged USAAF warplanes to seek sanctuary there—four crash-landed in southern Europe, and four ditched in the Mediterranean off Tunisia. Most of the B-17s that were shot down were from the unescorted third combat wing, including ten from the 100th Group—the beginning of a long series of disasters that would lead to the group being called the "Bloody Hundredth."

Jim Laurier

Outbound to Schweinfurt, August 17, 1943
(previous pages)

A Holland-based Fw 190 bearing the colorful markings of II./JG 1 makes a head-on attack on a B-17F formation from the 91st Bomb Group, 1st Bombardment Wing, which was leading the first of two task forces on its way to Schweinfurt on August 17, 1943. The commander of the wing, Brigadier-General Robert Williams, was the co-pilot on one of the aircraft in this formation, but both his aircraft and the lead aircraft survived the mission.

In the rear, German Bf 110G night fighters are breaking off their attack. The 91st Bomb Group B-17s are flying in fairly tight formation, which provided good defensive firepower, but one of the bombers has already been hit in the cockpit area.

The formation gradually fell apart later in the raid as losses left gaps in the formation. The 1st Bomb Wing lost 36 B-17s on this raid, and the 91st lost seven of their 34. (Artwork by Jim Laurier © Osprey Publishing)

Schweinfurt

Meanwhile, with the German controllers focused on the Regensburg raid, the German listening services monitoring Eighth Bomber Command were surprised to hear the radio transmissions from the English bases that signaled another large-scale American bombing raid preparing to take off.

The Regensburg force's turn to Africa briefly confused the German controllers, but they quickly switched their attention to the four combat wings of the 1st Wing, 230 B-17s on their way to Schweinfurt three-and-a-half hours behind the Regensburg force. The limited range of the 1st Bomb Wing B-17Fs forced them to take the most direct route to Schweinfurt and back, almost precisely the route to Regensburg the 4th Wing had flown and the route the German controllers were expecting the Regensburg raid to use on the way back.

The plan was for the B-17s to fly at their normal altitude between 23,000ft and 26,500ft, and the escorting group, as normal, would fly slightly above them. But as the lead combat wing approached the coast, its task force saw a cloud bank in front of them; so, deciding that his heavily laden bombers could not fly over the clouds, he elected to fly his entire B-17 force under them. The escort fighter group for the first combat wing approached the rendezvous point at

the assigned altitude and tried in vain to locate the bombers below the clouds. The escort group never found the first force and had to return without engaging the Germans. The German controllers quickly saw this and followed their normal policy of attacking the weakest formations, sending the Luftwaffe fighters, including some Bf 109s firing Wfr. Gr. 21 aerial rockets, to attack the low group and the lead group of the first combat wing.

The fighters broke off their attacks as the bombers approached Schweinfurt, but the bombing there was not as effective as at Regensburg, probably because the bombers flew at a higher altitude and those in the rear combat wings were hampered by smoke from the leading raids. Still, they did a great deal of damage. Plant records indicate 80 high-explosive hits on the two main ball-bearing plants and that 663 machines were destroyed or damaged. Losses in the ball-bearing department were especially serious; there, production dropped from 140 tons in July to 69 in August and just 50 in September, and despite heavy demand output did not increase until November 1943.

The P-47s of the 56th Fighter Group, scheduled to escort the returning bombers, had climbed out at a low, fuel-saving power setting and retained their external fuel tanks. They made the rendezvous point

While a head-on pass was the least dangerous way to attack a bomber formation, the formation still had a number of guns firing forward. Here an Fw 190 has been hit and damaged after making a head-on pass through a B-17 formation. (NARA)

Jim Laurier

Thunderbolt Interception, August 17, 1943
(previous pages)

While covering the return of the Schweinfurt raid of August 17, 1943, the 56th Fighter Group led by Colonel "Hub" Zemke flew at a very economical fuel setting and was able to fly deeper into Germany than P-47s had ever flown before. The group actually overflew the exiting B-17 force and came around behind a large force of German fighters. The P-47s shot down several single-seat fighters and also caught a group of German Bf 110G night fighters.

Here Lieutenant Frank McCauley from the 61st Fighter Squadron, flying his P-47D Rat Racer, shoots down a Bf 110G from I./NJG 4 at about 1530hrs, one of 21 of the night fighters the Germans lost that day. These German night fighters had attacked the raid both on the way in and on the way out, but they were manned by inexperienced crews that had not scored many night kills yet and their rear-firing defensive weapons consisted of only one or two small-caliber machine guns. Nevertheless, the night fighters were a very valuable commodity because of their expensive radar equipment, and the German night-fighter crews who rarely saw a bomber were awestruck by "the overwhelming strength of the enemy air forces attacking our country." (Artwork by Jim Laurier © Osprey Publishing)

Major Gerald W. "Jerry" Johnson 61st Fighter Squadron, 56th Fighter Group P-47D serial no. 42-7877 HV-D. This posed shot shows the ground crew and the 75-gallon drop tank. This tank was standard issue for both the P-39 Airacobra and Curtiss P-40, and was in use long before being used by the 56th Fighter Group. (littlefriends.co.uk)

on time, but with the extra gas they had saved they overflew the B-17 formation to a point 15 miles beyond the German border, much farther east than the P-47s had ever flown before. They were undetected by several formations of German attackers below them, who were concentrating on getting into position to attack, and the P-47s swung in behind the surprised formations and shot down 16 German fighters, including at least five Bf 110G night fighters. These Bf 110Gs were a critical loss, not only of experienced crews but also of the aircraft and their scarce, sophisticated radar equipment.

Counting the Cost

The overall cost of the two raids was 60 B-17s (the previous high was 26 on the June 13 raid), plus approximately 60 men dead and wounded in returning bombers. In the 1st Wing, 36 B-17s were lost, most from the leading wing. From the 4th Wing, 24 were lost to various causes.

To compound the 4th Wing's losses, because of the inadequate maintenance facilities in North Africa only 60 of the 115 Fortresses that reached Africa were ready to fly back immediately, and the lack of replacement parts and servicing equipment delayed the return of many of the other B-17s for some weeks.

The Schweinfurt raid undermined USAAF faith in the viability of self-defending bombers. It was quite clear from operations research in 1943 that escort fighters substantially reduced the bombers' loss rate. Was it possible to develop a fighter with sufficient range to escort the bombers deep into Germany? In response to the Schweinfurt raid, the USAAF finally reoriented its policy on escort fighters and began accelerated efforts to develop long-range fighters for the Eighth Air Force.

Eighth Bomber Command's September 1943 reinforcement

Beginning in the fall of 1943, USAAF commander General Arnold's decision to give Eighth Air Force priority resulted in a huge influx of new bombers; the number of aircraft in heavy bombardment groups was increased from 35 to 62 planes, and now groups could fly two group boxes on a single mission. Additionally, in early September the

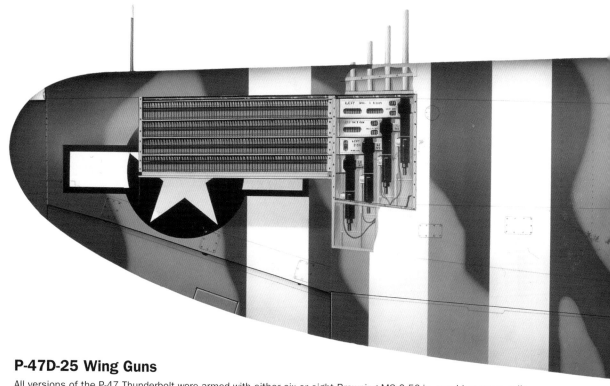

P-47D-25 Wing Guns

All versions of the P-47 Thunderbolt were armed with either six or eight Browning M2 0.50-in. machine guns, split three or four per wing. The wing magazines contained 425 rounds per gun, although this number had to be reduced to 267 rounds per gun from the P-47D-15 onwards if the fighter was carrying a bomb load of 1,000lb or additional fuel tanks affixed to its newly introduced underwing pylons (one per wing).
(Artwork by Chris Davey © Osprey Publishing)

Eighth's B-24 groups grew to four along with 16 B-17 combat groups. There were now six P-47 groups, two more than had been available on August 17, and there were also sufficient numbers of the very useful 75- or 108-gallon pressurized drop tanks.

A new Fortress model, the B-17G, began to reach squadrons in the form of replacement aircraft during September. It carried a Bendix remotely controlled "chin" turret, introduced on the YB-40 and found very useful for forward defense; it also gave the bombardier more room to operate.

On the German side, by mid-September 1943 the Luftwaffe was completely focused on defending the Reich and had drastically cut ground attack operations in the Soviet Union and the Mediterranean. The number of single-engine fighters facing the Eighth Air Force rose from approximately 300 in April to nearly 800 in October, about 65 percent of total German fighter strength.

Second Schweinfurt: Mission 115, October 14, 1943

Despite the recent heavy losses, with a forecast of good weather on October 14, Eighth Bomber Command scheduled a maximum effort return trip to Schweinfurt. All three bomb divisions were scheduled to fly the mission, and the Eighth hoped to send 360 B-17s and 60 B-24s, but losses from missions earlier in the month cut into this figure so only 291 B-17s actually launched. Since the route of the B-17s was beyond the normal combat radius of non-"Tokyo tank" B-17Fs, those planes had to carry one bomb bay fuel tank.

The force was dispatched in three groups, with 149 B-17s from the 1st Bombardment Division and 142 B-17s with Tokyo tanks from the 3rd Bombardment Division. The formations would cross enemy defenses roughly abreast, though some 30 miles apart, and then the courses would diverge slightly for deception. The plan called for the 1st Bomb Division to lead the train of bombers, followed by the 3rd Bomb Division, which was on a parallel course just ten miles to the south. As the B-17s approached Germany, almost 40 had aborted for various reasons. Because of the long distance to Schweinfurt, the B-17s had to fly a straight line to the target, which would make the German controllers' job easier. A third force of B-24s from the 2nd Bombardment Division was to fly a route to the south for a diversionary mission. Each force, including the B-24s, was assigned one group of P-47s to escort the bombers to the maximum fighter range.

The Germans were, as usual, alerted by their listening posts; the chief controller of the Holland center put his fighters on full alert and was calling down additional fighters 50 minutes before the American force approached the Dutch coast. By the time the B-17s crossed the coast, the Reichsluftverteidigung (RLV) had about 150 single-engine fighters ready, and every rocket-firing Bf 110 and Me 410 *Zerstörer* unit in Germany had been called to join in the fray.

German tactics repeated the successful pattern developed previously in late August when the twin-engine *Zerstörer* joined the force. Most of the rocket-firing *Zerstörer* units reached the bombers well before they arrived at Schweinfurt and made their first attacks from the rear, destroying or damaging a few bombers, but most

The 21cm Bordrakete became one of the most effective supplements to fighter armament in late 1943 to deal with US heavy bombers. Single-engine fighters like this Fw 190A-4/R6 received two launch tubes. (Author's collection)

importantly the rocket explosions spread out the formations of the combat boxes, thus making the attacks by the large number of single-engine fighters easier. Some single-engine fighters also carried rockets, usually in the ratio of one *Staffel* per *Gruppe*, and these made gun attacks after they fired their rockets.

All of the German pilots were under orders to keep attacking until forced to withdraw by damage or shortage of fuel or ammunition. Most of the single-engine fighters attacked in columns from the front, singling out the most scattered and vulnerable formations of the stream. The better *Jagdgruppen* reorganized and made repeated head-on attacks, but many formation leaders settled for beam attacks, which were less demanding for the German pilots, but were much less successful.

After leaving the target, the bombers made a wide turn south before taking the westerly route home in an attempt to confuse the enemy and stretch the range of his fighters, but the single-engine fighters continued to make heavy attacks.

In all, 60 B-17s were destroyed by the Luftwaffe in almost three-and-a-half hours of continuous attacks, and 17 more bombers were scrapped.

Those in charge of Eighth Air Force operations overestimated the degree of lasting damage inflicted on the Schweinfurt plants and it was generally felt, both in Eighth Air Force headquarters and in Washington, that the mission had been decisive.

Despite some efficiently executed and relatively effective bombing accomplished in the teeth of this concentrated opposition, the month's operations ended in discouragement and a decision to alter for the time being the conduct of the CBO insofar as it involved the American heavy bombers. At that point, Eighth Air Force was in no position to make further penetrations either to Schweinfurt or to any other objectives deep in German territory beyond the range of the P-47 escorts. The USAAF's doctrine of unescorted daylight bombing

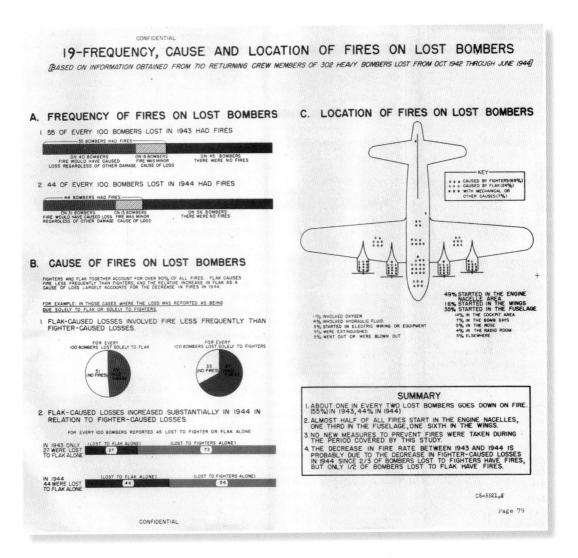

and self-defending bomber formations was dead. No more deep-penetration raids would be made into Germany until the bombers could be escorted all the way to the target. Eighth Air Force, which had never really managed air superiority over Germany, had for the time being lost even a pretense of it.

Morale at bomber bases was a major problem. The crews had been told time and again that the Luftwaffe fighter force was almost finished, but Fortress crews were currently incurring a casualty rate higher than any other branch of the US forces: during 1943, only about 25 percent of Eighth Air Force bomber crewmen completed their 25-mission tours—the other 75 percent were killed, severely

This graphic illustration comes from a report entitled *An Evaluation of Defensive Measures Taken to Protect Heavy Bombers from Loss and Damage: Operational Analysis Section, November 1944.* It revealed that one in every two bombers lost went down in flames with almost half of all fires started in the engine nacelle. (Author's collection)

wounded, or captured. It was difficult to persuade the men who survived Schweinfurt that the opposition encountered was the last effort of a beaten force. Almost certainly, if the bomber crews had known how few German fighters they were destroying, morale would have collapsed.

The value of fighter escort had been plainly demonstrated on many occasions—losses of Eighth Bomber Command per mission were averaging 1 percent when escorted, 7 percent when not escorted—and it had gradually been elevated to a position of paramount importance in planning future missions. The future of daylight strategic bombing would depend on the presence of fighter escorts with much longer range than the current P-47s, because fighter escort was the only answer to the deadly but relatively unmaneuverable twin-engine, rocket-firing German fighters which were peculiarly vulnerable to attacks by other fighters. No one knew this better than Army Air Force commander "Hap" Arnold, and on October 29 he ordered that all P-38 and P-51 production for the next three months was to be withheld from all other theaters and sent to the Eighth, showing the urgency of Eighth Air Force's need for long-range escorts.

1944: WINNING THE ARGUMENT
Preparing for D-Day

The raids against the ball-bearing industry around Schweinfurt in the summer and autumn of 1943 proved unexpectedly costly, and delayed the start of the final phase of the Operation *Pointblank* campaign. The solution was the use of long-range escort fighters such as the P-47D Thunderbolt and P-51B Mustang. The Luftwaffe remained convinced through the end of 1943 that improvements in fighter weapons and tactics would continue to cause such severe attrition against the USAAF daytime bombers that the campaign would be defeated.

By early 1944, the USAAF had accumulated sufficient heavy bombers and escort fighters to initiate the final phase of Operation *Pointblank*, codenamed *Argument*. In the final week of February 1944, the Eighth Air Force launched systematic bombing attacks on

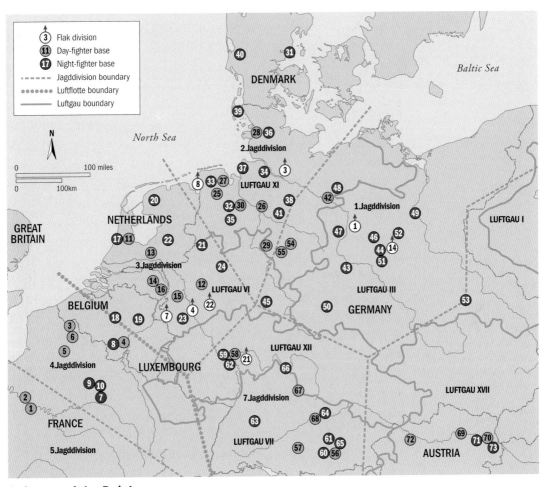

Defenses of the Reich

Shown here are the Reich's defenses against aerial attack in mid-February 1944.

the German aircraft industry, while at the same time staging a broader campaign against German day fighters by means of more aggressive fighter tactics.

The tactical aim of Operation *Argument* was to affect the Luftwaffe's "production-wastage differential." What this jargon meant was that the campaign had to suppress German fighter production as well as increase Luftwaffe fighter losses (wastage) in order to shrink the size of the German fighter force. This was a classic attrition strategy. With Allied intelligence raising growing doubts about the reliability of

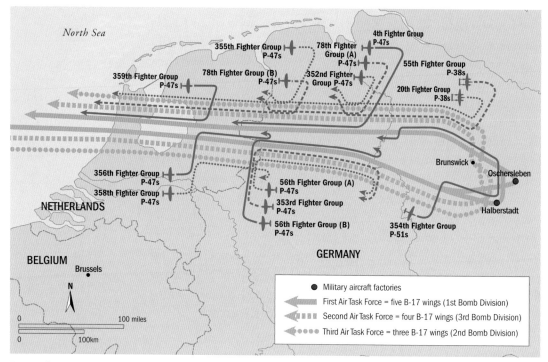

Escorting the Bombers

This map shows the fighter escort relay system used on a typical bombing mission, in this case against Oschersleben and Halberstadt, January 11, 1944. Shown here is the initial plan for the mission; weather conditions interfered with its actual execution. Because of the speed differential between the fighters and bombers, the fighter groups had to weave in their defensive zone to keep pace with the bombers.

bomber-gunner claims against German fighters, USAAF commanders sought other approaches to increasing the Luftwaffe's fighter attrition. General Arnold's 1944 new year's message to the Eighth and Fifteenth Air Force commanders concluded with the admonition: "This is a MUST—Destroy the Enemy Air Force wherever you find them, in the air, on the ground, and in the factories." While this might seem like a routine pep talk, it addressed one of the key tactical dilemmas facing the expanding deep-escort-fighter force. Should the fighters be confined to "close-escort" of the bombers, staying near the combat boxes and not pursuing the German fighters? Or should they be given free rein to chase down the fighters, even if it meant leaving the immediate vicinity of the bombers?

Major-General William Kepner, commander of Eighth Fighter Command, had been urging a more aggressive policy, a point of view apparently sanctioned by Arnold's letter. When Eighth Air Force's new commander Lieutenant-General James Doolittle visited Kepner's headquarters in early January 1944, he noticed a sign on the office wall that read: "The first duty of the Air Force fighters is to bring the bombers back alive." Kepner explained that the sign dated back to Hunter's days in command. Doolittle ordered the sign to be replaced by a new one reading: "The first duty of the Eighth Air Force fighters is to destroy German fighters." Doolittle amplified his intent by instructing Kepner that, "We'll still provide a reasonable fighter escort for the bombers, but the bulk of your fighters will go hunting for Jerries. Flush them out in the air and beat them up on the ground on the way home. Your first priority is to take the offensive." Doolittle's January directives fundamentally changed the dynamics of fighter combat during Operation *Argument* and had a decisive impact on its outcome.

"Big Week"

Mission 226 would kick off Operation *Argument*; this was what would eventually be called "Big Week." Operation *Argument* had 12 principal targets, all of which were major aircraft-assembly plants. The attack on February 20 was aimed at three clusters of these around Leipzig, Gotha, and Brunswick. The attack was aided by an RAF mission the night before against Leipzig, which helped exhaust the supply of Flak ammunition in that area. The 3rd Bombardment Division dispatched 314 B-17s to hit the Tutow plants in northeast Germany, while the 1st and 2nd Bombardment divisions sent out 417 B-17s and 272 B-24s to attack the plants in the Brunswick/Leipzig corridor. Fighter escorts totaled 835 aircraft, including 73 of the new P-51B fighters, but mainly comprised P-47 Thunderbolts. To further disrupt Luftwaffe fighter defenses, the heavy bomber force was preceded by two spoiling attacks by medium bombers of the Ninth Air Force against scattered targets along the Dutch coast.

The Luftwaffe response was poorly coordinated and many units of Luftflotte 3 failed to intercept the incoming force. The 1. Jagddivision was assigned to deal with the 3rd Bombardment Division attack toward Tutow, while the 2. and 3. Jagddivisions were assigned to

Thunderbolts streak into the attack. The P-47 and P-38 Lightning were the only fighters equipped with turbo-supercharged engines. This gave the P-47 exceptional performance at high altitude and gave its pilots a distinct advantage over their Luftwaffe counterparts. (Author's collection)

attack the main force. I Jagdkorps failed to group together any large attack formations and the fighters attacked in a disjointed fashion. Of the 362 Luftwaffe fighters taking off, only 155 managed to reach the US force. The Luftwaffe claimed 27 bombers and eight fighters against US reports of 26 bombers and six fighters lost or missing. However, German losses were high, totaling 28 fighters lost and 21 aircraft damaged beyond repair.

Operation *Argument* resumed on February 21, with RAF Bomber Command preceding the assault with a night attack on Stuttgart. The Eighth Air Force dispatched 861 bombers and 679 fighters against a variety of aircraft plants in the Diepholz–Achmer area. The Luftwaffe response was hampered by poor weather and only 282 fighters were launched. US losses were 23 bombers and eight fighters.

On the third day of Big Week, February 22, Eighth Air Force put up 799 bombers and 659 fighters, but poor weather over England forced the 3rd Bombardment Division to abort their mission to Schweinfurt, and ultimately only 255 bombers reached the target area around Oschersleben and Bernberg. This was the first mission where the Fifteenth Air Force was finally able to participate, operating from bases in Italy, sending 183 bombers toward Regensburg. In

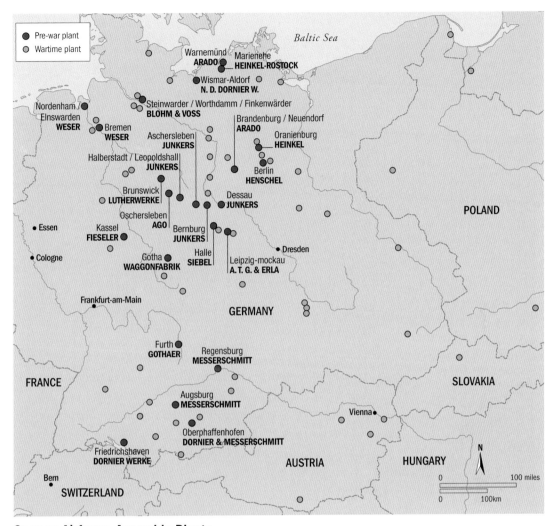

German Airframe Assembly Plants

Shown here are the locations of key targets for Allied bombing raids in 1944, in their efforts to cripple German military aviation production.

contrast to the two previous days, the weather conditions were good enough that I Jagdkorps was finally able to get its planes airborne in time to build up large attack formations, and they also took advantage of a gap in escort coverage, hitting the bombers hard. A total of 332 fighters took part, claiming 55 bombers and 11 fighters against actual total losses of 45 bombers and 12 fighters to all causes.

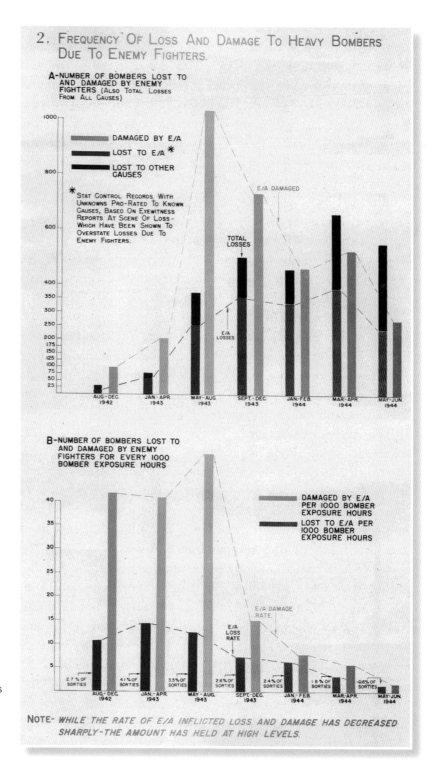

This graph clearly shows that losses of US bombers to Luftwaffe fighters remained high right into March of 1944. (Author's collection)

The next Eighth Air Force attack on February 24 was against the dreaded Schweinfurt area. Once again, the 3rd Bombardment Division staged a separate attack toward Rostock in northeast Germany while the 1st and 2nd divisions struck the primary targets at Schweinfurt and Gotha. The Fifteenth Air Force returned to Steyr; in all, some 923 bombers set off on the various missions. The German fighter response was intense and included a significant number of night fighters, totaling 336 fighters. The I Jagdkorps claimed 52 bombers and seven fighters against actual Eighth Air Force total losses of 46 bombers and ten fighters from all causes.

The attacks on February 25 were aimed primarily at southern Germany, with 754 bombers and 899 fighters from the Eighth Air Force and 176 bombers from the Fifteenth Air Force. A diversionary force was sent out toward the North Sea in hopes of distracting German fighters, and as a result both the 1. and 2. Jagddivisionen were alerted but not dispatched on intercept. Most of Eighth Air Force's losses that day were from Flak rather than fighters, with a total of 34 bombers lost to all causes. It was an especially successful mission from the bombing standpoint, causing extensive damage at the Regensburg and Augsburg plants.

The weather on February 26 again turned bad, ending the Big Week surge for the time being. In the week of attacks, the Eighth and Fifteenth air forces had conducted about 3,800 bomber sorties and dropped 10,000 tons of bombs. Bomber losses were lighter than anticipated, at 226 B-17s and B-24s, or about 6 percent; fighter sorties had totaled 3,673 with 28 losses, and total US aircrew losses were about 2,600 killed, missing, and captured. I Jagdkorps had never managed to seriously contest the attacks on the scale that they had accomplished in 1943, largely because of the presence of the USAAF escort fighters as well as the complications imposed by the winter weather. There had been only 1,412 Luftwaffe sorties, and losses had totaled 145 aircraft with 122 crew killed and 44 wounded—a loss rate of about 10 percent. Other units, including the 7. Jagddivision in southern Germany and elements of Luftflotte 3 in France and the Netherlands, had also taken part in the fighting but on a smaller scale. For example, the "Abbeville Boys," Jagdgeschwader 26 of Luftflotte 3, had seen considerable action on both February 24

Taken from the tail gunner's position, this color photo shows the B-17s of the 385th Bomb Group plowing through heavy Flak in January 1945. Smoke markers can be seen above the center B-17. The use of smoke markers indicates this was a "blind bombing" mission using H2S radar. (Author's collection)

and 25, and had claimed 32 bombers and eight fighters for a loss of 19 of their own fighters during Big Week. Total Luftwaffe fighter losses during Big Week were about 355, but even more critical was the loss of about 150 pilots.

The extent of the damage against the German aircraft plants was extensive, but not crippling. The Regensburg Messerschmitt plant was put out of action permanently; the Augsburg plant halted production for two weeks. The Leipzig plant had 160 new aircraft damaged, while at Gotha 74 aircraft were damaged or destroyed. Reich State Secretary Erhard Milch estimated that the attacks had cost the Luftwaffe the lost production of about 750 fighters.

Berlin—The Big City

Buoyed by Big Week's success, Doolittle selected Berlin as the next major target for the Eighth Air Force. While there were numerous aircraft-industry targets in the area, the main intent of the raid was to

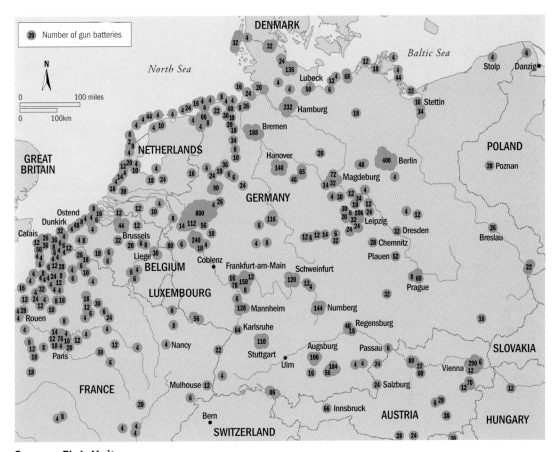

German Flak Units

Shown here are the dispositions of German Flak units in June 1944.

stir up the Luftwaffe in the hopes of accelerating the war of attrition. The first major attack was staged on March 6. Aside from some diversionary feints by Ninth Air Force medium bombers to draw away Luftflotte 3 fighters, the bombers' path was making directly for Berlin. A total of 814 bombers took off, of which 702 reached the target areas around Berlin. Their fighter escort was 801 Eighth Air Force fighters, plus additional support from the RAF and Ninth Air Force. The Luftwaffe answered with 528 sorties, with 369 fighters actually engaging in combat.

The air battles rivaled the intensity of the Schweinfurt missions six months earlier. The Berlin corridor was heavily saturated with Flak,

which discouraged fighter actions, though a number of German night fighters and scattered day fighters continued their attacks. Flak claimed 13 bombers and one fighter that day, and contributed to several other losses. By the end of the mission that afternoon, it had become the Eighth Air Force's bloodiest air battle on record, with some 69 B-17s and 11 escort fighters lost. Luftwaffe losses were 66 aircraft shot down or damaged beyond repair, or one out of every five that had engaged in combat. The losses were especially heavy in the twin-engine units, with the Bf 110 and Me 410 day fighters losing 40 percent of those participating and the Bf 110 night fighters losing nine out of 18. Both sides claimed the Berlin battle as a victory, with the German press trumpeting the loss of 140 American bombers. Actual bomb damage on the ground had been light, as cloud cover and combat interfered with targeting. Yet in spite of the heavy losses, the Eighth Air Force had scored a major propaganda victory, conducting an assault on the German capital in broad daylight. The loss rate at around 10 percent was heavier than average. The Eighth Air Force campaign against Berlin was relentless. Two days later, on March 8, 623 bombers attacked the Erkner ball-bearing plant in Berlin's southern suburbs. The attack followed the same path as before over northern Germany, and I Jagdkorps responded in the same fashion, first forming up a large *Gefechtsverband* near Brunswick from Jagdgeschwader 1 and Jagdgeschwader 11. The scale of the German attack was smaller than before because of the number of damaged aircraft, and only 282 fighters were launched. US losses were 40 bombers and 34 fighters; German losses were 42 fighters. On March 9, the bombers returned to Berlin and the Hanover area with 490 bomber sorties. This time, I Jagdkorps did not even attempt to respond, hampered by casualties and the thick cloud cover; US losses were 11 bombers to Flak and weather.

The next large operation was a deep attack against Augsburg in southern Germany on March 16, with 675 bombers and 868 escort fighters. This time both I Jagdkorps and the autonomous 7. Jagddivision responded with 266 fighter sorties. It was a very bad day for the Luftwaffe twin-engine fighters and Zerstörergeschwader 76 was jumped by Mustangs whilst forming up, losing 23 of its 77 fighters. Losses at the end of the day were 23 US bombers and ten

OPPOSITE Like a medieval castle, the "Holy Ghost" Flak tower in Hamburg stands as a mute testament to the considerable resources allocated to the *Flakwaffe* by Hitler during the war. These huge structures (also found in Berlin and Vienna) were in fact air raid shelters with Flak batteries on top of them. (Author's collection)

"Bandits, 1 O'clock Low" (previous pages)

An element of P-51B Mustang fighters of the 363rd Squadron, 357th Fighter Group, peel off to intercept a group of Fw 190 fighters attempting to intercept a B-17 formation above during the March 1944 air battles of Operation *Pointblank*. The P-51B in the foreground, *Glamourus Glen*, is flown by Flight Officer Chuck Yeager, who later went on to fame as the first pilot to break the sound barrier in the Bell X-1 rocket plane. The Mustang immediately above Yeager's is Captain Clarence "Bud" Anderson's *Old Crow*. Anderson ended the war with 16¼ victories.

Although the P-51B had an excellent radius of action, the addition of a pair of 75-gallon drop tanks enabled the Mustang to fly deep into Germany. It was the practice to keep these tanks in place until the fuel was exhausted, but the fighters would release the tanks on contact with enemy fighters because of the hazard they presented in a dogfight, both from their drag and their flammability. Compared with German fighters like the Fw 190, the P-51B was not especially well-armed, with four .50-cal. machine guns, but this was adequate as the P-51 was fighting enemy fighters, not heavy bombers. (Artwork by Steve Zaloga © Osprey Publishing)

A formation of B-17 bombers flies through heavy Flak. (Public Domain)

escorts; German losses were 46 fighters, and Zerstörergeschwader 76 was pulled out of combat. The Eighth Air Force returned to Berlin on March 22 in overcast weather and conducted radar bombing through the cloud; I Jagdkorps made no effort at all to intercept under these weather conditions and with the battered state of its force.

I Jagdkorps' commander, "Beppo" Schmid, later assessed the lessons of the March fighting: "American losses during Big Week had no effect whatsoever on American operations. American air forces captured air supremacy over the entire Reich except for the more distant east. The bombing of Berlin and Munich meant the collapse of German air power."

Beyond Operation *Pointblank*: Transportation vs Oil

The Combined Bomber Offensive and Operation *Pointblank* formally ended on April 1, 1944. This marked a command transition of the strategic bomber forces from control by the Combined Chiefs of Staff to control by Eisenhower's Supreme Headquarters Allied Expeditionary Force (SHAEF). Under the original scheme, USSTAF (United States Strategic Air Forces) switched from Portal's command to a new Allied Expeditionary Air Force (AEAF) command under Air Marshal Trafford Leigh-Mallory. Arnold and Lieutenant-General Carl Spaatz, commander US Strategic Air Forces, were not happy about the switch, both because of concerns about Leigh-Mallory's judgment as well as serious disagreements over tactics and strategy. Leigh-Mallory's leadership was further undermined by his strong disagreements with his fellow RAF commander, Arthur Harris of Bomber Command. While Spaatz understood that at some point the USSTAF would be taken off its strategic missions to support Operation *Overlord* (the Battle of Normandy), Harris was adamant that Bomber Command be reserved for strategic missions and that support for *Overlord* should be undertaken solely by the tactical air forces, which were better suited to the task. To mediate the disputes Eisenhower turned to Arthur Tedder, his RAF air deputy, who had served with him in the Mediterranean theater in 1943 and who served as Deputy Supreme Commander AEF for Operation *Overlord*.

Spaatz tried to convince Eisenhower and Tedder that the USSTAF had enough strength in the spring of 1944 to simultaneously engage in a continued strategic campaign into Germany while also conducting the necessary missions to support *Overlord*. The Ninth Air Force had been specifically deployed in Britain to conduct tactical missions, which gave the Eighth Air Force freedom to continue its strategic missions. At the heart of the AEAF's mission for the USAAF and RAF strategic bombers was the "Transportation Plan." It had been conceived by Professor Solly Zuckerman, and it aimed to sever the main rail links between Germany and the Normandy battlefield by concentrated attacks on rail choke points such as bridges and marshaling yards. Spaatz did not feel that the Transportation Plan represented the best use of the Eighth Air Force, and offered his own alternative, dubbed the "Oil Plan."

The Oil Plan was intended to be a continuation of Operation *Pointblank*, but with updated priorities. Since most of the aircraft-assembly plants had been bombed during *Pointblank*, the emphasis would shift to the German fuel industry, and especially to the synthetic-fuel plants that provided all of the Luftwaffe's high-octane aviation fuel. Destruction of 14 synthetic-fuel plants and 13 refineries would eliminate 80 percent of production, 60 percent of refining capability, and substantially reduce available German fuel supplies. Spaatz's resistance to the Transportation Plan was echoed from other influential corners, notably Field Marshal Alan Brooke, chief of the British Imperial General Staff. To complicate the debate further, in mid-April Churchill began to push for an acceleration of the campaign against the suspected German V-weapon "Crossbow" launch sites. These had already been targeted by the Eighth Air Force under its "Noball" program when weather over Germany prevented missions there. However, Churchill was pushing this mission as the top priority over Luftwaffe, oil, or transportation targets, to the consternation of Spaatz and Harris, who believed the attacks to be a complete waste of heavy bombers. Indeed, the devastating attacks on the original V-1 "ski" sites had forced the Luftwaffe to shift to other basing options, but construction continued at the ski sites to distract Allied bombers and cause them to continue to waste bombs attacking them.

In the end, the targeting decisions eventually became a mixture of all of these various objectives. Weather played a critical factor in any precision-bombing mission, and as often as not a bad-weather day

over Germany left alternate targeting opportunities in France. During the third week of April, after heated debate, Eisenhower gave Spaatz permission to begin his oil campaign.

The Oil Campaign, May 1944

After the April 20 agreement with Tedder, the Eighth Air Force had to wait until May 12 for sufficiently clear weather. The attack included 886 bombers from all three divisions and 735 Eighth and 245 Ninth Air Force fighters, targeting 13 separate fuel facilities.

The Luftwaffe fighters and Flak cost the attacking force 46 bombers and seven escorts, but Luftwaffe losses were severe, including 65 fighters. Leadership losses were also grave.

The May 12 attacks on the hydrogenation plants had been effective: the Zeitz plant was hardest hit and lost 16 weeks of output; the Brüx and Tröglitz plants were shut down and lost seven weeks' output while the Böhlen and Leuna plants lost half or more of their capacity. Speer reported to Hitler on May 19 that: "The enemy has struck us at one of our weakest points. If they persist at it this time, then we will soon no longer have any fuel production worth mentioning. Our one hope is that the other side has an air force general staff as scatterbrained as ours." Schmid was equally grim in his assessment, judging that, "On this day, the technological war was decided."

Regardless of the success in suppressing Luftwaffe fighters, German Flak remained a dangerous threat. This B-24, named *Little Warrior*, of the 862nd Bomber Squadron, 493rd Bomb Group, piloted by Lieutenant Jon Hansen, was hit in its #3 engine by Flak on a mission against the aircraft-engine plant near Fallersleben on June 29, 1944. The Flak damage ignited the fuel tanks and most of the crew was killed in the ensuing crash. A memorial to the crew of *Little Warrior* stands today outside the elementary school in McKees Rocks, Pennsylvania. (NARA)

The heavy Luftwaffe fighter losses in 1944 substantially reduced bomber losses in the autumn of that year, and Flak became a more significant factor in American aircraft loss. Here, a B-17G runs through a Flak barrage over Kassel on September 22, 1944. (NARA)

An attempt to attack the hydrogenation plants in Silesia in eastern Germany on May 13 was largely frustrated, but a massive May 28 attack of 1,341 bombers and 1,224 fighters against a large number of fuel-related targets and aircraft led to another major air battle. The day's attack was again costly on both sides, with 33 bombers and 12 fighters lost to Luftwaffe fighters and Flak; German losses were between 52 and 78 shot down or damaged beyond repair. The effect of the bombing on the oil plants was not as dramatic as on May 12, with only the Zeitz plant being severely damaged. Nevertheless, the May 28 battle showed the diminishing ability of the Luftwaffe to deal with bomber attacks.

By mid-June 1944, Allied intelligence estimated that German synthetic-fuel capacity had been reduced from 1,200,000 tons per month to 670,000 tons, and that the Wehrmacht required at least 1,000,000 tons per month for operational efficiency. Allied intelligence had recognized that it had finally found a vital target that was exceptionally vulnerable to bomber attack.

Operation *Overlord*

From the USAAF's perspective, Operation *Pointblank* had been a costly success. Although its goal was reached, it had not occurred in the way the USAAF had expected. The initial conception had been that "self-defending" bombers could devastate the German aircraft plants, ending fighter production and thereby winning air superiority. In fact, both of these tenets proved to be false. The "self-defending" bomber proved to be a failure in the face of tough Luftwaffe opposition. The senior leadership of the USAAF proved pragmatic and adaptable under the circumstances, abandoned their cherished doctrine, and vigorously supported a crash program to field a substantial deep-escort force by early 1944. The combination of fuel-extension programs for the P-47 and P-38 and the arrival of the superior P-51 were important ingredients in the eventual success of the escort fighter. However, they were not the only factor. Arnold, Doolittle, and Kepner also switched the tactical doctrine from close-bomber support to mixed tactics encompassing free-ranging attacks on German fighter formations and air bases. The results were dramatic and proved to be a tipping point in the air campaign over Germany.

The USAAF expected that precision-bombing attacks against German fighter-assembly plants could shrink or collapse the Luftwaffe fighter force. This proved to be a chimera. German fighter production actually increased from 1943 to 1944. This aspect of the USAAF plan was unsuccessful in part because Allied intelligence had little reliable intelligence on the German aircraft industry and was not aware of Milch's fighter-production expansion plan. Although Operation *Pointblank* failed to cut Luftwaffe fighter production, it did manage to place a limit on the expansion planned by Milch. For example, Milch's Program 224, from October 1, 1943, anticipated the production of 13,400 single-engine fighters in the first half of 1944 when actually only 6,650 to 9,485 were produced. The scale of German fighter production in 1944 is more obscure than generally recognized. The postwar US Strategic Bombing Survey on the aviation industry indicated that German fighter production more than doubled from 1943 to 1944, going from 11,738 to 28,529

Minus its drop tanks, this 360th Fighter Group P-51D serial no. 44-15056 has just completed another long-range escort mission in April 1945. The group consisted of the 359th, 360th, and 361st Fighter squadrons. Even with the bubble canopy this Mustang still has a rear-view mirror attached on the top of the forward canopy bow. (Author's collection)

An atmospheric view from the Martlesham Heath control tower of the 356th Fighter Group, 1944. The P-51Ds nearest the camera sit in sandbagged revetments. The threat of Luftwaffe attack by this point in the war was next to zero, making the revetments obsolete. (littlefriends.co.uk)

according to Speer's ministry's data. What has not been as widely noted was that a separate report by the Military Analysis Division found that German statistics on fighter production were exaggerated for internal political reasons and probably overstated German fighter production by as much as 30 percent. Accounting tricks made the fighter program seem like a miracle to Hitler, but the purported increase in new fighters manufactured did not translate into comparable growth in operational-fighter strength.

The results on the Luftwaffe were dramatic. Luftwaffe leadership was unprepared for escort fighters that could range so deeply into Germany. The Luftwaffe single-engine fighter force suffered catastrophic losses from the last quarter of 1943, with 1,052 fighters lost, 2,180 in the first quarter of 1944, 3,057 in the second quarter of 1944, and a staggering 4,043 fighters in the third quarter of 1944. To put this in some perspective, the Luftwaffe lost more single-engine fighters in the West from July to September 1944 than they lost in two whole years on the Eastern Front from September 1942 to September 1944.

Luftwaffe fighter-pilot losses were grim. For example, 462 crewmen were lost in May, including 275 dead and 185 wounded, or about three out of every five. When Feldmarschall Hugo von Sperrle canvassed his command in July 1944, he found that with rare exceptions only group and squadron commanders had operational experience of over six months. Of the remainder, a small percentage had been in combat for three months, but the majority had been in combat for only eight to 30 days.

The effects of the air battles over Germany in January–May 1944 were evident in the skies over Normandy on D-Day, June 6, 1944. Luftflotte 3 in France had been held back from some of the worst May 1944 air battles in hopes of conserving its strength for the expected invasion. Nevertheless, its paltry forces could do nothing in the face of the massive scope of Allied missions on D-Day, which totaled about 13,700 sorties. The Allies had total air superiority and the Luftwaffe fighter force was almost completely ineffective against this vast armada. The fighter units of Luftflotte 3 on D-Day claimed to have shot down 24 Allied aircraft out of the approximately 130 lost that day to all causes; Luftwaffe fighter losses were 16. The emaciated state of the Luftwaffe fighter force in the West was largely attributable to the Operation *Pointblank* air battles of the previous several months. It took Luftflotte 3 the remaining three weeks of June to match the number of sorties that the Allies had conducted on D-Day alone, a 20-fold difference in sortie rates.

Luftwaffe strength in France increased in June and July as more units were pushed forward from the Reich defense force. However, the Luftwaffe never managed to seriously challenge Allied air supremacy in the summer and autumn battles either over France or Germany. While the Luftwaffe sometimes staged major surge operations, for example the attacks on the Seine River crossings in mid-August 1944, they were never able to seriously contest Allied air dominance. In mid-August, Hitler was so frustrated at the ineffectiveness of the Luftwaffe Reich-defense force that he instructed Luftwaffe Generalmajor Adolf Galland to deploy the Luftflotte Reich units to the west in a tactical role, and told Speer to cut fighter production in favor of Flak. The German war industries were in an irreversible descent to annihilation.

1945: CRIPPLING NAZI GERMANY

January 1945 marked the start of the Eighth's fourth year of operations, and it seemed as if the end of the war was in sight. The following month, Prime Minister Winston Churchill and President Franklin D. Roosevelt agreed on massive air attacks on the German capital and other cities such as Dresden and Chemnitz. These cities were not only administrative

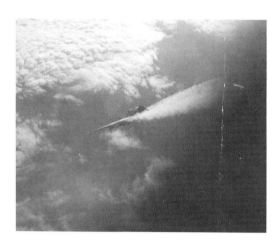

B-17 42-97170 *Julie Mae* collided with B-17 42-97833 *Silver Dollar*, both of 379th Bomb Group, over France on December 9, 1944. *Julie Mae*, seen here, was cut in half with no survivors. *Silver Dollar* was heavily damaged but managed to land on an Allied airfield in France. (Author's collection)

centers controlling military and civilian movements, but also the main communication centers through which the bulk of the enemy's war traffic flowed.

Spaatz had set the wheels in motion with the February 3 raid on Berlin. The cities of Magdeburg and Chemnitz were bombed three days later, but the most devastating raids of all fell upon the old city of Dresden in eastern Germany, starting with an 800-bomber mission by the RAF on the night of February 13. Two waves of "heavies" produced firestorms and horrendous casualties among the civilian population. The next day, 400 US bombers attempted to stoke up the fires created by RAF Bomber Command, while a further 900 attacked Chemnitz, Magdeburg and other targets. Although Eighth Air Force crews were to return to the pottery city of Dresden again in March and April, the Allied air forces' top priority remained the oil-producing centers.

On February 22, 1945, Operation *Clarion* (the campaign to destroy the German communications network) was launched. More than 6,000 Allied aircraft from seven different commands were airborne that day, and they struck at transportation targets throughout western Germany and northern Holland. All targets were selected with the object of preventing troops being transported to the Eastern Front, now only a few miles from Berlin.

By April, bomber crews were now hard-pressed to find worthwhile targets, and the planners switched attacks from inland targets to coastal areas. Beginning on April 5, the weather over the Continent improved dramatically, and the B-17s were sent to U-boat pens on the Baltic coast.

April 16 saw General Spaatz announce an end to the strategic mission of the Eighth Air Force. The strategic air offensive against Germany is credited with crippling the Third Reich's ability to continue the war. For nearly three years, by day and night, the Allies had pulverized Germany's cities and factories, paralyzed its transport system, terrorized and killed its civilians, and eventually smashed its armies as they defended their ever-shrinking territory. They had truly become "Masters of the Air."

Trolley Runs

On April 26, 1945, the crews of the Mighty Eighth flew their final sorties over a Germany that had been largely reduced to rubble. Adolf Hitler committed suicide in his Berlin bunker, Soviet tanks rolled into Berlin, and hostilities came to an end in Europe on May 7, 1945. The Eighth Air Force promptly mounted a new campaign, the aim of which was to provide "all ground (non-rated) personnel with an opportunity of seeing the results of their contribution in the strategic air war against Germany."

Known as the "Trolley Runs," these flights began in early May 1945. Flying Fortresses and Liberators took thousands of ground crew on extensive sightseeing tours of the ruins of marshaling yards, aircraft plants, and cities. "Many of us never imagined there could be such destruction," said Staff Sergeant John Foster of the 93rd Bomb Group, who had flown missions in both the Eighth and Fifteenth air forces. "All the time we thought they were beating the hell out of us, we were putting them out of business."

In total, over 2,000 ground crew took part in these runs, flown by the Eighth Air Force's most experienced pilots. Safety was a key concern, and pilots were ordered to maintain an altitude of 1,000ft for the whole flight and were not permitted to circle any particular locations. The flights were also accompanied by an observer plane. However, several fatalities did occur on the runs, the result of crashes and mid-air collisions.

The ruins of Cologne, Germany, from the air in 1945. (US Army)

Crews of the 92nd Bomb Group pose for the camera before the B-17 *Flagship* during a decoration ceremony at Alconbury, England, on July 3, 1943. (NARA)

CHAPTER 3

ORGANIZATION OF THE EIGHTH AIR FORCE

Air and Ground Units

The Eighth Air Force was activated at Savannah, Georgia, January 28, 1942. In February, a small detachment of officers arrived in England to make initial arrangements for the housing and basing of groups to follow, and by June 1942, aircraft crews and ground personnel had begun to arrive in the UK. On August 17, 1942, the first operational mission with its own aircraft was carried out by the Eighth Air Force, the first of 459 days on which heavy bombers and fighters struck at enemy targets.

At peak personnel strength, the Eighth Air Force numbered more than 200,000 officers and men. At peak operating strength, it numbered 40½ heavy bomb groups, 15 fighter groups, two photo/recon groups, one scouting group, one emergency rescue squadron, and two fighter training groups from bases in the UK. At this strength, a typical mission consisted of 1,400 heavy bombers escorted by 800 fighters, consuming 3,500,000 gallons of aviation gasoline, expending 250,000 rounds of 50-cal. ammunition, destroying 25 German aircraft in the air and on the ground for the loss of four US fighters and five bombers, and dropping 3,300 tons of bombs on enemy targets, of which on visual

A P-51 Mustang being unloaded at the Liverpool docks. Next step would be final assembly at Burtonwood, test flight, and then delivery to a squadron. Between 1943 and 1945, over 11,500 aircraft were processed through the Burtonwood base. (Author's collection)

missions 40 percent fell within 1,000ft of the assigned MPIs (Mean Points of Impact) and 75 percent within 2,000ft.

AIR UNITS

The squadron was the smallest unit with both tactical and administrative responsibilities, and the unit with which airmen most closely identified. Squadrons were classified as bombardment (very heavy, heavy [B-17 and B-24], medium, and light) and fighter (single-engine, two-engine, night, fighter-bomber).

A single common model of aircraft was assigned to a given squadron. Heavy Bombardment squadrons had 12 B-17 or B-24s, Fighter squadrons initially had 16 aircraft, but 25 by 1944.

A new B-17/B-24 heavy bomber base would accommodate the following:

- One Bomb Group of four flying squadrons plus a Service Group or Squadron
- 72 B-17/B-24s, plus reserves
- Average base personnel: 2,500
- 144,000 gallons of aviation fuel storage
- 3,000 tons of bombs of various sizes.

A fighter base could accommodate the following:
- One Fighter Group of three flying squadrons, plus a Service Group or Squadron
- 75 to 108 P-38s, P-47s, or P-51s including reserves, and 75 to 108 pilots
- Average base personnel: 1,200
- 72,000 gallons of aviation fuel storage
- 1,000 tons of bombs.

The group, roughly analogous to a ground battalion, was normally commanded by a lieutenant-colonel. Groups were made up of two to four squadrons, usually with the same model of aircraft, though some composite groups existed with mixed types. Bomb groups usually had four squadrons while fighter groups had three. The group was the basic air unit for planning combat missions; e.g. three bombardment groups, escorted by two fighter groups, might be assigned to a specific bombing mission. An entire group might be based at a single field, in which case its squadrons' technical and service divisions might be centralized under group control.

Two or more groups could be organized into a wing. The wing was principally a tactical planning headquarters, but also had administrative and support functions.

The division was employed in only limited instances, particularly in the Eighth Air Force, where the 1st, 2nd, and 3rd Bombardment divisions each controlled four wings. These divisions, commanded by brigadier-generals, contained common model aircraft: the 1st and 3rd with B-17s and 2nd with B-24s. A heavy bombardment squadron had 67 officers and 360 enlisted men, but fewer than 170 personnel were on flying status. The 1944 single-engine fighter squadrons had 39 officers and 245 enlisted men.

GROUND CREWS AND PERSONNEL

Of the over 2,000,000 personnel assigned to the USAAF at war's end (down from a peak 1944 strength of 2,372,292), the vast majority were involved with keeping aircraft flying and supporting the proportionally small numbers of actual flyers.

Lieutenant Richard G. Thieme's 505th Fighter Squadron, 339th Fighter Group P-51D 44-14705 6N-W *Boomerang* undergoing maintenance. Crucial to any fighter squadron was the number of aircraft ready and available for operations. Poor serviceability rates meant lower combat effectiveness. Quality maintenance personnel were just as important as a good fighter pilot. (littlefriends.co.uk)

Many unit histories tend to gloss over the work of the non-flying personnel with a few words of faint praise, despite their critical contribution to overall mission effectiveness. Yet a pre-occupation with combat accounts comes at the price of an incomplete understanding of what it took for a combat unit to succeed, especially in mid-20th-century mechanized warfare.

Lewis Lyle, though, spoke up for his ground-based comrades in the 303rd Bomb Group throughout the war when he paid them this warm tribute: "The ground echelon of our group never let us down during the three-and-a-half years of our wartime existence. The support we had at every level, from the cooks, drivers, guards, clerks, administrators, and our chaplains, plus the intelligence, armament, bomb loading and supply personnel, was outstanding. And who could ever forget the magnificent support we received from the depot group and the line maintenance people?"

Ground units assigned or attached to the Eighth Air Force provided a wide variety of support functions and included quarter master supply, ordnance supply and maintenance, signal, transportation, medical, chemical, weather, engineer, and military police units. There were well over 150 types of AAF ground units, and more than 30 types of Army Service Forces units attached to the AAF.

The Mental Toll

As flying operations increased from late 1942, the physiological effects of constant combat began to appear. Men became jumpy and anxious, and the terms "Focke-Wulf jitters" and "Flak happy" became common terms. Eighth Air Force flight surgeons quickly observed that the absence of a fixed, limited tour of duty would invariably lead to fatigue, anxiety, and emotional breakdown. Colonel Grow, Surgeon of Eighth Air Force, realized in 1942 that morale was beginning to sag and was "not all that it should be to obtain the maximum efficiency in operational missions."

No immediate action was taken and, during the winter of 1942-43, morale sank to disturbing levels. Finally, in March 1943, a study entitled *Morale in Air Crew Members, 8th Air Force Bomber Command* recommended a definite and fixed combat tour of duty be established. In response, General Ira Eaker directed bomber crews to fly 25 combat missions and fighter pilots were limited to 150 missions or 200 operational flying hours before being taken off combat operations. This didn't last long and in August 1944 a combat tour of duty for a bomber crew was increased to 35 missions.

Bomber crews quickly did the math and realized that if the average loss rate was 5 percent per mission, they would not survive 25 missions.

By December 1942, evidence of mental stress, combat fatigue, and more serious psychological disorders began to appear. On the recommendation of Eighth Air Force Surgeon, Colonel Grow, rest homes were soon established. Those diagnosed with combat fatigue would be sent to these homes for an average of seven days' rest and recreation. By December 1944, there were 17 rest homes in operation.

In the case of extreme flying fatigue or mental breakdown, crews were sent to the 5th General Hospital, where they would receive psychiatric and psychological care. In Europe, 3,067 neuropsychiatric cases resulted in removal from flying, of which, 1,042 were permanent.

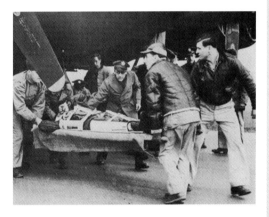

Casualties are removed from an Eighth Air Force bomber in 1943.

Medical Units

Every air base had a serviceable dispensary and sick bay building with bed space for 20–45 patients. The flight surgeons and corpsmen of the medical dispensary were the first on scene to care for the wounded when the bombers returned. Many were respected for the compassion they brought to their work. The mildly ill and slightly wounded could stay on base and receive treatment until fit for duty. The more seriously ill were usually transported to the general hospitals. For emergency cases that could not be transported long distances, RAF emergency medical hospitals were made available.

Death and injury in the air came in many forms. Enemy fighters and Flak wounded and killed thousands of aircrew. But bullets and shrapnel were not the only enemies. Anoxia (oxygen starvation) and frostbite were common and if not addressed quickly would lead to death, in the case of anoxia, or the loss of fingers and toes due to frostbite. For those who couldn't survive the journey home, crews had no choice but to push them out of the aircraft with their parachutes on and hope the Germans would treat them.

The Ground Echelon in Action

The best way to understand the contribution of the group's ground echelon was to see it in action. As with all US Army units in World War II, it comprised group headquarters, with four S-designated sections: S-1, personnel; S-2, intelligence; S-3, operations; and S-4, supply and maintenance. In January 1944, there were 79 officers and enlisted personnel attached to 303rd Bomb Group HQ, but they represented the tip of the iceberg. In addition to squadron-level functions, such as armament, ordnance, communications, and technical supply, numerous special duties squadrons existed to take care of the unit's personnel and materiel needs.

Working with parallel organizations in each squadron, S-1 handled group personnel matters. A typical S-2 staff of an Eighth Air Force bomb group consisted of the group intelligence officer, the group photo interpreter, a senior NCO In Command, an NCO for the map room and the escape and evasion materiel, as well as one or two additional NCOs. Supplementing this small crew were the intelligence officers and staff from the four combat squadrons who had desks in the group office. Each squadron usually had two officers and four NCOs, so there were adequate numbers to operate on a 24-hour basis. At first glance, it might appear as if the organizational structure was contrary to effective management, with the personnel answering to both the S-2 officer and their squadron commander, but in practice this was no hindrance to effective operation in the 303rd Bomb Group. Dedication to a common mission outweighed parochial ties. Duties were assigned and performed by mission functions rather than by squadron designation.

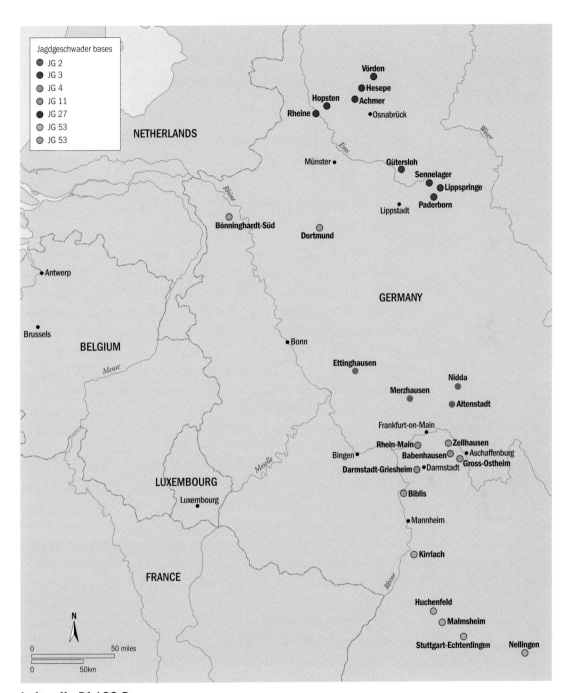

Luftwaffe Bf 109 Bases

Shown here are the main German Bf 109 bases in January 1945.

To walk through a typical mission, it would start with the receipt of the field order from operations. The briefing officers would prepare their notes, maps, photos, and other material, while the NCOs would post the routes on the maps, prepare the mission kits for the bombardiers and navigators, make up the escape and evasion kits, and be ready to assist in the briefings. Usually, there was a separate briefing for pilots, bombardiers, navigators, and gunners. All would be advised of the importance of the target, Flak and enemy fighter threats, and recommended escape and evasion procedures. In addition, the S-2 briefing for bombardiers would include detailed target identification information and bomb-run landmarks beginning at the initial point.

When the aircraft returned from the mission, the S-2 personnel became interrogators. It was then their job to obtain as much information as possible from tired crews who were often more anxious to hit the sack than talk about the mission. It required tact and understanding when probing for the details that went into the reports required by higher headquarters in just a few hours' time. There was always a mission summary report, which had to be compiled, and very important for future operations was the Flak report. The reports concerning crew comments and fighter claims were no less important.

Carlton M. Smith was a lieutenant serving as group Photo Interpreter (PI) on the S-2 staff. He recalls what happened next:

> As soon as the strike photos were received from the photo laboratory, the PI plotted the bomb patterns of each squadron, determining their centers, and comparing them to the assigned mean point of impact. From this, a degree of bombing accuracy—range and deflection—could be recorded. The last phase of the report was a damage assessment. The report was sent immediately to the group commander, but it was also of much interest to the bombardiers, and many made post-mission stops at the PI desk to review the photos. As the PI, I became close to many of the bombardiers because of this common interest, and it was a natural for me to do the bombardier briefings and target identification classes.

The dedication of the 303rd's S-2 staff is underlined by the fact that a number of them flew on combat missions so that they could better

understand the way their efforts assisted the aircrews. Carlton Smith, for example, flew five such missions.

The group S-3 section was responsible for detailed mission planning. Working with the operations sections of the individual squadrons, they would "put the mission together," allocating squadron aircraft and crews to the effort. Usually, three out of four squadrons would fly a mission unless it was a "maximum effort," which meant that everything would fly. The S-3 section would work from the field order, analysing it and deciding just how the group would accomplish its part of the operation within established procedures and guidelines. Lead crews selected for the mission would be brought into the planning process as early as possible, rising well before the regular aircrews. It was not uncommon for individual operations officers who were rated as pilots to put themselves down as group or squadron leaders. Mel Schulstad, for example, flew many missions as an operations officer during the later stages of the war.

Most visible in its functioning was group S-4, supply and maintenance. Its role was a supervisory one, closely related to that of the four squadron S-4 organizations—ensuring that there were enough B-17s available in operational condition to fill the mission rosters. S-4 responsibility included not just supply and maintenance, but also engineering and armament. This was a task of extraordinary difficulty,

A fine study of a Spitfire PR. XI of the 7th Photo Group on the ramp at Mount Farm. Painted in British Photo Recon Unit Blue, the Mk XI had a top speed of 422mph. The aircraft was unarmed, relying on its speed and high-altitude performance to avoid interception. (Author's collection)

given the technical complexity, for that time, of the B-17's different systems. Listing just a few areas—engines, propellers, superchargers, radio equipment, radar navigation and bombing equipment such as *Gee* and H2X, oxygen systems, instruments, electrical systems, hydraulics, bombsights, and automatic flight-control equipment (AFCE), not to mention armament and ordnance—gives some sense of the task's magnitude. All systems had to operate perfectly for the mission to succeed and to give the aircrews a fighting chance to return.

Group S-4 was assisted in this challenge by a large ground staff, and this organization was comprised not only of the flying squadron S-4 staffs and individual aircraft ground crews, but by a host of ancillary support squadrons resident at Molesworth, many of whose responsibilities were blurred. As Quentin Hargrove, who ended the war as group S-4, recalled: "There was an overlap of functions, but nobody really cared about that. You just got on with what you needed to do. Everybody pitched in and it all got done somehow."

Ordnance, Supply, and Maintenance

At the flying squadron level, the technical supply section, to which Sgt Zimba belonged in the 427th Bomb Squadron, were supply "jacks-of-all-trades," responsible for ensuring squadron personnel had everything from personal flight equipment, such as oxygen masks, Mae Wests, and electrically heated "blue-bunny" suits, to aircraft spares. The armament section maintained all the 50-cal. guns and their sights, both for turrets and hand-held flexible ones. They were also in charge of loading the ammunition and bombs before each mission. The ordnance section was responsible for fusing the bombs before a mission, and otherwise ensuring that their squadron had the ordnance it needed. The 863rd Chemical Company handled all incendiary bombs and similar munitions for the group.

B-17Gs of the 91st Bomb Group taxy out at Bassingbourn.
The two olive drab Fortresses are B-17Gs from the 324th Bomb Squadron.
A natural-metal P-51D can also be seen. (Author's collection)

In these functions the flying squadrons were aided in 1943 by the 1681st Ordnance Supply and Maintenance Company, which was responsible for the dual task of bomb and ammunition supply to the squadrons, as well as the maintenance of all base vehicles. The 1681st likewise maintained aircraft machine guns, was responsible for the cleaning and oiling of guns, and passed out Flak suits to combat crewmen. It also repaired the bicycles of base personnel and made many other repairs to base facilities and personal items of others at the base.

The group's supply office was responsible for procuring everything needed to allow the air echelon to function. But there was nothing more important than supplying the critical spare parts necessary to get an aircraft back in the air, so that it no longer had AOG—aircraft-on-ground, not-in-stock—status. Special tracking and supply procedures were in force to ensure the AOG list was kept as short as possible.

Each heavy bomber and fighter was assigned a crew chief and maintenance crew. They were responsible for the service and maintenance of an assigned aircraft. Each man had a specialty, including supercharger, powerplant, fabric and dope, electrical instruments, autopilot and fire control, gyro, optical, hydraulic and mechanical instrument technicians, machinists, parachute and propeller specialist, sheet metal workers, welders, and woodworkers. For every one man in the air, it required four on the ground. For the crew chief and his men, every mission was just as personal as it was to the men in the fighters and bombers. They took great pride in their work, knowing their attention to detail could mean the difference between life and death for the crew tasked with flying these aircraft. After working tireless hours and once the planes had taken off, they could relax in a way as they began to "sweat it out." In those hours, they would catch some sleep, play cards, write letters, or grab a bite to eat. And when the distant throb of engines could be heard, they all headed to the landing field to count the returning aircraft.

The squadron ground crews were responsible for normal maintenance and repairing "routine" damage, such as bullet or cannon shell holes in the aircraft's skin. More serious repairs and overhauls were handled by Sub Depot units that had extensive specialty shops, such as the structures, electrical, and supercharger shops, to name just a few. Repairs to entire airframes, both new and old, were carried out in the larger hangars.

Aircraft maintenance was often a brutal job, done outside in all weather. The tempo of war often meant round-the-clock work. Engine changes carried out in the open were common, although specialized hangars were used for major engine repair and larger airframe replacement and maintenance. Field modifications were common. As Luftwaffe head-on fighter attacks increased, some enterprising armament chiefs responded by adding more guns to the nose of their B-17Fs and B-24Ds.

Aircraft mechanics assigned to the Eighth Air Force lived on base in hastily constructed Nissen huts with 14–16 men. Not only did they have to work outdoors, but staying warm in these huts during the winter was another battle.

Maintenance was a dangerous business that required strict attention to detail. Add fuel, bombs, compressed oxygen, and live ammunition and it was a lethal mix. Accidents were common and did have devastating effects. While preparing for a mission, the 95th Bomb Group lost an entire ground crew when a B-17 blew up. Nineteen men were killed and four B-17s destroyed.

P-38 pilot Arthur L. Thorsen of the 55th Fighter Group recalls a memorable return to base:

> I landed at Wormingford and taxied to my hardstand where Sergeant Harmon and the rest of my crew waited for me. The ground crews are very special people. They watch you take off for a mission, then wait in the dispersal area for your return, greeting you with broad smiles of relief. All of the pilots are touched by this display of faithfulness and affection, and though few of them will comment on it, the warm feeling between pilot and crew is there, nevertheless.
>
> When I shut down my engines and cut switches, I began to tremble, first mildly, then growing in intensity. I was bathed in sweat and soon realized I was too weak to crawl out of the cockpit. Sergeant Harmon and Sergeant Shieny had to help me out of the cockpit, then off the wing and onto the waiting truck that would take me back to the 38th Squadron pilot's room.

It was a sad fact of war that not every aircraft returned. The loss of a bomber or fighter was a devastating blow for the ground crews.

On December 27, 1943, three B-17s of the 100th Bomb Group (serial nos. 42-3474, 42-6094, and 42-3772) were destroyed after colliding while taxiing. Accidents and mid-air collisions were not uncommon, causing the loss of hundreds of B-17s. (Author's collection)

Friends you had seen just hours before had simply vanished. For the planes that did make it back, the work would begin all over again. Replacement aircraft and crews would arrive and be introduced to their new crew chief. Some ground crews experienced the loss of more than one aircraft. And as the tempo of operations picked up in the summer and fall of 1943, it was not an uncommon occurrence.

The battle damage sustained by B-17s and B-24s was far greater than had been anticipated. A Bomber Command study revealed that 588 aircraft suffered battle damage between October 21, 1942 and March 31, 1943. To assist the base-level mechanics, mobile repair units were created, consisting of 16–19 specialists equipped with a truck, a jeep, and two trailers. Stocked with tools and equipment needed for the job, these mobile units could perform on-the-spot repairs. By the end of 1943, Eighth Air Force had 50 mobile repair units in operation.

Fire and Facilities

The ground echelon was also responsible for preventing aircraft being damaged by an ever-present threat—fire. Because Molesworth was initially under British administrative control, firefighting duties were performed by the resident RAF fire equipment school. Later, the American 2097th Engineers Fire Fighting Platoon was responsible for all base fire-fighting activities. The firemen extinguished fires on burning B-17s, haystacks in fields near Molesworth, dispersal tents, Nissen huts, and other base facilities. Several B-17s were saved when the 2097th quickly extinguished aircraft fires and prevented potentially disastrous explosions. Sometimes, of course, a B-17 could neither be saved nor repaired, in which case it was salvaged and the carcass consigned to the "bone yard."

The other part of the ground echelon's mission was to look after that most vital element—the men. The mission of the huge 3rd Station Complement, which comprised 185 men in 1944, was to make Molesworth a comfortable place to live, and to improve base working facilities. To this end, the utilities section employed carpenters, electricians, engineers, painters, and handymen. They maintained existing facilities, constructed new buildings, remodelled old ones, built roads, repaired runways, and kept water and electricity flowing throughout the base. The unit operated barber shops, tailor shops, the gymnasium, and many other facilities that made life more bearable for the troops.

Eighth Air Force airmen chat as they drink coffee served to them by workers in the Red Cross Clubmobile "New York" in Alconbury, England, February 13, 1943. (US Air Force)

The 3rd Station Complement had a separate control tower section, which was responsible for the radio equipment used for communicating with group aircraft and for the maintenance of the flare path, caravan, beacon, and searchlights. There was also a communications section which installed and maintained the telephone and teletype systems essential for the base operations.

The 1114th Quartermaster Company obtained fuel for both base vehicles and aircraft, which included not just the group's B-17s, but also two P-47s and a number of utility machines. The quartermasters dealt with rationing boards to get more coal for the barracks, and were responsible for laundry and shoe-repair services. They also had the important job of providing clothing and food for base personnel. Other units providing support services were the 1199th Military Police Company, the 3rd Provisional Gas Detachment, the 18th Weather Squadron, Detachment 107, the 202nd Finance Section, and the Eighth Air Force Dental Detachment (At Large).

Rest and Religion

Group officers' and enlisted men's mess facilities and clubs were located in communal sites near squadron areas, with each contributing mess personnel. The main officers' club had an attractive bar, as did that of the enlisted ranks. There were also times for lighter moments at the base, whether in the form of parties, games, or other activities only distantly related to military affairs.

Day-in, day-out, the bomber crews' return was the one event that gripped the ground echelon when the time drew near. All eyes would be watching the sky in the hope that the full complement of B-17s dispatched that morning would come home. After their return, there was little time for reflection, especially if another raid was scheduled for the next day. The ground crews would work around-the-clock to get their B-17s repaired and ready for the next effort. Perhaps a crew chief or an entire ground crew would pause briefly to point with pride to their B-17's mission tally for a photographer. But soon the crew chief would start the portable "putt-putt" power-unit needed to bring the B-17's four R-1820 engines to life and choreograph the engine-start sequence with the pilots. Then the whole ground crew would stand amid the ordered chaos of their support equipment to

wish their Fortress and her crew luck as they taxied off on another raid against the Third Reich.

With the reality of death ever-present, especially when a B-17 brought back crewmen killed in action, it was the duty of the group's chaplains to accompany a detail of the deceased's friends on a burial party. The dead would be laid to rest at a nearby site. Many of those who died were transferred after the war to the Cambridge American War Cemetery.

Fathers Edmund James Skoner and "Chappie" Slawson were often inventive in devising ways of helping the men endure the trials of combat. Perhaps the best story told about Slawson involves his practice of scratching crewmen's names on pennies and handing them out with the admonition that they return the coins to him. According to one account, the sole-survivor of a ditched B-17 held onto his penny, and with it the will to survive, because the chaplain had told him that morning, "Bring this penny back to me. I'll be praying for you." The man didn't want to disappoint "the old chap."

B-24s of the 458th Bomb Group form up over England alongside the group's assembly ship. These aircraft were brightly painted for easy recognition and were used to help the squadrons get into formation before heading out over the English Channel or North Sea. (Author's collection)

EIGHTH AIR FORCE ORDER OF BATTLE, JANUARY 1945

The Eighth Air Force reached its peak strength in January 1945, and the order of battle and tables below provide a snapshot of this key moment in its history.

Eighth Air Force HQ Bushey Park

Eighth Air Force Bomber Command HQ High Wycombe

1st Air Division
1st Combat Bombardment Wing
91st Bomb Group
322nd Bomb Squadron, 323rd Bomb Squadron, 324th Bomb Squadron, 401st Bomb Squadron
381st Bomb Group
532nd Bomb Squadron, 533rd Bomb Squadron, 534th Bomb Squadron, 535th Bomb Squadron
398th Bomb Group
600th Bomb Squadron, 601st Bomb Squadron, 602nd Bomb Squadron, 603rd Bomb Squadron

40th Combat Bombardment Wing
92nd Bomb Group
325th Bomb Squadron, 326th Bomb Squadron, 327th Bomb Squadron, 407th Bomb Squadron
305th Bomb Group
364th Bomb Squadron, 365th Bomb Squadron, 366th Bomb Squadron, 422nd Bomb Squadron
306th Bomb Group
367th Bomb Squadron, 368th Bomb Squadron, 369th Bomb Squadron, 423rd Bomb Squadron

41st Combat Bombardment Wing
303rd Bomb Group
358th Bomb Squadron, 359th Bomb Squadron, 360th Bomb Squadron, 427th Bomb Squadron
379th Bomb Group
524th Bomb Squadron, 525th Bomb Squadron, 526th Bomb Squadron, 527th Bomb Squadron
384th Bomb Group

544th Bomb Squadron, 545th Bomb Squadron, 546th Bomb Squadron, 547th Bomb Squadron

94th Combat Bombardment Wing
351st Bomb Group
508th Bomb Squadron, 509th Bomb Squadron, 510th Bomb Squadron, 511th Bomb Squadron
401st Bomb Group
612th Bomb Squadron, 613th Bomb Squadron, 614th Bomb Squadron, 615th Bomb Squadron
457th Bomb Group
748th Bomb Squadron, 749th Bomb Squadron, 750th Bomb Squadron, 751st Bomb Squadron

2nd Air Division
2nd Combat Bombardment Wing
389th Bomb Group
564th Bomb Squadron, 565th Bomb Squadron, 566th Bomb Squadron, 567th Bomb Squadron
445th Bomb Group
700th Bomb Squadron, 701st Bomb Squadron, 702nd Bomb Squadron, 703rd Bomb Squadron
453rd Bomb Group
732nd Bomb Squadron, 733rd Bomb Squadron, 734th Bomb Squadron, 735th Bomb Squadron

14th Combat Bombardment Wing
44th Bomb Group
66th Bomb Squadron, 67th Bomb Squadron, 68th Bomb Squadron, 506th Bomb Squadron
392nd Bomb Group
576th Bomb Squadron, 577th Bomb Squadron, 578th Bomb Squadron, 579th Bomb Squadron
491st Bomb Group
852nd Bomb Squadron, 853rd Bomb Squadron, 854th Bomb Squadron, 855th Bomb Squadron
492nd Bomb Group
856th Bomb Squadron, 857th Bomb Squadron, 858th Bomb Squadron, 859th Bomb Squadron

Idiots' Delight was the first B-17 of the 94th Bomb Group to survive 50 missions; not once turning back due to mechanical failure. The first mission was flown on July 14, 1943, and the 50th was March 22, 1944. The 94th suffered huge casualties during this period; 80 B-17s were lost. On June 19, 1944, *Idiots' Delight* was hit by Flak flying over the Pas de Calais. The pilot, Theodore A. Milton, was forced to ditch the plane in the Channel, where nine of the ten crew lost their lives. (Author's collection)

20th Combat Bombardment Wing
93rd Bomb Group
328th Bomb Squadron, 339th Bomb Squadron,
330th Bomb Squadron, 409th Bomb Squadron
446th Bomb Group
704th Bomb Squadron, 705th Bomb Squadron,
706th Bomb Squadron, 707th Bomb Squadron
448th Bomb Group
712th Bomb Squadron, 713th Bomb Squadron,
714th Bomb Squadron, 715th Bomb Squadron
489th Bomb Group
844th Bomb Squadron, 845th Bomb Squadron,
846th Bomb Squadron, 847th Bomb Squadron

96th Combat Bombardment Wing
458th Bomb Group

752nd Bomb Squadron, 753rd Bomb Squadron,
754th Bomb Squadron, 755th Bomb Squadron
466th Bomb Group
784th Bomb Squadron, 785th Bomb Squadron,
786th Bomb Squadron, 787th Bomb Squadron
467th Bomb Group
788th Bomb Squadron, 789th Bomb Squadron,
790th Bomb Squadron, 791st Bomb Squadron

3rd Air Division
4th Combat Bombardment Wing
94th Bomb Group
331st Bomb Squadron, 332nd Bomb Squadron,
33rd Bomb Squadron, 410th Bomb Squadron
385th Bomb Group
548th Bomb Squadron, 549th Bomb Squadron,

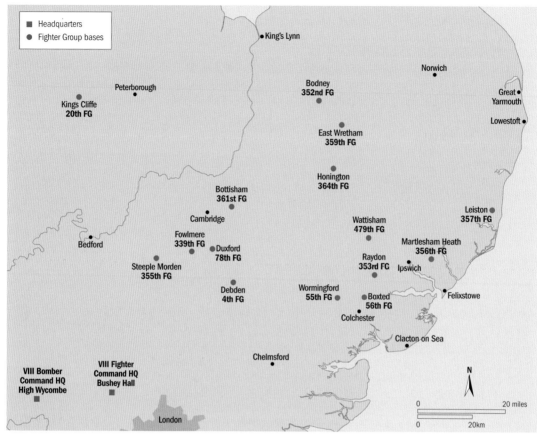

Eighth Fighter Command Bases

Eighth Fighter Command's fighter groups were based in East Anglia so that they could be as close to targets in occupied Europe as possible. Most of these airfields were built from scratch especially for the USAAF in a massive construction program launched in 1942.

550th Bomb Squadron, 551st Bomb Squadron
447th Bomb Group
708th Bomb Squadron, 709th Bomb Squadron,
710th Bomb Squadron, 711th Bomb Squadron

13th Combat Bombardment Wing
95th Bomb Group
334th Bomb Squadron, 335th Bomb Squadron,
336th Bomb Squadron, 412th Bomb Squadron
100th Bomb Group
349th Bomb Squadron, 350th Bomb Squadron,

351st Bomb Squadron, 418th Bomb Squadron
390th Bomb Group
568th Bomb Squadron, 569th Bomb Squadron,
570th Bomb Squadron, 571st Bomb Squadron

45th Combat Bombardment Wing
96th Bomb Group
337th Bomb Squadron, 338th Bomb Squadron,
339th Bomb Squadron, 413th Bomb Squadron
388th Bomb Group
560th Bomb Squadron, 561st Bomb Squadron,

562nd Bomb Squadron, 563rd Bomb Squadron
452nd Bomb Group
728th Bomb Squadron, 729th Bomb Squadron,
730th Bomb Squadron, 731st Bomb Squadron

4th Combat Bombardment Wing (Provisional)
486th Bomb Group
832nd Bomb Squadron, 833rd Bomb Squadron,
834th Bomb Squadron, 835th Bomb Squadron
487th Bomb Group
836th Bomb Squadron, 837th Bomb Squadron,
838th Bomb Squadron, 839th Bomb Squadron

93rd Combat Bombardment Wing
34th Bomb Group
4th Bomb Squadron, 7th Bomb Squadron, 18th
Bomb Squadron, 391st Bomb Squadron
490th Bomb Group
848th Bomb Squadron, 849th Bomb Squadron,
850th Bomb Squadron, 851st Bomb Squadron
493rd Bomb Group
860th Bomb Squadron, 861st Bomb Squadron,
862nd Bomb Squadron, 863rd Bomb Squadron

325th Photo Reconnaissance Wing
25th Bomb Group
642nd Bomb Squadron, 653rd Bomb Squadron,
654th Bomb Squadron
7th Photo Group
13th PRS, 14th PRS, 22nd PRS, 27th PRS
802nd RCN Group

Special Operations
482nd Bomb Group (Pathfinders)
812th Bomb Squadron, 813th Bomb Squadron,
814th Bomb Squadron
801st Bomb Squadron
803rd Bomber Squadron

Total Aircraft and Crew Strength Heavy Bombers, January 1945 (peak strength)	
Aircraft B-17 and B-24	
Assigned to Air Force	2,799
On hand Operational Tactical Units	2,179
Fully operational in Operational Tactical Units	1,750
Crews	
Assigned	3,564
Available	2,295
Effective strength for combat	1,651

Eighth Fighter Command HQ, Bushey Hall

65th Fighter Wing
4th Fighter Group
334th Fighter Squadron, 335th Fighter Squadron,
336th Fighter Squadron

56th Fighter Group
61st Fighter Squadron, 62nd Fighter Squadron,
63rd Fighter Squadron

355th Fighter Group
354th Fighter Squadron, 357th Fighter Squadron,
358th Fighter Squadron

479th Fighter Group
434th Fighter Squadron, 435th Fighter Squadron,
436th Fighter Squadron

66th Fighter Wing
78th Fighter Group
82nd Fighter Squadron, 83rd Fighter Squadron,
84th Fighter Squadron

339th Fighter Group
503rd Fighter Squadron, 504th Fighter Squadron, 505th Fighter Squadron

353rd Fighter Group
350th Fighter Squadron, 351st Fighter Squadron, 352nd Fighter Squadron

357th Fighter Group
362nd Fighter Squadron, 363rd Fighter Squadron, 364th Fighter Squadron

67th Fighter Wing

20th Fighter Group
55th Fighter Squadron, 77th Fighter Squadron, 79th Fighter Squadron

55th Fighter Group
38th Fighter Squadron, 338th Fighter Squadron, 343rd Fighter Squadron

352nd Fighter Group
328th Fighter Squadron, 486th Fighter Squadron, 487th Fighter Squadron

356th Fighter Group
359th Fighter Squadron, 360th Fighter Squadron, 361st Fighter Squadron

359th Fighter Group
368th Fighter Squadron, 369th Fighter Squadron, 370th Fighter Squadron

361st Fighter Group
374th Fighter Squadron, 375th Fighter Squadron, 376th Fighter Squadron

364th Fighter Group
383rd Fighter Squadron, 384th Fighter Squadron, 385th Fighter Squadron

Scouting Force
1st Scouting Force
2nd Scouting Force
3rd Scouting Force

Rescue Group
5th Emergency Rescue Squadron

Flying Training
495th Fighter Group
551st Fighter Training Squadron, 552nd Fighter Training Squadron
496th Fighter Group
554th Fighter Training Squadron, 555th Fighter Training Squadron

Total Aircraft and Crew Strength Fighters, January 1945 (peak strength)	
Aircraft P-47 and P-51	
Assigned to Air Force	1,484
On hand Operational Tactical Units	1,262
Fully operational in Operational Tactical Units	1,031
Crews	
Assigned	1,747
Available	1,267
Effect strength for combat	1,009

OPPOSITE TOP P-51D serial no. 44-14783 CG-C of the 3rd Scouting Force in the winter of 1944. Based at Wormingford, the unit was active from August 1944 until May 1945. (littlefriends.co.uk)

OPPOSITE P-47D serial no. 42-8586 5F-S of the 5th Emergency Rescue Squadron. Each P-47 was equipped with two droppable life rafts on the wings, a single 100-gallon drop tank, and behind that four smoke markers. Armament consisted of four 50-cal. machine guns. (littlefriends.co.uk)

Captain Donald S. Gentile, 336th Fighter Squadron, 4th Fighter Group. P-51B serial no. 43-6913 VF-T *Shangri-La*. Gentile had joined the RAF in 1941 and served in the Eagle Squadron; in April 1944 he was credited with 27¾ kills in USAAF service plus two in RAF service. (littlefriends.co.uk)

CHAPTER 4

AIRCRAFT OF THE EIGHTH AIR FORCE

Bombers, Fighters, Reconnaissance

What the Eighth Air Force accomplished in World War II was staggering. It terms of men, aircraft, and logistical organization required to mount daily bombing and fighters operations, it boggles the mind. Without the industrial might and leadership of the United States, it would not have been possible. Between 1942 and 1945, 459 days of bombing operations were carried out (with related fighter, photo, and special operations), 46,456 combat crews and fighter pilots became casualties, 59,644 battle-damaged aircraft were repaired by maintenance/ground personnel, 732,231 tons of bombs were expended, and 99,256,341 rounds of ammunition were linked together.

BOMBERS
Boeing B-17 Flying Fortress
B-17E
The USAAF's Eighth Air Force launched its bomber war against Nazi Germany with the Boeing B-17E. The first examples of this

magnificent and quite majestic four-engined bomber rolled off the production line in September 1941 and arrived in England in July 1942. Seven tons heavier and 40 percent faster than Boeing's original Model 299, it represented an extensive redesign and improvement over the earlier C and D variants, with a major aerodynamic reworking of the tail section and rear fuselage areas in order to improve stability for bombing. Most evident was the distinctive, low, sweeping fillet that pulled back from halfway along the fuselage as part of an extended tail assembly.

The fuselage of the B-17 was formed from an all-metal, semi-monocoque structure constructed of Alclad fastened with alloy rivets, and within which was built a number of bulkheads separating four sections. These comprised the forward section housing the bombardier-navigator's and pilots' compartments, the center section containing the bomb bay, the rear fuselage section, and the tail section. Internally, there was a maximum cross-section height of 103in. and a maximum width of 90in.

The B-17E had a semi-monocoque wing with a span of 103ft 9in. (1,486ft wing area), and the aircraft was 73ft 10in. in length. Power was provided by four up-rated 1,200hp Wright Cyclone R-1820-65s, which increased maximum speed to 323mph at 25,000ft—an improvement over the B-17C/D. The wings held three fuel tanks in their inboard sections and nine outboard, with a total capacity of 2,780 US gallons. Normal range was 2,000 miles. Empty, the aircraft weighed 32,250lb.

The extreme rear fuselage had also been extended and enlarged to accommodate a tail gun turret, mounting twin 50-cal. Browning M2 machine guns for anticipated defense against fighter attack from the rear. These were hand-operated by a gunner in a sit-kneel position. Additionally, a dorsal, 360-degree-turn, power-operated turret built by Sperry was installed into the upper fuselage immediately aft of the cockpit, while a remotely controlled Bendix ventral turret, fitted with a periscope sight to be used by a gunner in a prone position, was installed in the underside of the central fuselage aft of the bomb bay. Both these turrets also fielded twin Brownings, turning the B-17E into a proper "Flying Fortress," armed with eight 50-cal. guns in total and a single 30-cal. nose-mounted weapon in a framed nose cone.

B-17s forming up on their way to their target. One very discouraging thing for German civilians was to see, on a daily basis, American bombers in a seemingly impeccable "Nuremberg Rally formation." (Author's collection)

There were two major disadvantages that stemmed from this design, however. Firstly, the Bendix turret proved unsatisfactory, and secondly, the resultant drag from the turrets and the enlarged tail assembly reduced top speed by some 6mph.

Although the B-17E was a most welcome addition to US air power, by January 1942 the Boeing plant at Seattle, which had received an order for 512 E-models in the summer of 1940, was producing only around two to three machines per day. And while, on paper, the USAAF boasted 14 heavy bomb groups, only three were fully equipped with B-17s. It seems that agreements signed with Douglas and Lockheed-Vega did little to overcome the slow rate of production.

The B-17E first saw operational service with the USAAF against the Japanese in the Philippines shortly after Pearl Harbor, and also in India, from where missions were flown against the enemy advance through Burma. In early 1942, B-17s flew from northern Australia and then over the Southwest Pacific, where they met with considerable success in antishipping attacks.

B-17/B-24 Total Efforts, August 17, 1942–May 8, 1945	
Heavy bombers (B-17 and B-24)	
Bombing effective sorties	266,872
Bomb tons on target	
Germany only	520,267.7
All targets	691,470.2
B-17s and B-24s missing in action	4,145
Category E (damaged beyond economical repair)	1,556

The steady destruction of the Luftwaffe fighter force made the Eighth Air Force increasingly brazen in its camouflage practices, completely foregoing camouflage paint on many aircraft later in 1944, such as these B-17Gs of the 532nd Squadron, 381st Bomb Group. (NARA)

However, there were tactical lessons learned. Japanese fighter pilots had quickly identified that the head-on attack against the B-17E exploited its weakest point of defense, while Fortress crews soon came to learn that the ventral turret was actually quite impractical. Thus, the nose armament was beefed up by removing the 30-cal. gun and replacing it with one or two 50-cal. guns, while crews elected to remove the ventral turret to save on weight. But none of these early operations could be termed "strategic bombing" of the kind that would be needed in the coming European war.

The B-17 had been conceived essentially as a medium bomber whose range and endurance had been optimized in a trade-off against the aircraft's bomb load, which stood at just 4,000lb—the British Avro Lancaster of comparable size could carry a payload of 14,000lb. The bomb bay doors of the B-17 were a modest 11ft long, compared with those of the Lancaster which measured 33ft.

Forty-nine B-17Es were eventually ferried to the UK for the 97th Bomb Group. Before leaving the US, the aircraft had their side gun windows enlarged and, on arrival on the other side of the Atlantic, further modifications were carried out that included improvements to the aircraft's radio. Some shortcomings were also noted in oxygen, bomb rack, lighting, fire extinguisher, and life raft equipment.

The B-17E did not enjoy a long period of service, being "moved aside" to make way for the F-model, the improved performance of which made joint operations between the two types problematic. Apart from performing a small number of combat missions, the type was relegated to an operational training role with the Combat Crew Replacement Center (CCRC) at Bovingdon in early 1943. By the summer of that year, B-17Es were being used for training, liaison, ambulance, transport, or target-towing duties. Nevertheless, the E-model formed an admirable platform for the development of the renowned variants that would follow it.

B-17F

The USAAF's first truly combat-ready version of the Fortress, refined following experience in the Pacific and from early operations conducted over England with the RAF (which had used both the D- and E-models as the Fortress I and II, respectively) and the Eighth Air Force, the B-17F actually differed very little from its immediate predecessor. In fact, the F-model's main distinguishing external feature was its new frameless nose cone. Internally, however, some 400 minor changes had been made. These included re-engineering the leading-edge contours of the cowlings of the four 1,200hp Wright R-1820-97 radial engines to avoid the new Hamilton Standard "paddle blade" propellers striking them when feathered, as well as improvements to the oxygen system (which suffered from inadequate supply and freezing), landing gear, and brakes. Enhancements were

The YB-40 in Action (previous pages)

The YB-40 was a converted B-17F with added armament, including dual waist guns and an extra power turret in the radio compartment. It also had a turret below the nose, a modification that was successfully adopted by later B-17s.

During the 48 sorties completed in mid-1943 by the 12 YB-40s assigned to the 92nd Bomb Group, gunners on board the bomber escorts claimed five German fighters shot down, two more probably destroyed, and a handful damaged. Two of the victories and one of those damaged came on the June 25, 1943 raid on Blohm & Voss's plant at Oldenburg, this mission proving to be the high point during the YB-40's brief operational career in the ETO with the Eighth Air Force. (Artwork by Adam Tooby © Osprey Publishing)

also made to the bomb racks and ball turret (the least favored position in the aircraft, where excess ice and oil played havoc with the guns), and an automatic pilot/bombsight link was installed.

The first F-models were delivered by Boeing Seattle in late May 1942, with Douglas at Long Beach and Lockheed-Vega following during the summer. By August 1943, all three plants accounted for an average output of 400 aircraft per month.

In terms of armament, the lessons learned in the Pacific resulted in the fitting of a 50-cal. Browning M2 in each of two newly created Plexiglas observation windows either side of the nose, to be used by either the bombardier or the navigator. These additions meant that the B-17F (by this stage the most heavily armed bomber in service) carried 12 or 13 machine guns. However, not all machines benefited from this modification, and many soldiered on into early 1943 with the nose adapted to accommodate a 50-cal. gun with a mounting able to absorb the increased recoil.

YB-40

When America entered the war, there was real doubt about the technical feasibility of developing a truly long-range escort fighter. The RAF and Luftwaffe thought it was impossible (though the Japanese Zero had a range of over 1,200 miles), but in mid-1942 the USAAF began to consider that the Tactical School doctrine of the self-protecting bomber

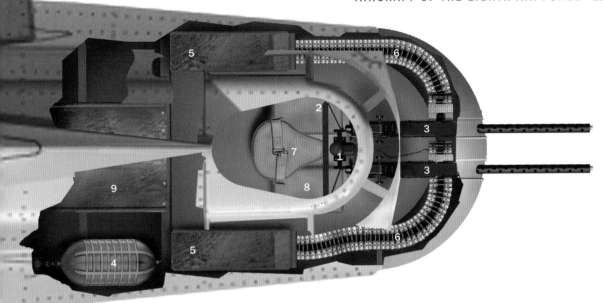

B-17G Cheyenne Tail Turret

1. Gunsight
2. Bulletproof glass shield
3. Twin 0.50-in. Browning M2 machine guns
4. Oxygen supply
5. 0.50-in. ammunition boxes
6. 0.50-in. ammunition feed belts
7. Gunner's seat and seat belts
8. Gunner's knee pads
9. Wooden catwalk

(Artwork by Jim Laurier © Osprey Publishing)

formations might be flawed, and in September 1942 the Army Air Force converted a B-17F into an "escort fighter" for a formation defense role. Designated the YB-40, it had two additional power turrets, one over the radio room and one in a remotely controlled installation under the nose, and dual manually operated gun positions replaced single guns in waist windows, giving the aircraft a total of 14 50-cal. machine guns. It also carried much more ammunition and additional armor plate around the crew stations.

Eaker was enthusiastic about the YB-40 idea, much more so than about increasing the range of Eighth Air Force's fighters with external tanks and, in May 1943, 13 experimental models were sent to the 327th Squadron, 92nd Group for combat trials. For two months, from late May 1943 through late July 1943, YB-40s flew combat missions, but it proved to be an abject failure. The YB-40 was too heavy to keep up with normal B-17 formations after they dropped their bombs, and while it had more guns, they fired mostly to the side and were of little help since most Luftwaffe passes were from the front or rear. The most

B-17G Cheyenne Tail Turret (opposite)

1. Gunsight
2. Bulletproof glass shield
3. Hand grips for twin 0.50-in. Browning M2 machine guns
4. Light
5. Defrost tubes for Plexiglas
6. Interphone jack
7. Oxygen regulator
8. Oxygen gauges
9. Oxygen hoses
10. Interphone jack box
11. 0.50-in. ammunition boxes
12. 0.50-in. ammunition feed belts
13. Gunner's seat and seat belts
14. Gunner's knee pads
15. Heated flight suit electrical outlet
16. Portable oxygen bottle
17. Switch panel
18. Wooden catwalk
(Artwork by Jim Laurier © Osprey Publishing)

troublesome aspect of the YB-40 was its flying characteristics, particularly its tendency to fly tail-heavy due to the added weight in the rear section. On many missions, YB-40s flew in the "Purple Heart Corner," also known as the "coffin corner," but after a few missions it was clear they would not be the solution to the escort issue. However, the chin turret of the YB-40 proved very effective and was quickly adopted for late-model B-17Fs and for the B-17G.

B-17G
The B-17G was the last production model of the B-17 series, with first examples being delivered to the USAAF from September 1943. These were in turn deployed on operations conducted by the Eighth Air Force the following month, early aircraft taking part in the second Schweinfurt raid alongside B-17Fs. Effectively an organic development of the F-model, the G is perhaps best identified by its Bendix "chin" turret, which was fitted with twin 50-cal. Browning M2s, and intended as an antidote to Luftwaffe head-on fighter attacks.

The Fields of Fire of a B-17G

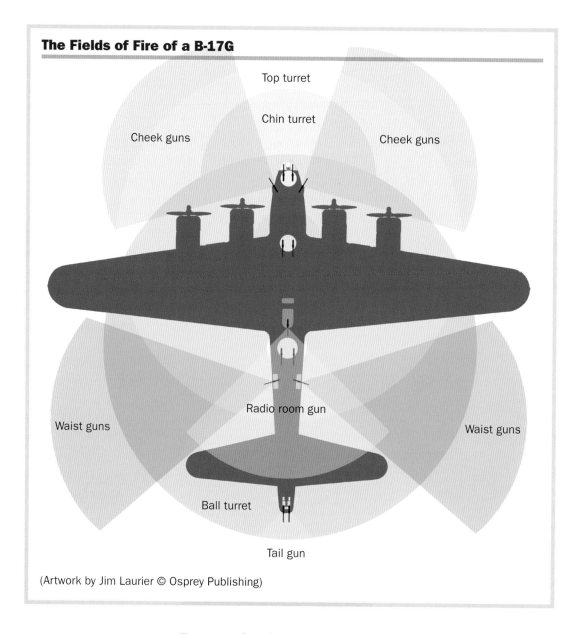

Top turret

Chin turret

Cheek guns

Cheek guns

Radio room gun

Waist guns

Waist guns

Ball turret

Tail gun

(Artwork by Jim Laurier © Osprey Publishing)

First introduced on some of the last B-17Fs, the chin turret was designed to be operated under remote control by the bombardier, but its installation forced the removal of the direction-finding loop originally housed in a streamlined fairing. This equipment was re-installed just forward of the bomb bay and a little to the left of the fuselage centerline.

The Sperry upper turret was replaced by a Bendix type that offered improved visibility and control. The earlier design of the tail turret, which featured a tunnel opening at the very end of the fuselage, was changed for a new Cheyenne turret—named after the town in Wyoming where it had been designed at the United Air Lines Modification Center—which provided larger windows, giving better visibility, a greater field-of-fire and a reflector sight for the tail gunner. This was a great improvement over the former turret's 30-degree traverse and primitive ring and bead sight positioned outside and beyond the much smaller gunner's window. The guns were moved nearer the gunner and the mounting protected by a semi-circular cover.

In its usual form, the B-17G brandished no fewer than 13 50-cal. Browning M2 machine guns, two each in the chin, upper, ball, and tail turrets, with further such weapons in the nose cheek positions and waist windows.

B-17G Specifications

Powerplant:	4 x 1,200hp Wright-Cyclone GR-1820-97 engines
Maximum Speed:	280mph at 20,000ft
Range:	1,140 miles (with maximum bomb load)
Maximum Bomb Load:	12,800lb
Armament:	13 x 50-cal. Browning machine guns
Service Ceiling:	26,500ft

Consolidated B-24 Liberator
XB-24 prototype

The USAAF's second heavy bomber in the ETO was the B-24 Liberator. In 1938, at the request of the French *Armée de l'Air*, Consolidated had secretly commenced design work on a four-engined bomber. At the same time, the USAAC had begun searching for a new heavy bomber to complement the B-17. With war in Europe on the horizon, US President Franklin D. Roosevelt secured backing from Congress in January 1939 to spend $300,000,000 on the acquisition of new military aircraft. With the B-17 by then already four years old, the USAAC issued a request for a new bomber capable of attaining a speed of 310mph and a ceiling in excess of 30,000ft while carrying a four-ton bomb load up to 3,000 miles.

XB-24 prototype 39-556 (later serial-numbered 39-680). The longer-legged Liberator would prove itself in combat in the ETO, where its rugged construction and heavy bomb load made the aircraft popular with crews. (Author's collection)

Consolidated combined their earlier design work on the French bomber with a completely new wing, which would be the key to the aircraft's operational success in myriad roles. Conceived by aeronautical engineer David R. Davis, the new "Davis" aerofoil promised high lift, less drag, and long range at a high cruising speed. Compared with the B-17, the B-24 would have a quicker gestation period. On March 30, 1939, Consolidated was awarded a contract for a single prototype XB-24. One month later, the USAAC ordered seven YB-24 service test aircraft, and by August 10, it had committed to a further 38 B-24As.

On December 29, 1939, the XB-24 (39-680) made its first flight from Lindbergh Field in San Diego. Powered by four Pratt & Whitney R-1830-33 Twin Wasp engines, the new bomber, with its Davis wing, had a longer range than the B-17 but its maximum speed (at 273mph) was appreciably slower than expected. Although the French would be the second nation to order the B-24, the country's capitulation to German forces in June 1940 meant the order was never fulfilled. Britain duly took over all outstanding French aircraft contracts, obtaining six YB-24s (designated LB-30As) and 20 B-24As (LB-30Bs) from 1941.

Like the B-17, the early versions of the B-24 were deficient in armament. In December 1941, the first of nine C-models incorporating a Martin powered turret in the dorsal position and a tail turret, both with two 50-cal. machine guns, and a single 50-cal.

ventral gun, was delivered. Production soon switched to the B-24D, which was the first model to be produced in quantity. Capable of hauling up to 8,000lb of ordnance, its nominal range with a 5,000lb bomb load was 2,300 miles. Combat experience with the B-24D led to the creation of the H-model, which incorporated the Emerson A-15 nose turret and improved Consolidated A-6B tail turret. The B-24H was quickly followed by the near-definitive Liberator, the B-24J—it was also the most-produced variant, with 6,678 examples completed. Both the H- and J-models were equipped with a retractable Sperry ball turret.

Three B-24Ds practice formation flying. The early D model, like the B-17E and F, did not have adequate nose gun armament. This was rectified with a powered turret in the G, H, J, and L/M models. (Author's collection)

B-24D Liberator Nose Compartment (opposite)

1. Map case	15. Bombardier's seat
2. Oxygen regulator	16. Center Browning M2 0.50in. machine gun
3. Left ammunition box	17. Right Browning M2 0.50in. machine gun
4. Clock	18. Flexible ammunition feed belt
5. Airspeed indicator	19. Defroster hose
6. Outside air temperature indicator	20. Cabin heater
7. Altimeter	21. Right ammunition box
8. Left Browning M2 0.50in. machine gun	22. Receptacle for flying suit heating plug
9. Flexible ammunition feed belt	23. Portable oxygen bottle
10. Bomb selector and control panel	24. Compass
11. Bomb control quadrant	25. Light
12. Center gun firing switch	26. Bombardier's intercom control
13. Invalometer	27. Alarm bell
14. Norden bombsight	(Artwork by Jim Laurier © Osprey Publishing)

The final versions to see combat were the B-24L/M models, which had been modified to address the excessive weight gain, degraded performance, and poor visibility. Lighter tail and ventral ball turrets rectified many of the weight-related issues.

B-24D

Built in greater quantity than any other American combat aircraft, the Liberator has often been overshadowed by the more famous B-17. Dimensionally similar to the Flying Fortress, the Liberator was easily recognizable thanks to its long, thin Davis wing, twin rudders, tricycle landing gear, and box-like fuselage.

Powered by four Pratt & Whitney R-1830-43 engines, each rated at 1,200hp, the D-model of the Liberator was only the second American heavy bomber to see combat over Europe. While more demanding to fly than the B-17E/F, the B-24D had a superior range and bigger bomb load. Maximum speed was 303mph at 25,000ft. With a more spacious bomb-bay, the B-24D could carry up to 8,800lb of ordnance. This was reduced to 5,000lb when covering distances of up to 2,300 miles. Like the B-17E, the B-24D was equipped with self-sealing fuel tanks and armor plating for each crew station. Although the armament installed in the D-model varied during the aircraft's production run, typically, most examples were fitted with ten 50-cal. M2 machine guns. Only

Plan and Profile Views of B-24D Fields of Fire

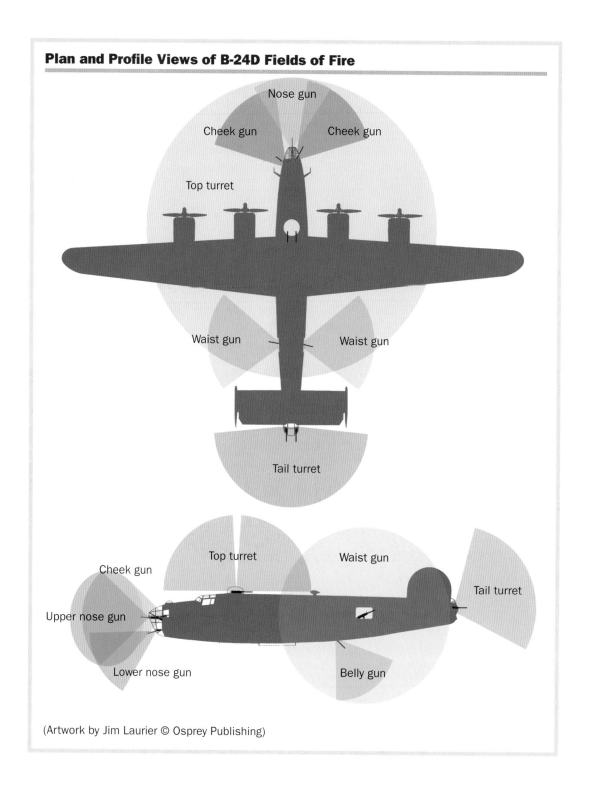

Nose gun

Cheek gun

Cheek gun

Top turret

Waist gun

Waist gun

Tail turret

Top turret

Waist gun

Cheek gun

Tail turret

Upper nose gun

Lower nose gun

Belly gun

(Artwork by Jim Laurier © Osprey Publishing)

four of the latter were turret-mounted, split evenly between the Martin A-3 dorsal and Consolidated A-6 tail turrets.

B-24Ds began to reach the USAAC in January 1942, and by the time production of this variant ended, 2,696 had been built.

B-24G-1

Just 405 G-1s were built, this variant effectively being a B-24D with an A-6 turret in the nose to offer the aircraft better protection from head-on attacks by German fighters. B-24G-1s served primarily with Fifteenth Air Force units in Italy.

B-24H

The H-model was the first major production model equipped with the Emerson A-15 turret in place of the B-24D's 24-panel "greenhouse" nose glazing. More than 50 other airframe changes were also made, with the more obvious ones being a redesigned bombardier's

Two B-24H Liberators of the 446th Bomb Group head toward their target. The B-24 never won the acclaim crews felt it deserved. It was always in the shadow of the prettier, but "short legged," B-17, even after it became the most numerous military aircraft ever manufactured in the United States. (Author's collection)

compartment (as a direct result of the turret installation), improved visibility from the dorsal and tail turrets, and Plexiglas-paneled, laterally offset, waist gun positions. The D-model's R-1830-43 engines were retained, however. A total of 3,100 B-24Hs were built.

B-24J

Built in greater numbers (6,678) than any other Liberator variant, the J-model went into series production from August 1943. A shortage of Emerson turrets meant that most B-24Js were fitted with modified A-6 turrets instead. Although very similar to the H-model, the B-24J was in many ways inferior to its predecessor. Drag from the front turret and an overall increase in weight to 65,000lb made it 5,000lb heavier than the D-model. This in turn meant that the aircraft was slower (even with its upgraded Pratt & Whitney R-1830-65 engines) and had to fly at a lower altitude than previous models.

B-24J Specifications

Powerplant:	4 x 1,200hp Twin Wasp R-1830-43 or 65 engines
Maximum Speed:	270mph at 20,000ft
Range:	990 miles (with maximum bomb load)
Maximum Bomb Load:	12,800lb
Armament:	10 x 50-cal. Browning machine guns
Service Ceiling:	26,500ft

B-24L/M

Concerned by the drop in performance of the heavily armed B-24H/J, the USAAF asked Consolidated to build a lighter version of the Liberator. The company responded with the B-24L, which was 1,000lb lighter than the preceding model through the removal of the Sperry ventral ball turret and replacement of the hydraulically powered Consolidated A-6B rear turret with the manually powered M-6A. The B-24M was similar to the L-model, with additional weight savings and a redesigned flight deck canopy to improve the pilot's vision for formation flying. The A-6B turret, in lightweight form, was reintroduced, as was the Sperry ball turret. Finally, the waist-gunner positions were also left open. A total of 1,667 B-24Ls and 2,593 B-24Ms were completed in 1944–45.

FIGHTERS

Spitfires
Supermarine Spitfire

The first fighter to see operational service in the Eighth Air Force was the British-designed Supermarine Spitfire. It would serve both as a fighter and in the photo reconnaissance role. The Spitfire Mk V would initially equip the 4th, 31st, and 52nd Fighter groups and 21 Mk XIs would be assigned to the 7th Photo Group.

Spitfire Mk V

The Spitfire V was simply a Mk I/II airframe fitted with the new Merlin 45, 46, 50, or 50A engine. The Merlin 45 was the less complex version of the Merlin XX, designed to power the Mk III. The supercharger's second stage (for improved low-altitude performance) was removed and replaced by a new single-speed, single-stage supercharger. The Merlin 45 was rated at 1,440hp on take-off and was easy to mass produce. Other engine improvements included a new carburetor that allowed for negative G maneuvers and prevented interruption of fuel flow to the engine. Pilots soon found the Merlin 45-powered Spitfire V ran at excessively high oil temperatures. The original Spitfire I/II engine cooling system was not powerful enough, so a larger matrix had to be fitted to the cooler. This, in turn, required a larger air intake. The new oil cooler intake was enlarged and made circular in shape. The Spitfire I/II's fabric-covered ailerons were also replaced by examples made from light alloy.

Spitfire Mk VB EN951 MD-U of "Eagle Squadron" 133 was the aircraft of Squadron Commander Don Blakeslee. Arguably the most influential American fighter leader in the ETO, Blakeslee began his combat career flying Spitfires with No. 401 Squadron RCAF. (Author's collection)

The first Spitfire Vs built were fitted with the A-type wing that housed eight 30-cal. Browning machine guns. Armor plating was also increased and now weighed 129lb. Top speed for the Spitfire VA was 375mph at 20,800ft. Just 94 were built.

The Spitfire VB would ultimately be the most numerous Mk V variant. It featured the B-type wing, housing two Hispano 20mm cannon, with 60 rounds per weapon, and four 30-cal. Browning machine guns with 350 rounds per gun. Armor was increased in weight to 152lb. A total of 3,911 Spitfire VBs would be built, 776 by Vickers Supermarine, 2,995 in Castle Bromwich, and 140 by Westland.

Spitfire VB Specifications

Powerplant:	1,470hp Merlin 45
Maximum Speed:	371mph at 20,000ft
Range:	470 miles
Service Ceiling:	35,000ft
Armament:	2 x 20mm Hispano IIs cannon, 4 x 30-cal. Browning machine guns

The Spitfire VC introduced the "universal" C-type wing first tested on the Spitfire III prototype. The "universal wing" was designed to reduce manufacturing time and allowed for three different armament options. The "C" wing featured either eight 30-cal. machine guns, two 20mm cannon and four 30-cal. machine guns, or four 20mm cannon. The Hispano Mk II cannon were now belt-fed from box magazines, doubling the ammunition per weapon to 120 rounds. Early build Spitfire VCs were delivered with four 20mm cannon, but two of these weapons were usually removed once the fighter was in front-line service. Later, production would shift back to the B-type wing, with two 20mm cannon and four 30-cal. machine guns.

The Spitfire VC's airframe was also re-stressed and strengthened. The new laminated windscreen design seen on the Mk III was introduced, as were metal ailerons and a stiffened undercarriage with wheels moved 2in. forward. Armor was increased to 193lb.

To increase the Spitfire VC's ferry range, a 29-gal fuel tank was installed behind the pilot. This, combined with a 90-gal slipper tank (rarely seen on the Channel Front), meant that the Mk VC could carry up to 204 gallons of fuel. This gave it a ferry range of approximately 700

miles. When fitted with four 20mm cannon, the Spitfire VC had a top speed of 374mph at 19,000ft. Although some Mk VCs saw combat on the Channel Front, most served in overseas theaters including the Middle East, Burma, and Australia. Some 2,647 Spitfire VCs would be built, 478 by Vickers Supermarine, 1,494 in Castle Bromwich, and 495 by Westland.

Spitfire PR MK XI of the 7th Photo Group. With a maximum cruise speed of 387mph at 31,300ft, the PR Mk XI was extremely hard to intercept, making it one of the most successful photo reconnaissance aircraft of World War II. (Author's collection)

First Victory

The first taste of real action for the USAAF Spitfire groups came on August 19, 1942, when the 31st Fighter Group formed part of the fighter cover for the large-scale raid on the French port of Dieppe, which was to see some of the heaviest air fighting of the war. In company with Nos 130 and 131 RAF squadrons, a dozen Spitfires of the 309th Fighter Squadron left Westhampnett early for Dieppe. Over the beachhead, they were attacked by a swarm of Fw 190s, and in the ensuing dogfight Lieutenant Samuel F. Junkin, Jr. managed to shoot one down to claim the first fighter victory for the USAAF in Europe. However, moments later he was attacked and wounded by a second Focke-Wulf and forced to bale out—Junkin was rescued by a torpedo boat that also picked up squadron mate Lieutenant Collins.

Spitfire PR Mk XI

The Spitfire Mk XI was designed from the outset as a high-speed, high-altitude photo reconnaissance aircraft. The Mk XI was essentially a Mk

IX Spitfire modified for the photo reconnaissance role with two vertically mounted F52 cameras with 36in.-focal-length lens behind the cockpit. All the guns and armor were removed to allow for the increase in fuel capacity. The 14th Photographic Squadron operated the type from November 1943 until April 1945. Powered by either the Merlin 61, 63, or 70 engine developing 1,655hp, it had a top speed of 422mph. Cruising speed was 369mph with a ceiling of 40,000ft.

Republic P-47 Thunderbolt

The new P-47 Thunderbolt fighter, unlike most of its contemporaries, employed an air-cooled radial engine in the shape of the recently developed Pratt & Whitney R-2800, developing 2,000hp. Designed as a high-altitude interceptor, the P-47 featured turbo-supercharging for the engine, which gave it top speeds in excess of 400mph at the then very high altitudes of 25,000 to 30,000ft. In comparison with the P-39 and P-40, the P-47 was a giant both in size and weight.

The P-47 Thunderbolt began to arrive in the United Kingdom in late December 1942. The first P-47 group, the 4th Fighter Group, turned in their Spitfires and became operational with the P-47 in early March 1943, but they were not impressed. In April 1943, the P-47 was tested against the Fw 190, and the tests found that while

The Republic XP-47B Thunderbolt shown here was a single prototype subvariant of the P-47B. Powered by a R-2800-35 engine and a Curtiss four-bladed constant speed propeller, it achieved a top speed of 412mph at 25,800ft. (Author's collection)

P-47 External Tanks

The use of external fuel tanks was the most important tactical development for Eighth Fighter Command, but their long-delayed development and deployment was a sad story that cost many American bomber crewmen their lives, the result of the flawed doctrine of the self-protecting bomber promulgated by the Air Corps Tactical School.

The idea of external fuel tanks was not new—the Army Air Corps had experimented with external fuel tanks for tactical aircraft in the late 1930s—but in May 1939 General Arnold, a product of the Air Corps Tactical School, issued an order forbidding their use because of a suspected fire hazard. However, when the war began, and the USAAF was faced with the problem of moving fighters long distances, General Arnold modified his position. On February 20, 1942, he authorized the development and manufacture of external fuel tanks for fighters. An unpressurized paper 200-gallon belly "bath-tub" for the P-47 began to arrive in theater in March, but it was only intended for ferry purposes and jettisoning the tanks was difficult and intended only for emergencies. The P-47 groups also found that only 100 of the advertised 200 gallons were really usable, and since the tanks were unpressurized, the fuel would not feed above 20,000ft.

Finally, at the beginning of September 1943, the first British-made 108-gallon steel tanks and 108-gallon paper tanks became operational. The P-47s first used them on their September 27 mission to Emden, even though there was only 4in. ground clearance under these tanks and they could not be used on "rough" airfields.

Eighth Fighter Command also ordered 75-gallon all-steel, teardrop-shaped centerline fuel tanks designed for the P-39 fighter. They were shipped at great cost to the United Kingdom and modified for use on the P-47 in late August after the Schweinfurt–Regensburg raids; they proved very effective.

This cine-film still shows the large 200-gallon drop tank first used in 1942. This garishly painted tank belonged to Captain Eugene W. O'Neill's 62nd Fighter Squadron P-47C serial no. 41-6347. (littlefriends.co.uk)

the Thunderbolt showed exceptional performance above 20,000ft because of its turbo-supercharger, the 60ft of air ducting for the supercharger and the Thunderbolt's heavy weight gave it poor acceleration, and the Focke-Wulf outclimbed and outmaneuvered it easily. When the P-47s first began to fly combat missions, they rarely engaged German fighters, so the maintenance teams had a chance to solve the Thunderbolt's early problems with radios and the pilots had an opportunity to develop escort tactics. This allowed them to gain both confidence and experience without heavy combat.

Once they began to escort American bombers, the P-47 groups' tactics made them a favorite of the bomber crews. The RAF Spitfires flew at very high altitude, where they outperformed the German fighters but were often too late to prevent the initial German attack. The P-47s flew the three squadrons of the group above the bombers, with the center squadron 2,000–3,000ft above the others, which in turn flew 3,000–4,000ft higher than the bombers. The center and highest squadron acted as "top cover" protection for the lower squadrons, whose job it was to intercept enemy fighters making for the bombers. This gave the Germans the initiative, but also ensured that they would be intercepted prior to their first pass.

The P-47's major limitation was range. Its 2,000hp Pratt & Whitney engine used fuel rapidly—100 gallons per hour on a combat mission, whereas the standard RAF fighter, the Spitfire IX, used 45 gallons per hour—giving it a combat radius of action of less than 200 miles. It was this range limitation that made the P-47 ineffective for the first half of 1943, but the introduction of various types of jettisonable external fuel tanks, beginning in late July, allowed the Thunderbolts to extend their combat radius somewhat so they could escort the bombers and keep the rocket-firing German *Zerstörer* at bay. However, they still were range-limited, and the German controllers quickly recalibrated to keep the rocket fighters out of their range.

P-47C

Similar to the P-47B, the P-47C-1-RE (RE was factory designation for Farmingdale) was fitted with a 2,300hp R-2800-59 that featured an A-17 turbo-supercharger regulator. Aircraft also had a slightly longer forward fuselage, which had been extended 8in. at the firewall (increasing overall length from 35ft to 36ft 1in.) to create a better center of gravity and make the engine accessories compartment roomier and easier to work in. This variant also had the provision for a belly mounted bomb or drop tank. The first P-47C was completed on September 14, 1942, and a total of 602 were eventually built.

P-47D-1 through to D-10

The D-1-RA (114 built) was the first P-47 model to emerge from the new Evansville, Indiana plant from December 1942—RA was the Evansville factory designation. It was essentially similar to the C-5. The D-1-RE had additional cowling flaps, improved pilot

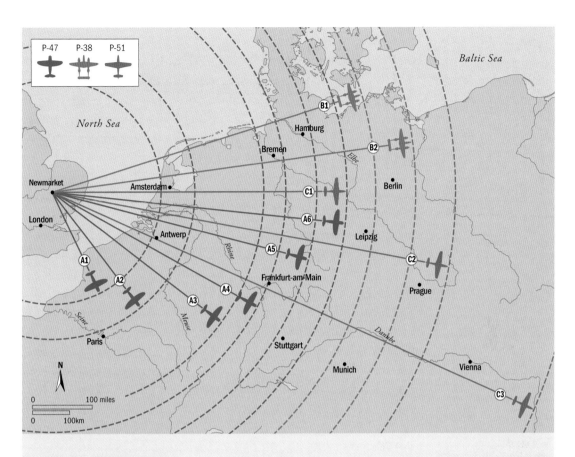

US Escort-fighter ranges

	Range (Miles)	With Drop Tanks	Date
P-47			
A1	175	none (P-47C)	May 1943
A2	230	none (P-47D)	June 1943
A3	340	75-gallon belly	July 1943
A4	375	108-gallon belly	August 1943
A5	425	150-gallon belly	February 1944
A6	475	2 x 108-gallon wing	February 1944
P-38			
B1	520	none	November 1943
B2	585	2 x 108-gallon wing	February 1944
P-51			
C1	475	none	January 1944
C2	650	2 x 75-gallon wing	March 1944
C3	850	2 x 108-gallon wing	March 1944

armor, and a new radio mast—all 105 were built at Farmingdale. The D-2-RA (200 built) was similar to the D-1-RE, as was the D-2-RE (445 built), which also featured minor upgrades to the fuel system. Some 100 D-3-Ras were then constructed, and these were similar to the D-2-RE. The D-5-RE (300 built) was based on the D-1-RE, but with modifications to the aircraft's fuel and hydraulic systems. The D-4-RA (200 built) was similar to the D-5-RE. The D-6-RE (350 built) was effectively a D-1-RE with two-point shackles for a bomb or a drop tank under the fuselage. The D-10-RE (250 built) was also based on the D-1-RE, but with further improvements to the hydraulic system and the fitment of a General Electric C-23 turbo-supercharger.

P-47D-11 through to D-23

The D-11-RE (400 built) was fitted with a 2,300hp R-2800-63 engine that featured water injection, as was the identical Evansville D-11-RA (250 built). The D-15-RE (496 built) introduced single stations for a bomb or drop tank beneath each wing panel and an increased payload that meant it could carry two 1,000lb or three 500lb bombs. The D-15-RA (157 built) was identical in specification. The D-16-RE (254 built) was based on the D-11-RE, but it could run on 100/150 octane fuel—just 29 D-16-Ras of a similar specification were built. The D-20-RE (250 built) was powered by a

This P-47D serial no. 42-26641 LM-S belonged to Lieutenant-Colonel David C. Schilling of the 62nd Fighter Squadron. The artwork on the nose depicts "Hairless Joe" from the Dogpatch cartoon strip. The P-47D with the bubble canopy offered an excellent all-round view and was a big improvement over the birdcage design of the earlier P-47Ds. (littlefriends.co.uk)

2,300hp R-2800-59, and it also had a raised tailwheel strut, General Electric ignition harness, and other minor airframe modifications— Evansville built 187 D-20-Ras to an identical specification. Delivered in natural metal finish, the D-21-RE (216 built) had manual water injection control for the engine, but was otherwise similar to the D-11-RE. The D-21-RA (224 built) was the same as the D-21-RE. The D-22-RE (850 built) featured the 13ft Hamilton Standard paddle-blade propeller and an A-23 turbo-supercharger regulator. Featuring the same engine modification, the D-23-RA (889 built) was fitted with a Curtiss Electric 13ft paddle-blade propeller.

P-47D-25 through to D-40

The D-25-RE (385 built) was the first P-47 fitted with a teardrop canopy and cut-down rear fuselage. The aircraft also had an increased supply of oxygen and some of its fuselage-located systems repositioned to allow its fuel capacity to be increased to 270 US gallons.

P-47M-1

Farmingdale hastily constructed the M-1-RE (130 built), featuring a 2,800hp R-2800-57 with an uprated CH-5 turbo-supercharger. The aircraft was also fitted with airbrakes in the wings, but was otherwise identical to the D-30-RE. All were sent to the 56th Fighter Group in the autumn of 1944, where dorsal fins were fitted in the field.

P-47D-25 Specifications

Powerplant:	2,300hp R-2800-59
Maximum Speed:	429mph at 27,800ft
Range:	475 miles (without drop tanks)
Service Ceiling:	42,000ft
Armament:	8 x 50-cal. Browning machine guns

Lockheed P-38 Lightning

The Lightning had been reintroduced to the Eighth Air Force in the late summer of 1943, seasoned stateside operators of the P-38 in the shape of the 20th and 55th Fighter groups commencing their work ups to operational flying in the middle of September.

P-47D-25 cockpit (opposite)

1. Rudder trim tab control
2. Aileron trim tab control
3. Elevator trim tab control crank
4. Cockpit spotlight
5. Wing flap control handle
6. Landing gear control handle
7. Gun safety switch
8. Fuel selector valves
9. Supercharger control
10. Throttle
11. Microphone push-to-talk button
12. Propeller control
13. Mixture control
14. Hydraulic handpump
15. Main switch box
16. Circuit breakers
17. Dive flap controls
18. Canopy open/close switch
19. Control switch box for constant speed propeller
20. Ammeter
21. Master battery switch
22. Ignition switch
23. Airspeed indicator
24. Clock
25. Rear radar warning lamp
26. K-14A gunsight
27. Rearview mirror
28. Landing gear warning lights
29. Directional gyro turn indicator
30. Artificial horizon
31. Carburetor air temperature gauge
32. Turbo rpm gauge
33. Fuel pressure warning lights
34. Oil and fuel pressure temperature gauge
35. Defroster control lever
36. Engine primer
37. Oil temperature gauge
38. Cowl flap control lever
39. Control column
40. Rudder pedals
41. Altimeter
42. Turn and bank indicator
43. Accelerometer
44. Rate of climb indicator
45. Suction gauge
46. Engine hours gauge
47. Compass
48. Fuel warning light
49. Fuel contents gauge
50. Gun firing button
51. Manifold pressure gauge
52. Hydraulic and oxygen pressure gauges
53. Engine starter switches
54. Tachometer
55. Recognition light switches
56. Oxygen regulator
57. Flare pistol port cover
58. Crystal filter selector switch
59. Cockpit vent control
60. Tailwheel lock
61. VHF radio control box
62. Command transmitter control box
63. Identification light switches
64. IFF radio destroyer buttons
65. Command receiver control box
66. Pilot's seat

(Artwork by Chris Davey © Osprey Publishing)

Few would dispute that in aerial combat the Merlin-engined North American P-51 Mustang was the dominant US single-engined fighter of World War II. Even the most devoted P-38 veteran would acknowledge the Mustang's ability to master most piston-engined opponents, at least under certain conditions. The P-51 was a truly

The prototype Lockheed XP-38 was a sleek and futuristic-looking fighter. The P-38 was originally designed as a bomber interceptor and was never intended to be a long-range escort fighter. But like all fighters in World War II, it was given roles the original designers never envisioned. (Author's collection)

great air superiority fighter, and its performance was clearly superior to the P-38.

A consummate leader, Colonel Hubert Zemke's record with the 56th and 479th Fighter groups was near legendary, so his opinion on USAAF fighters in the ETO should be respected. Having said that, his disdain for the P-38 is based on disputable facts, and should be taken with a degree of reserve. Basically, he considered the Lightning to be an obsolescent failure in the ETO because of its mechanical troubles at altitude, its frail construction, and its apparent low survivability.

Zemke's scathing comments about the P-38 included the tail buffeting that took place in high-speed dives, and the fact that at high speeds airflow over the cockpit and wing center section became turbulent.

Like his commanding officer, Robin Olds was also a P-51 enthusiast, but he was not as anti-P-38 as Zemke—he achieved ace status in the Lightning after all. "Mutual admiration" best describes the relationship between Colonel Zemke and the young Olds. Zemke was aware of the spirited, youthful Olds from the youngster's days as a "military brat" (he was the son of Major-General Robert Olds, who commanded the 2nd Bomb Group in the late 1930s) and firebrand who had gained his wings just prior to his graduation from West Point. Olds reciprocated the feeling, considering Zemke to be a great fighter leader and group commander.

P-38J-10 of Captain Robin Olds, 434th Fighter Squadron, June 1944

Olds flew four P-38s between May and September 1944, and this first aircraft lasted him through the D-Day operations of June 1944. (Artwork by Chris Davey © Osprey Publishing)

In the 1970s, Brigadier-General Robin Olds (an ace flying both the P-38 and P-51) gave his opinion on the two types of fighter aircraft that he had flown with the 434th Fighter Squadron in World War II. He wrote:

> The P-38 was a wonderful fighter in many respects, and having been weaned on it, I loved it, up to a point. It was fast, easy to fly (once you really knew it), and would turn with the best of them, providing you had an exceedingly strong right arm. It was honest in most respects, giving ample stall warning under all flight conditions, and easy to recover if you ignored it. With proper power management, it had fine endurance, and could cover the bombers all the way in and out again. Its four 50-cal. machine guns and its single 20mm cannon gave it good firepower. It was acceptably rugged and could absorb a respectable beating and still get you home.

P-38H

With the production of the P-38H, engine power was increased to 1,425hp with the introduction of the Allison V-1710-89/91. The H-model was the first Lightning to be fitted with fully automatic engine controls, along with new turbo-superchargers and automatic oil radiator flaps. These improvements gave the Lightning more power at high altitude and a maximum speed of 402mph at 25,000ft. The M1 20mm cannon was replaced by the M2 version and the underwing bomb capacity for both racks was raised to 1,600lb. A total of 601 P-38H models were produced, with 90 being converted to the F-5B photo reconnaissance model.

**P-38J-10 42-67926 of Captain Lindol F. Graham,
79th Fighter Squadron, March 1944**

Graham "made ace" in this fighter during a confused aerial clash involving several P-38s
and a formation of Bf 110s on February 20, 1944 southwest of Brunswick. He claimed
two Messerschmitt "twins" destroyed. (Artwork by Tom Tullis © Osprey Publishing)

P-38J

This 55th Fighter Squadron
P-38J serial no.
42-104239 KI-P belonged
to Major Martin L. Low.
This P-38 suffered a forced
landing on June 12, 1944.
The new improved J model
had chin radiators, flat
bulletproof windscreen,
power-boosted ailerons,
and increased fuel
capacity.
(littlefriends.co.uk)

Introduction of the P-38J was a big step forward for the aircraft. Up to
this point, the basic contours of the Lightning, and its engine nacelles,
had remained virtually unchanged. With the new J-model, however,
"beard" or "chin" intakes had been installed directly below the propeller
spinners. Earlier versions of the P-38 had been afflicted by compressed
air cooling problems created by the turbo-supercharging. If the air
being fed to the latter was not cool enough, it duly restricted engine
power at higher altitudes and created explosive backfires.

With the J-model, the old method of passing the compressed air
through hollow passageways (intercoolers) fitted within the leading
edge of the wings was replaced by core-type radiators located below

the engines and sandwiched between the oil radiator intakes. The core-type radiators were very efficient, and with the elimination of the leading edge ducting, more space was created for additional fuel tanks—capacity was duly increased to 410 gallons internally. Although the new chin radiators created more drag, they finally allowed the Lightning to use full engine power at altitude. The P-38J, equipped with the same engines as the H-model, was the fastest Lightning of them all, with a top speed of 420mph at 26,500ft.

P-38J Specifications

Powerplant:	Two 1,435hp Allison V-1710-89/91 engines
Maximum Speed:	420mph at 26,500ft
Range:	1,040 miles (without drop tanks)
Service Ceiling:	44,000ft
Armament:	1 x 20mm Hispano M1 cannon, 4 x 50-cal. Browning machine guns

North American P-51 Mustang

The story of the P-51 Mustang is one founded on superlative airframe and engine design, perseverance, collaboration, urgent strategic requirement, industrial might, and excellent execution—with a measure of what might be called aeronautical serendipity.

In April 1940, British Purchasing Commission (BPC) officials visiting America sought a new long-range fighter to supplement the Spitfire and Hurricane. When they approached North American Aircraft with an invitation to produce the Curtiss 11-87 (P-40D) in quantity under license for the RAF, the California-based company suggested instead that it build a brand new and infinitely superior fighter using the same 1,150hp Allison V-1710-39 engine. The BPC accepted the proposal, but a 120-day limit for the construction of a prototype was imposed.

North American's only previous experience in fighter design and construction was limited to the near-identical NA-50 and NA-68, both of which were little more than reworked, single-seat trainers fitted with guns in the wings. Just 13 examples of these aircraft had been built for the Peruvian and Royal Siam air forces in 1939. Nevertheless, North American Aircraft Company president J. H.

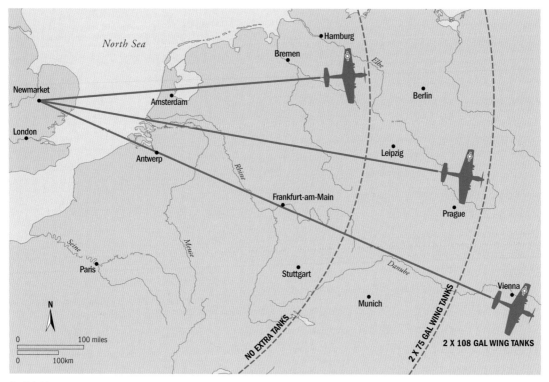

P-51 Ranges

This map shows the ranges which P-51 Mustangs could extend to.

"Dutch" Kindelberger was confident that his company could produce an aircraft that answered the needs of the RAF. He and his team of engineers had studied early accounts of air combat in Europe, and these had influenced the design of a new fighter that North American already had on its drawing board prior to the BPC visit.

With the BPC contract signed, the design team, headed by Lee Atwood, Raymond Rice, and German-born Austrian Edgar Schmued (the latter having previously been employed by Dutch aircraft manufacturer Fokker), hastily began work on the new fighter, which was designated the NA-73X—"73" was North American's model number and "X" denoted its experimental status.

The NA-73X prototype was assembled in 117 days, although when the aircraft was rolled out of the company's Mines Field facility its 1,100hp Allison V-1710-39 (F3R) engine was not yet installed and the prototype was fitted with wheels borrowed from an AT-6 basic trainer. The NA-73 was one of the first fighters to employ a low, square-cut, laminar-flow airfoil, which had its maximum thickness well aft. The aircraft duly boasted the lowest-drag wing fitted to any fighter yet built. Drag was further reduced by streamlining a radiator scoop into the underside of the fuselage behind the pilot, whilst keeping the fuselage cross-section to the least depth possible.

On May 4, 1940, the US Army released the new design for sale to Britain, provided that two of the initial batch of fighters be transferred to the USAAC for tests. After 320 NA-73s were ordered by the BPC 19 days later, the fourth and tenth aircraft were allotted the Army Air Corps designation XP-51 in a contract approved on September 20, 1940. Four days later, the BPC increased its purchase of these fighters to 620 examples.

When the Mustang entered service, the Allison was found to perform well at low-to-medium altitudes, but from 11,300ft power would start to drop off at full throttle and by 15,000ft performance had ebbed away rapidly. The RAF accepted this, and duly deployed the aircraft in tactical fighter and reconnaissance roles rather than in higher-altitude fighter/air superiority missions—the latter were left to the Spitfire V/IX.

The North American XP-51 Mustang, protoype to the P-51. Equipped with the Allison V-1710-39 engine and its full armament of four 30-cal. and four 50-cal. machine guns, XP-51 achieved a top speed of 379mph at 13,000ft in December 1941. (Author's collection)

The story remained the same for the first Allison-engined Mustangs, known as the P-51 and P-51A, delivered to the USAAF from the spring of 1943, initially for service with the Ninth Air Force.

EIGHTH AIR FORCE ENEMY AIRCRAFT CLAIMS	
In the air destroyed	5,222
Probables	348
Damaged	1,568
On the ground destroyed	4,250
Probables	23
Damaged	2,886
P-47, P-38, P-51, Spitfire missing in action	2,048
Category E (damaged beyond economical repair)	778

Enter the Merlin

Crucially, that same year in an important revision, the Allison V-1710 was replaced by a license-built Packard Merlin engine adapted from the two-stage British Merlin 61. In Britain, serendipity played its hand. On April 30, 1942, following a request from the commanding officer of the Air Fighting Development Unit, Rolls-Royce factory pilot Ronald W. Harker had made a brief flight in an RAF Mustang I at Duxford, in Cambridgeshire, and was instantly impressed. He enthusiastically noted that it was 35mph faster than the Spitfire VB at similar power settings, and with double the range. When questioned after the flight on how the fighter could be made even better, Harker opined that the only natural improvement he would recommend was the installation of a Merlin 61 engine.

P-51B

When the Packard Merlin engine was fitted into the Mustang to produce the ensuing P-51B, which first flew on May 5, 1943, the Americans had a fighter with an impressive top speed and rate of climb, together with a range capability that would allow the Mustang to fly 300 miles from its base and back. Such performance numbers meant that the P-51B more than adequately fulfilled Eighth Fighter Command's need for a long-range escort fighter. Furthermore, the B-model Mustang was not as "thirsty" as the P-38 Lightning or P-47 Thunderbolt, and was also less expensive to produce.

Executive Officer of Eighth Fighter Command's 4th Fighter Group, Lieutenant-Colonel Don Blakeslee, was assigned to the 354th Fighter Group to oversee the group's introduction to combat in the European Theater of Operations. He became a firm advocate for the P-51B:

The P-51 Mustang was a little slow in coming to us in England, but I knew the first time I flew it that it was the plane to do the job. When the P-47s arrived in late 1942, they were a great improvement, but still not the full answer range-wise. The P-38 was supposed to be the USAAF's best long-range fighter, but there were no P-38 groups in the ETO before late 1943. Things began to change when we were told we had to gain air superiority over the Luftwaffe before an invasion could take place. The German pilots would not tangle with us as often as we wanted, therefore making it difficult to destroy them. Then, in December, the 354th Fighter Group began operations with Mustangs and, finally, in early 1944, the Eighth Air Force began receiving them. We now had plenty of fuel to loiter around the bombers, chase the Luftwaffe, or go to the deck and strafe at will. No area of the ETO was out of reach.

A P-51B serial no. 42-106886 5Q-O of the 504th Fighter Squadron, 339th Fighter Group. The Merlin-powered P-51 was faster than the Spitfire Mk IX, the Bf 109G-6, and Fw 190A-8. (littlefriends.co.uk)

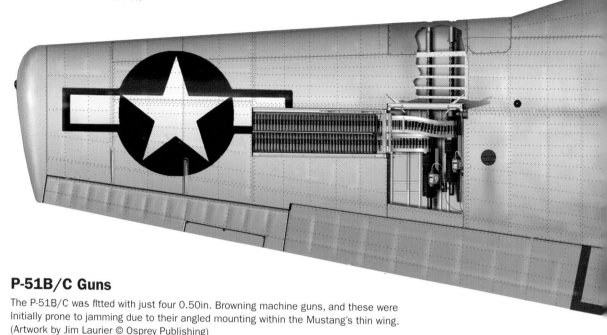

P-51B/C Guns

The P-51B/C was fitted with just four 0.50in. Browning machine guns, and these were initially prone to jamming due to their angled mounting within the Mustang's thin wing. (Artwork by Jim Laurier © Osprey Publishing)

The appearance of the P-51B in significant numbers must have sent a shiver of concern down the spines of Luftwaffe fighter pilots, and by March 1944 the four Mustang fighter groups in England were being credited with a "kill" rate of 13 enemy aircraft destroyed per 100 sorties—a figure that easily exceeded those for the P-38 and P-47 squadrons of four and three, respectively. There was almost universal agreement among senior USAAF commanders that as many fighter squadrons as possible, if not all, should be equipped with P-51s.

A total of 1,988 B-models were built at Inglewood, the last 550 becoming P-51B-7s to -10s. The addition of an 85-gallon fuselage fuel tank increased the fighter's total internal fuel capacity to 269 US gallons and the normal range to 1,300 miles. This modification was also made in the field to earlier P-51B/Cs. Some 274 P-51Bs were allocated to the RAF as Mustang IIIs.

P-51C

Generally similar to the P-51B, 1,750 C-models were built at North American's new Dallas plant. Both the B- and C-models differed from earlier versions by having a strengthened fuselage and redesigned ailerons, and they were initially powered by the Packard Merlin V-1650-3, followed by the V-1650-7 Merlin 68. The latter had a war emergency rating of 1,695hp at 10,300ft, and produced a maximum speed of 439mph at 25,000ft. The sea-level climb rate was 3,900ft/min. Maximum weight with a 2,000lb bomb load was 11,200lb. Armament was four 50-cal. machine guns in the wings, with a total of 1,260 rounds of ammunition. The RAF received 636 P-51Cs (Mustang IIIs). A total of 71 USAAF P-51B/Cs were modified as F-6C tactical reconnaissance aircraft.

P-51D

The major production version, with a total of 7,956 built, the D-model introduced the bubble canopy to improve the pilot's field of view, a modified rear fuselage, and six 50-cal. machine guns. Fifty P-51Ds were supplied to the nationalist Chinese Air Force and 40 to the Royal Netherlands Air Force in the Pacific Theater of Operations (PTO). A modification of this series resulted in ten TP-51D trainers being built with radio equipment relocated and an additional seat, with full dual controls, behind the pilot seat. One TP-51D was further modified for use as a high-speed observation post for the Supreme Allied Commander, General Dwight Eisenhower, who flew in it to inspect the Normandy beachheads in June 1944.

This early P-51D serial no. 44-13763 E9-O belonged to the 376th Fighter Squadron. The early D models did not have the fin fillet added, but were later modified in the field. (littlefriends.co.uk)

P-51D Cockpit (opposite)

1. Landing gear control lever
2. Elevator trim tab control wheel
3. Carburetor hot air control lever
4. Carburetor cold air control lever
5. Rudder trim tab control
6. Aileron trim tab control
7. Coolant radiator control
8. Oil radiator control
9. Landing light switch
10. Florescent light switch, left
11. Flare pistol port cover
12. Arm rest
13. Mixture control lever
14. Throttle quadrant locks
15. Throttle control
16. Propeller pitch control
17. Selector dimmer assembly
18. Instrument light
19. Rear radar warning lamp
20. K-14A gun sight
21. Laminated glass
22. Remote compass indicator
23. Clock
24. Suction gauge
25. Manifold pressure gauge
26. Airspeed indicator
27. Directional gyro turn indicator
28. Artificial horizon
29. Coolant temperature
30. Tachometer
31. Altimeter
32. Turn and bank indicator
33. Rate of climb indicator
34. Carburetor temperature
35. Engine temperature gauge
36. Bomb release levers
37. Engine control panel
38. Landing gear indicator lights
39. Parking brake handle
40. Oxygen flow indicator
41. Oxygen pressure gauge
42. Ignition switch
43. Bomb and rocket switch
44. Cockpit light control
45. Rocket control panel
46. Fuel shut-off valve
47. Fuel selector valve
48. Emergency hydraulic release handle
49. Hydraulic pressure gauge
50. Oxygen hose
51. Oxygen regulator
52. Canopy release handle
53. Canopy crank
54. IFF control panel
55. IFF detonator buttons
56. VHF radio control box
57. Rear radar control panel
58. VHF volume control
59. Florescent light switch, right
60. Electrical control panel
61. Circuit breakers
62. BC-438 control box
63. Cockpit light
64. Circuit breakers
65. Rudder pedals
66. Control column
67. Flaps control lever
68. Pilot's seat
69. Flare gun storage

(Artwork by Jim Laurier © Osprey Publishing)

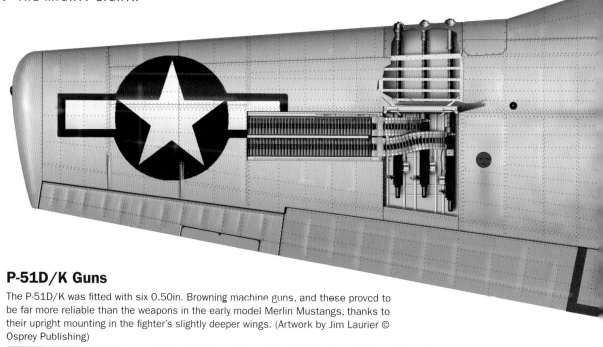

P-51D/K Guns

The P-51D/K was fitted with six 0.50in. Browning machine guns, and these proved to be far more reliable than the weapons in the early model Merlin Mustangs, thanks to their upright mounting in the fighter's slightly deeper wings. (Artwork by Jim Laurier © Osprey Publishing)

P-51D Specifications

Powerplant:	1,470hp V-1650-7 Packard Merlin
Maximum Speed:	440mph at 30,000ft
Range:	950 miles (without drop tanks)
Service Ceiling:	41,900ft
Armament:	6 x 50-cal. Browning M2 machine guns

P-51K

The 1,500 generally similar examples differed only in the replacement of the Hamilton-Standard airscrew by an Aeroproduct propeller and a slightly modified canopy with a blunter rear. Weighing 11,000lb loaded, the P-51K was not fitted with rocket-mounting stubs, and it had an inferior performance to the P-51D. 163 were completed as F-6K tactical reconnaissance examples. 594 were allocated to the RAF.

PHOTO-RECON AND RECONNAISSANCE

A limited number of aircraft were created for photographic reconnaissance (PR) and mapping tasks. They were designated with the prefix "F" (phonetically, for "photo").

K-14 Gunsight View

Introduced in the spring of 1944, P-51 Mustangs were fitted with the K-14 gunsight. Instead of the typical cross hairs one might expect, the K-14 projected a center dot of yellow light surrounded by six diamond-shaped dots. The basic idea was to maneuver until the dot could be placed on the enemy target, using the twist grip on the throttle handle to adjust the reticule of diamonds. (Artwork by Jim Laurier © Osprey Publishing)

One hundred and thirty-six tactical reconnaissance aircraft were modified from the P-51D production contract to create the F-6 variants. A total of 281 were allocated to the RAF. The cameras could be mounted in the rear of the fuselage, to the left of the pilot, and facing downward out of the bottom of the fuselage. Most of these photo-aircraft retained their armament.

On April 20, 1941, Major-General Hap Arnold, Chief of the USAAC, Major Elwood Quesada, General Arnold's aide, and later to control Ninth Fighter Command in England, and other senior officers were present at Hatfield when the Mosquito prototype (W4050), in the hands of Geoffrey de Havilland, Jr., was demonstrated to Lord Beaverbrook, Minister of Aircraft Production. The Americans

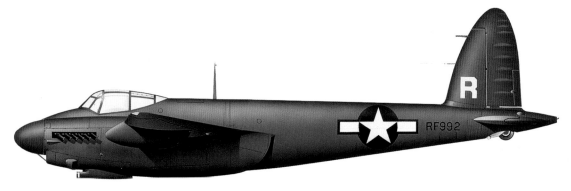

PR XVI RF992/R, 654th Bomb Squadron, 25th Bomb Group, 325th Photographic Wing, March 1945

On March 20, 1945, this aircraft, flown by Lieutenant Roger W. Gilbert and Lieutenant Raymond G. Spoerl, was attacked over Germany by Me 262s. Although its left wingtip was blown off, Gilbert brought RF992 home safely to RAF Watton. (Artwork by Chris Davey © Osprey Publishing)

were greatly impressed by the Mosquito's performance, and had long been interested in setting up production in Canada and Australia. However, in America, the Material Division of the AAC placed little importance in the Mosquito, expecting that the F-4 (P-38) Lightning would be capable of carrying out US Photo Reconnaissance needs.

In the summer of 1942, Colonel Elliott Roosevelt brought two squadrons of F-4 Lightnings and a squadron of B-17F "mapping Fortresses" to Britain. Given a B IV Mosquito for combat evaluations, Roosevelt discovered that the Mosquito outperformed his F-4s, and had five times the range. Demand for the Mosquito was so great only 200 reached the USAAF. On April 22, 1944, the 802nd Reconnaissance Group was formed at Watton, in Norfolk comprising the 652nd Heavy Weather Squadron (B-17s and B-24s) and two Mosquito units, the 653rd Bomb Squadron (Weather Reconnaissance, Light) and 654th Bomb Squadron (Reconnaissance Special, Heavy) using Mosquito PR XVIs. The 802nd would later be redesignated as the 25th Bomb Group in August 1944.

Mosquito Mk XVI Specifications

Powerplant:	Two 1,710hp Rolls-Royce Merlin 76/77 engines
Top Speed:	408mph
Cruising Speed:	250mph
Service Ceiling:	38,500ft
Range:	2,450 miles

The 653rd performed weather scouting and reconnaissance missions over occupied Europe, while the 654th assisted blinding bombing by taking H2X screen shots and flew high-altitude daytime reconnaissance missions. And from late 1944 until the end of the war, both squadrons flew special "Greenpea" missions which involved dropping strips of aluminum foil (chaff) in front of the lead bomber formations to confuse German radar-guided Flak batteries.

Altogether, the 25th Bomb Group flew 3,246 missions, with the 653rd Bomb Squadron losing 24 PR XVI Mosquitos, including 13 on operations, and the 654th 27 Mosquitos, 16 of them operationally.

A Mosquito Mk XVI of the 25th Bomb Group (Recon). The Mosquito was one of the most versatile aircraft of World War II. With a top speed of 401mph at 25,200ft and a maximum cruising speed of 352mph at 18,800ft, the Germans found it extremely difficult to intercept and it was the one aircraft they hated the most. (Author's collection)

Captain Donald S. Gentile (second from right) of 336th Fighter Squadron next to his P-51B 43-6913 VF-T *Shangri-La*. Don is pictured among the armorers servicing the 50-cal. guns on the starboard wing. Stoppages in combat drew the most criticism from pilots flying the B-model Mustang in combat in 1943–44. The P-51B was fitted with just four 50-cal. machine guns—two in each wing. Its laminar airfoil section was too thin to accommodate the weapons in the normal upright position, so they were canted over about 30 degrees. Thus, the ammunition feed trays had to curve slightly upward and then down again to enable link-belted rounds to enter the gun at the right angle. Gun jams were almost inevitable if the weapons were fired while the pilot was maneuvering at anything beyond 1.5g. (littlefriends.co.uk)

CHAPTER 5
THE TOOLS OF BATTLE
Training, Formations, Technology, Armament, Tactics

From the opening of its operations in August 1942 to the end of that year, the Eighth Air Force's Eighth Bomber Command, commanded by Brigadier-General Ira C. Eaker, had been "blooded" in 30 daylight missions flown from its airfields across eastern England to maritime, industrial, airfield, and railway targets in France and the Low Countries. On most occasions, the bombers enjoyed RAF fighter escort. Eighth Bomber Command had been progressively reinforced and expanded throughout the second half of 1942 to the point where it numbered six bomb groups—four equipped with B-17Fs and two with B-24Ds. On January 20, 1943, Eaker handed Prime Minister Winston Churchill a memorandum in which were outlined his reasons for the pursuance of such daylight attacks. "By bombing the devils around the clock," Eaker wrote, "we can prevent the German defenses from getting any rest."

This was just what Churchill wanted to read, and the very next day, during the Allied leaders' conference in Casablanca, the air commanders were informed that, given a force of 300 heavy bombers flown by trained crews, General Eaker believed he could attack any target in Germany by day with less than four percent loss. Smaller numbers would naturally suffer more severely. Despite all problems and currently effective limitations, he stoutly maintained that,

"Daylight bombing of Germany with airplanes of the B-17 and B-24 types is feasible, practicable and economical."

A month later, on April 17, the Eighth Air Force unveiled its new, more concentrated type of defensive flight formation for the war against Germany. In the first such deployment, two "combat wings" comprising 107 B-17s in six "boxes"—the largest force thus far assembled—were despatched on this date to bomb the Focke-Wulf plant at Bremen. Just after the "heavies" had commenced their bomb run, the Fw 190s of I. and II./JG 1 closed in at speed and mauled the B-17s for an hour. In determined, well-coordinated head-on attacks, JG 1 accounted for 15 Flying Fortresses destroyed, including an entire squadron—the heaviest losses sustained to date in a single mission. For their part, the American gunners excessively claimed 63 fighters shot down and another 15 "probables." Just one German aircraft was actually lost in combat.

Despite these setbacks, Eaker acknowledged that his bombers had proven their ability to successfully penetrate the German defenses, but that continued success depended on the quick expansion of his command. He asked for a further 944 B-17s by July; 1,192 by October; 1,746 by January 1944; and 2,702 by April. In the short term, however, May 13, 1943 saw the arrival of six new bomb groups to strengthen Eighth Bomber Command. Eaker recorded that it was "a great day."

TRAINING
Bomber Crew Training

Even before war had engulfed Europe, the United States was quietly making moves to expand its armed forces. The USAAC had laid plans to expand aircrew training to 1,200 pilots a year by 1941, and this figure was later revised upwards to 7,000 a year and again to 30,000 in 1941. The US government also knew that it was only a matter of time before the country was at war with Germany. Secret meetings between senior US and British staff officers in January and March 1941 established a course of action whereby American warships, troops, and aircraft would be committed to the campaign against the Axis powers in the European theater.

Aircrew training for the USAAF essentially followed the same pattern as for the RAF—Primary Flying School, Basic Flying School, Advanced Flying Training, and Transition Flying Training. The first step, however, was different. Would-be aircrew initially undertook a five-week basic military course. Here, aviation cadets went through a five-week regime that included exhaustive physical, psychological, and mental tests to determine their suitability for the flying program, and to determine which speciality was best for them as potential pilots, bombardiers, or navigators.

INSTRUCTION

TODAY IS NOT A JOB

IT'S A RESPONSIBILITY

WE'RE AT WAR

GENERAL, U. S. ARMY,
COMMANDING GENERAL,
ARMY AIR FORCES

A message to the new airmen found on the inside of the *Basic Flying Instructor's Manual*. (Author's collection)

America's full entry into the war on December 7, 1941 saw the rapid expansion of the USAAF and President Franklin D. Roosevelt's support for the acquisition of heavy bombers. It was a formidable training challenge. The new B-17 and B-24 required a crew of ten men—two-thirds larger than the standard crew for the B-18 and North American B-25 Mitchell medium bombers. It was estimated that more than 500 separate skills were required to execute a "routine" bombing mission. The commanding general of the newly renamed USAAF was fully aware of this, Lieutenant-General "Hap" Arnold stating in 1942 that, "This is an age of specialization. No rational man can hope to know everything about his profession."

American bombers also adopted the two-pilot system (British bombers had one pilot, with a flight engineer to assist), which meant twice as many aviators had to be trained. By 1944, the minimum number of hours required to produce a qualified pilot was as follows—Primary, 60 hours; Basic, 70 hours; Advanced, 75 hours. Those chosen for multi-engined types accumulated 70 hours flying twin-engined trainers like the Beechcraft AT-7 Navigator, AT-10 Wichita, AT-11 Kansan, and the Cessna AT-17 Bobcat. Based on their performance in these types, trainees were then selected for medium or heavy bombers, transports, or twin-engined fighters.

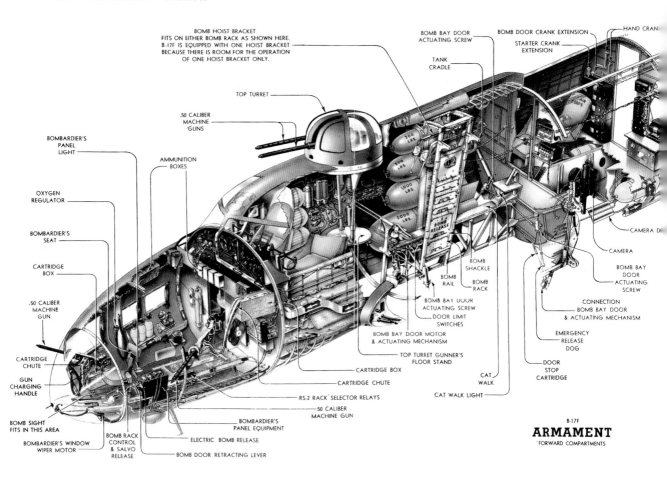

BOMB HOIST BRACKET
FITS ON EITHER BOMB RACK AS SHOWN HERE.
B-17F IS EQUIPPED WITH ONE HOIST BRACKET
BECAUSE THERE IS ROOM FOR THE OPERATION
OF ONE HOIST BRACKET ONLY.

TOP TURRET

.50 CALIBER
MACHINE
GUNS

BOMBARDIER'S
PANEL
LIGHT

AMMUNITION
BOXES

OXYGEN
REGULATOR

BOMBARDIER'S
SEAT

CARTRIDGE
BOX

.50 CALIBER
MACHINE
GUN

CARTRIDGE
CHUTE

GUN
CHARGING
HANDLE

BOMB SIGHT
FITS IN THIS AREA

BOMBARDIER'S WINDOW
WIPER MOTOR

BOMB RACK
CONTROL
& SALVO
RELEASE

ELECTRIC BOMB RELEASE

BOMB DOOR RETRACTING LEVER

BOMBARDIER'S
PANEL EQUIPMENT

.50 CALIBER
MACHINE GUN

RS-2 RACK SELECTOR RELAYS

CARTRIDGE CHUTE

CARTRIDGE BOX

TOP TURRET GUNNER'S
FLOOR STAND

BOMB BAY DOOR MOTOR
& ACTUATING MECHANISM

DOOR LIMIT
SWITCHES

BOMB BAY DOOR
ACTUATING SCREW

BOMB
RAIL

BOMB
RACK

BOMB
SHACKLE

CAT
WALK

CAT WALK LIGHT

BOMB BAY DOOR
ACTUATING SCREW

BOMB BAY DOOR CRANK EXTENSION

STARTER CRANK
EXTENSION

HAND CRAN

TANK
CRADLE

CAMERA D

CAMERA

BOMB BAY
DOOR
ACTUATING
SCREW

CONNECTION
BOMB BAY DOOR
& ACTUATING MECHANISM

EMERGENCY
RELEASE
DOG

DOOR
STOP
CARTRIDGE

B-17F
ARMAMENT
FORWARD COMPARTMENTS

This lavish cutaway illustration of the forward section of the B-17F comes from the *Familiarization and Inspection Manual* for the B-17F. These types of illustrations helped crews get to know the inner workings of their aircraft. The first F-models were delivered by Boeing Seattle in late May 1942, with Douglas at Long Beach and Lockheed-Vega following during the summer. By August 1943, all three plants accounted for an average output of 400 aircraft per month. (Author's collection)

Wearing their newly minted silver pilot's wings, aviators earmarked for heavy bombers commenced learning how to fly the type. During Transition Flying Training they received 105 hours of four-engined training, after which pilots reported to their unit training group. There, they would hone their formation flying, navigation, and bombing skills prior to being posted to an operational squadron.

Navigator and bombardier training also required a great deal of specialization and time. In 1942, navigator cadets received 403 hours of ground school and 100 hours in the air during a course that lasted 15 weeks. Bombardier training was shorter, as the early demand for crews meant that courses had to be cut to just nine weeks. Three-quarters of the training consisted of ground classes in theory, bombsights, and procedures, with bombardiers also honing their skills with the A-2 bombing simulator prior to taking to the air. After dropping between 120 and 145 practice bombs during qualification and 55 to 80 during the tactical training phase, the bombardier was considered ready. Both navigators and bombardiers also initially received some gunnery school training in the use of the flexibly mounted 30-cal. or 50-cal. weapons. However, by mid-1942, the gunnery schools were so jammed with new recruits that many bombardiers and navigators arrived in England having never previously fired a weapon.

Air Gunnery

Before the appearance of P-47s with drop tanks from the autumn of 1943, and later P-51s, which could escort B-17s to deep penetration targets in Germany, the Flying Fortress' defense was its guns, and their correct use was vital to the survival of air crew when under fighter attack. This was illustrated in stark terms by the Las Vegas Army Airfield (LVAAF) Year Book of the same year, which recorded the role of the gunner:

> The protection they provide is vital to success of long-range bombing. On this ability of self-protection, long-range bombing is built. Each bomber, alone, must be able to hold its own against fighters. Everything depends on the ability of one special class of men, the aerial gunners. They have to be good or they are dead, and heavy bombardment is dead with them. The five men who handle the guns in a bomber crew of nine are trained as mechanics, radio operators, cameramen. Many of them have never fired a gun. In order to make them first-rate gunners, the Air Forces give them the toughest six weeks of training in the Army.
>
> At the special schools, they learn their deadly business. Taught precision on miniature ranges with 0.22-cal. rifles, they learn to lead and swing while shooting trap and skeet. They fire machine guns, find out the trick of the turrets, have special training on altitude flying, and when their course is finished, they are assigned to operational training units ready for combat.

At the beginning of the war, the USAAC had no training facilities for aerial gunnery, but in the summer of 1941, a group of officers was sent to England to seek guidance on how to set up such a school. Subsequently, future B-17 air gunners would arrive at the Flexible

A gunner poses in a fully loaded Martin top turret. On average, during the second half of World War II, 600 gunnery students graduated from the Las Vegas Army Air Field (LVAAF) every five weeks, although during 1943 the school graduated 9,117 gunners. By September 1944, 227,827 gunners had been trained. (Author's collection)

Gunnery School north of Las Vegas, which provided training in moveable, as opposed to fixed, guns of the type to be found on a heavy bomber. The first thing that struck most trainees arriving at the base was the searing heat and the inhospitable Nevada landscape. As one man recalled, "All you can see is desert sand and mountains, mile upon mile." Here, future gunners would practice using air rifles for marksmanship, shooting at clay pigeons on the ground and from moving trucks, before firing machine guns on the ground. The student then graduated to the ground turret, firing machine guns at towed flags. Finally, they would fire in the air from B-34s and B-26s. Most of the course was dedicated to the 50-cal. Browning M2, which was the weapon gunners would use in the skies over Europe. Trainees were taught how to strip a gun down and then—under test conditions—reassemble the 80 or so parts blindfolded. When about two-thirds of the way through the course, trainees were transferred to another facility in the same state at Indian Springs, where there would be a brief period of airborne gunnery training on AT-6 Texans using ammunition filled with different-colored paint to assess individual accuracy and scoring. Finally, they would return to Las Vegas and be introduced to the B-17.

On average, during the second half of World War II, 600 gunnery students graduated from the LVAAF every five weeks, although during 1943 the school graduated 9,117 gunners. By September 1944, 227,827 gunners had been trained.

So it was that upon transfer to the ETO, gunners *seemed* highly skilled, and knew their aircraft inside and out. Initially, however, it had not been easy in England. The truth was that general standards of nose and waist position air gunnery were poor—despite high claims made during the initial clashes with the Luftwaffe—and incidents of damage from friendly fire were not uncommon. The effective use of a heavy, reverberating 50-cal. machine gun in a 200mph slipstream against a small, fast-moving target presented enormous challenges.

Following the arrival of the first bomb groups from the US in 1942, Eaker and Eighth Bomber Command set up further intensive gunnery training courses on land and coastal ranges procured from the British, such as those near Snettisham and in Cornwall, and by acquiring a handful of target-towing aircraft. Nevertheless, the overall standard of air gunnery remained disappointing for the rest of the year.

A B-24 equipped with the Emerson A-15 Nose Turret test fires its guns. The nose turret on the B-24 was not a complete success, but offered more protection against head-on attacks than the single 50-cal. gun in the B-24D. (Author's collection)

Even as late as November 1944, the Eighth Air Force conceded that, "There appears to be a serious weakness in nose gunnery. This is seen in the steady growth of the percentage of nose attacks, since enemy fighters may be expected to attack weak spots. There are explanations of this weakness: (1) the navigators and bombardiers have other primary duties, and tend to neglect their duty as gunners; (2) a high percentage of the navigators and bombardiers have had no gunnery training whatsoever."

However, by the time new B-17 groups arrived in numbers in England for the Eighth Air Force during the winter of 1943–44, operational training had reached considerably higher standards in the US. Much of it was handled by Combat Crew Replacement Centers (CCRC), although ad hoc forms of training continued to be meted out at unit level. In April 1944, inventive gunnery officers at Kimbolton, for example, constructed their own timber rig in a blister hangar into which were fitted chin, ball, and top turrets, and nose gun positions from wrecked B-17s. Target images were then projected into a screen, while elsewhere on the airfield a B-17 top turret was fitted onto the back of a truck. The latter would then be driven along a perimeter track and the new gunner would practice his aim against friendly aircraft flying over the airfield.

Early in the war, the rapid expansion of the USAAF and the demand for new personnel to man recently formed squadrons resulted in far too many poorly trained crews. To address the problem, the USAAF adopted the RAF use of finishing schools and set up its own Operational Training Units (OTUs).

Fighter Pilot Training

While the future cream of the Jagdwaffe's fighter force was receiving a blooding in the skies over Spain in the late 1930s, across the Atlantic in the USA, the USAAC had finally recognized that it would face monumental problems in developing a tremendously expanded air arm should the war that now seemed inevitable in Europe escalate into a worldwide conflict. In early 1939, USAAC chief of staff General "Hap" Arnold realized that US military forces had to plan for the possibility of involvement in the European war. He and other

P-51K-5 Mustang of Major Leonard "Kit" Carson, 362nd Fighter Squadron, December 1944

This aircraft, serial no. 44-11622, belonged to 357th Fighter Group, and was based at Leiston, Suffolk. (Artwork by Jim Laurier © Osprey Publishing)

senior officers in the USAAC duly devised a scheme that would facilitate the training of 1,200 pilots by the end of 1939, increasing to 7,000 in 1940 and 30,000 in 1941. The USAAC could not accomplish this task alone, however, so Arnold's scheme called for the establishment of civilian-operated training schools.

The latter would be responsible for the primary training phase of flight instruction, with civilian schools providing all services and facilities, bar the aircraft, but with USAAC control of the methods and manner of the instruction. In the spring of 1939, eight successful civilian pilot training school owner-operators agreed to become contractors to the USAAC to provide primary pilot training for 12,000 pilots per month. The program that Arnold recommended was to take up to 36 weeks to complete, with 12 weeks each for primary, basic, and advanced pilot training (ultimately, these training sessions would be conducted in ten-week periods to save time).

By July 1939, nine civilian schools were giving primary phase flying training to USAAC Aviation Cadets. Within 12 months, nine more schools were in operation, and by the end of 1940, Arnold's ambitious expansion program would be training more than 30,000 pilots a year. One such school was Darr Aero Tech, located some four miles southwest of Albany, New York, which by September 14, 1940 had its first class of 50 cadets conducting training flights with its 15 USAAC-supplied Stearmans.

For many would-be fighter pilots, their first introduction to a single-seat fighter aircraft was the P-39 Airacobra. This P-39N 42-8873 serial no. 134 belonged to the 363th Fighter Squadron, 357th Fighter Group. (littlefriends.co.uk)

By early 1942, the bulk of the US training program was being carried out by the Technical Training Command and Flying Training Command (renamed USAAF Training Command in 1943). By 1944, the standard USAAC program for the minimum number of flying hours required to produce a qualified pilot was 65 hours in Primary training, 70 in Basic training and 75 in Advanced training. Primary training consisted of 225 hours of ground school instruction and 65 hours of flight training to produce cadets that could fly single-engined, elementary aircraft. Most recruits had never even driven a car before, let alone flown an aircraft, but they were expected to fly solo after just six hours of tuition. Potential pilots who reached the Primary stage arrived via Classification and Pre-Flight Training.

College Training Detachments were established by the USAAF in early 1943, and everyone entering the Aviation Cadet Program from then until war's end was assigned to one of these detachments for a period of between one and five months, depending on the scores the recruits achieved on a battery of tests administered at both Basic Training and at the College Training Detachment.

By 1942, the USAAF had four Classification and Pre-Flight Centers in Nashville (Tennessee), Maxwell Field (Alabama), San Antonio (Texas), and Santa Ana (California). Classification consisted of general education tests, 50 questions per test, multiple-choice, physiomotor tests (to measure coordination), and a 64-point physical examination. Those who did not "wash out" awaited cadet classification for pilot pre-flight training. The latter normally lasted seven to ten weeks, during which time cadets attended academic classes, marched in formation, and took part in PT and drill, pistol shooting, and aquatic training, where they learned ditching procedures. Cadet pilots studied armaments and gunnery, with 30 hours spent on sea and air recognition, 48 hours on codes, 24 hours on physics, 20 hours on mathematics, and 18 hours on maps and charts. All who were successful moved on to the next stage of flight training. Potential pilots were now given the chance to learn to fly.

An average of 600 potential pilots attended each Primary training school, students spending 94 hours on academic work in ground school, 54 hours on military training, and 60 hours in 125–225hp PT-13/17 or PT-21/22 open-cockpit biplanes, or PT-19/23/26 low-wing monoplanes.

The standard primary school flight training was divided into four phases. The first was the pre-solo phase, which saw students taught the general operation of a light aircraft, proficiency in landing techniques, and recovery from stalls and spins. The second phase covered a pre-solo work review and development of precision control by flying patterns such as elementary figure 8s, lazy 8s, pylon 8s, and chandelles. In the third phase, students developed a high proficiency in landing approaches and landing. Finally, the fourth phase focused exclusively on aerobatics.

During this training, at least half of the flights were made with an instructor and the remainder would see the pilot flying solo. Each cadet had to make at least 175 landings. Those who soloed went on to basic flying training school, where they undertook a ten-week course. Here, a further 70 hours was flown in a 450hp BT-13/15 basic trainer (later replaced by the AT-6, because the BT was considered to be too easy to fly), 94 hours spent in ground school, and 47 hours conducting military training.

In ground school, five major topics were covered; aircraft and equipment (understanding the aircraft and how everything worked, including engines and mechanical theory); navigation (preparation for cross-country flights); aircraft recognition (both "friendly" and hostile); principles of flight; and radio codes and radio communication for pilots. A Link Trainer was also available for use by rated pilots, and this introduced cadets to the art of instrument flying.

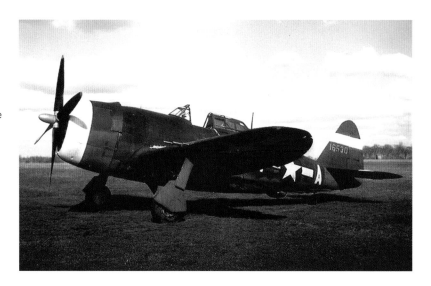

P-47C 41-6530 VM-A of 551st Fighter Training Squadron, 495th Fighter Training Group at Atcham, Shrewsbury in 1944. This is where pilots fresh from the United States would be introduced to Eighth Fighter Command's tactics and doctrine. (littlefriends.co.uk)

By the end of basic school, trainees would have learned to fly an aircraft competently. Further training taught them to pilot a warplane the USAAF way. Before the end of basic training, trainees were classified—on the basis of choice and instructors' reports—for single-engine training (fighter pilots) or twin-engine training (bomber, transport, or twin-engined fighter pilots). There were two final stages in the training phase prior to a pilot reaching the front line—advanced flying training and transition flying training. Advanced flying training was a ten-week course (single-engine and twin-engine), involving 70 hours flying, 60 hours ground school, and 19 hours military training. Single-engine trainees flew 600hp AT-6s during this period, and also used the aircraft to undertake a course in fixed gunnery.

At the end of advanced training, the graduate was awarded the silver pilot's wings of the USAAF and given the rank of flight officer, or commissioned as a 2nd Lieutenant. Transition flying training followed, pilots learning to fly the type of aircraft they would take into combat. Fighter pilots received a five-week transition course, with single-engine pilots flying ten hours in aircraft like the P-39, P-40, P-47, or P-51. Gunnery was part of fighter transition training.

At the conclusion of transition training, pilots reported to unit training groups, where they were welded into fighting teams. Between December 1942 and August 1945, 35,000 day-fighter crews were trained. All fighter units were supplied by the Operational Training

Finger-Four Formation

The "finger-four" formation, broadly resembling the fingers of an outstretched hand, was often adopted by P-51 Mustang squadrons to allow control and maximum visibility while on combat patrol. The No. 2 aircraft flew roughly 100ft below and behind the flight leader for optimum maneuverability. The second element flew 100ft behind the flight leader. These two aircraft would cross below on all turns. (Artwork by Bounford.com © Osprey Publishing

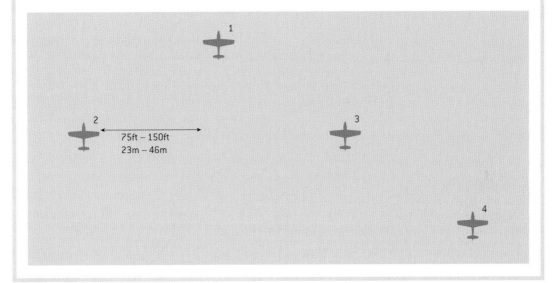

Unit program. Simultaneously, a replacement unit training program (90-day course) within the four domestic air forces provided replacements for overseas aircrew who had been lost in combat or rotated home for reassignment.

Six months were initially required after the formation of a cadre to complete the organization and training of a new group. By 1943, preparations to move an air unit overseas had been cut to just over four months. It normally took almost 120 days and 17 separate actions by HQ officers to move the unit to its port of embarkation.

Training Ground Crew

Well-trained aircrew were not the only personnel needed for combat. To get a single heavy bomber into the air required a small army of men. The B-17 and B-24 consisted of as many as 12,000 individual

B-17Gs of the 323rd Bomb Squadron, 91st Bomb Group head to their target, in March 1944. Forming up into combat formation required a great deal of time and discipline. For the pilot, maintaining place in formation was exhausting and required a good deal of skill. (Author's collection)

parts, and many of these needed replacement at some stage due to wear and tear or battle damage (the latter caused primarily by Flak). A typical heavy bomb group (equipped with either B-17s or B-24s) was comprised of a group headquarters with 25 officers, one warrant officer, and 57 enlisted men, and four squadrons of 12 aircraft each. Each of the squadrons was manned by 67 officers and 360 enlisted air- and ground crew. The total complement for one bomb group was 48 combat crews, consisting of 293 officers, one warrant officer, 1,487 enlisted men, and 48 aircraft.

The instruction of enlisted men for ground duty was the USAAF's largest single training endeavor. No fewer than 34 separate skills were required, and 80 different types of course were taught, including communications (radio, radar, telegraph, telephone), aircraft maintenance and repair, armament and equipment, meteorological, photography, motor transport, and Link Trainer operation. By the end of the war, an astonishing 670,000 aircraft maintenance specialists had been trained—the equivalent of 44 infantry divisions' worth of troops.

FORMATIONS
Bomber Formations

It was quickly obvious to Eighth Bomber Command in 1942 that fighter attack would be the biggest threat to the American day bomber formations, so the bombers would have to fly in close formation for mutual support and to concentrate their firepower. But while these large numbers of bombers flying in formation would give adequate protection against fighter attacks, they would increase Flak hazards and at the same time reduce accuracy by enlarging the resulting bomb pattern, since the formations bombed together.

There were many experiments trying to develop effective formations but, by late April 1943, Eighth Bomber Command had developed a compact staggered formation that stacked low squadrons downward in one direction and high squadrons upward in the opposite direction. Later, a third element of three bombers was added to the 18-plane box, placed in the most exposed squadron for additional support. This resulted in a 21-plane wedge-shaped configuration that remained standard through September 1943.

To build an even larger formation for defense, three of the boxes were brought together into a "combat wing box," which covered a very large area roughly 2,000ft by 7,000ft—and there could be two or three combat wing boxes in a wedge-shaped formation if there were enough aircraft available. This was even more difficult to fly, but again there was no alternative.

The combat wing boxes usually flew in a column with four to six miles between each combat wing, with fighter escort, when available, above the boxes. However, if a combat wing lagged, the escorts could lose visual contact, and if there was too much space the German controllers could see that and would attack the combat wing that was out of position.

There were many objections to such large and closely flown vertical formations, which were difficult to fly, unwieldy, and very difficult to keep together, especially in turns. Turbulence from leading bombers added to the difficulty of maintaining formation. The lowermost and uppermost elements, trailing at the end of the formation, were in an exposed position and German fighters concentrated on them, with the result that the low squadron in the low group was called "Purple

USAAF Combat Wing Formation

The standard USAAF Combat Wing formation fielded 54 B-17s (sometimes mixed with B-24s) in three "boxes" of bombers (in high, lead, and low positions), each consisting of three six-aircraft squadrons echeloned into lead, high, and low. In turn, the squadrons were formed of two three-ship flights (high and low). Such a formation, despite requiring considerable assembly time and disciplined flight control, ensured a high level of mutual protection and defense, although the bombers flying in the second flights of the low squadrons were most vulnerable.

(Artwork by Bounford.com © Osprey Publishing)

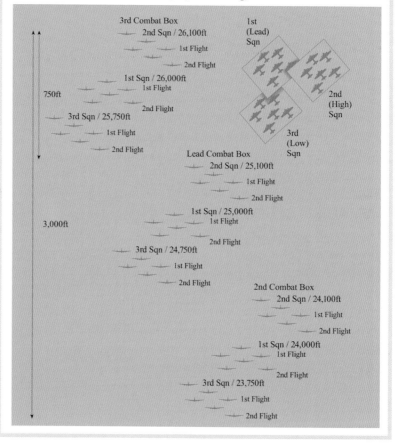

Heart Corner," after the decoration presented to wounded servicemen. Still, objectively, no matter what the formation, there was always going to be an outside corner that was more vulnerable than the center of the formation.

In the end, the combat wing box's defensive firepower was deemed more important than maneuverability, and it was felt that the staggered "combat box" formation gave maximum fields of fire for mutual defensive support.

The key to success for a combat box was how tight the formation was—that usually determined whether or not the Germans attacked. A well-organized box with the groups and squadrons tight was not what the German controllers or attacking pilots were interested in attacking. They wanted disorganized formations, scattered and/or out of position.

Formation Bombing and Lead Crews

Eighth Air Force Bomber Command had to develop procedures to strike the German targets with enough accuracy while keeping the bombers in their tight defensive formation. Additionally, while German fighters were the main threat, Flak was a danger over the target. Flak handicapped effective bombing operations not so much by destroying or damaging bombers but rather by forcing the bombers to bomb from high altitudes, which reduced accuracy.

The German fighter defenses made it obvious that each bomber could not spread out and make its own bomb run, and as early as January 1943, formation bombing—entire formations dropping their bombs in unison when the lead bomber dropped his—was tried successfully. In March 1943, the Operational Research Section of Eighth Bomber Command strongly recommended adopting this technique. In July 1943, Eighth Bomber Command's leadership agreed, and ordered that the combat wings begin to plan to use formation bombing, despite the fact that it would be clumsy to maneuver the large formations onto the bombing run and that the resulting bomb pattern would scatter more widely than was the optimum for the desired accuracy.

To make formation bombing work, the wings needed well-coordinated teams of pilot, navigator, and bombardier, and these had to be developed. To that end, Eighth Bomber Command directed the establishment of special "lead crews" in each squadron at each station. Squadrons had to identify their best bombardiers and they joined with

Wearing newly issued Flak vests, Captain Leonard Cox (right) and his unidentified co-pilot pose in front of B-17F 42-29921 *Oklahoma Okie* of the 324th Bomb Squadron, 91st Bomb Group at Bassingbourn, in Cambridgeshire, on June 16, 1943. The vest's job was to protect the wearer's chest and back from low-velocity shrapnel, and their belated issuing to all crews was a tacit admission by the USAAF that Flak was here to stay. (Author's collection)

a specially selected pilot and navigator. These lead crews alone would be responsible for identifying the target, leading the unit on the bomb run, locating the release point, and giving the order to release; and the lead crew pilot was chosen for his ability to fly smoothly and make changes gradually to keep the formation together. Only three other planes in each group—one wingman of the lead plane and the leaders of the high and low squadrons—carried bombsights, in case the leader was shot down. The mission of the other crews was to stay in tight defensive formation and release when the leader released.

The lead crews underwent intensive training so that they could act as group or squadron lead crews on combat missions. They often carried an additional navigator, and usually the tail gunner's position was occupied by an officer pilot who advised the pilot on the state of the formation. Finally, the lead crews were only to participate in combat as a lead crew, and their tour would be shortened by five missions. In addition to these crews, two very reliable B-17 aircraft in each squadron were designated as "lead bombers" and equipped with every approved device for accurate bombing of a target as it became available.

The critical moment in the entire mission was the few seconds immediately before the lead bombardier released the bombs, when he had to perform his final sighting operation and locate the bomb release point. This meant that the lead bomber had to be held as nearly as possible on a steady course without slips, skids, or changes in altitude, and Eighth Bomber Command decided that a mechanical instrument could hold this precise position better than a pilot, who might be distracted by Flak or attacking fighters. This AFCE, an automatic pilot that regulated target approach and bomb run, was developed and first used successfully on March 18, 1943. The AFCE allowed the bombardier to control the aircraft on the bomb run with mechanical precision by the synchronized sighting and pilotage, and enabled him to provide a steadier bombing run than could be achieved even by veteran pilots. Soon all the specially designated "lead" B-17s received the AFCE.

TECHNOLOGY
Radar Bombing

The Luftwaffe was deadly, but the biggest impediment to Eighth Bomber Command bombing was weather. Clouds split up combat wing boxes and dispersed the closely knit formations, and more importantly they could blanket targets, making it impossible to bomb. In desperation, in the late summer of 1943 Eighth Bomber Command turned to the RAF, whose night bombers had a number of blind-bombing and navigational aids including *Gee*, a navigational aid using signals from ground stations; *Oboe*, a short-range precision navigation device; and *H2S*, an airborne radar scanner that showed a rough terrain image below the aircraft.

Both *Oboe* and *H2S* were in short supply and the RAF was reluctant to lend Eighth Bomber Command these systems, ostensibly because of fear of them falling into enemy hands (though the RAF was losing dozens every night), but finally, in August 1943, both were given trial installations on B-17s. The *H2S* was preferred by Eighth Bomber Command and several *H2S* systems were installed in the B-17's nose compartment, with the scanner encased in a large plastic bath under the nose. A special unit was formed to fly lead position in a combat wing with all bombers dropping on its release with British smoke marker bombs to mark the release point for following formations. Later, an American version of the *H2S*, the *H2X*, was brought into service.

By December 1943, each of the three bombardment divisions had their own Pathfinder squadron and, as more radars became available, they were gradually deployed at wing and group level.

Electronic Countermeasures

Another electronic aid adopted in 1943 was the AN/APT-2 Carpet I radar jammer. This transmitter was designed to mask a bomber formation from Luftwaffe *Würzburg* fire-control radars by radiating electronic noise in the radar's operating frequency. When the Luftwaffe attempted to develop electronic counter-countermeasures (ECCM) in 1944, the USAAF deployed the APQ-9 Carpet III, which could conduct both barrage jamming and more focused spot jamming. A number of other electronic-warfare devices were fielded in 1943–44 to disrupt Luftwaffe fighter radios, GCI networks, and other communication and sensor nodes.

Chaff

Chaff is a radar countermeasure. Aircraft could spread a cloud of small, thin pieces of aluminum which would swamp radar screens with multiple returns, in order to confuse and distract.

The use of chaff by the Eighth Air Force did not occur until December 20, 1943. By October 1944, special chaff-dispensing formations of six to 12 B-17 or B-24s were regularly being sent ahead of the main force to screen the leading formations.

By late 1944, the Mosquitos from 653rd and 654th Bomb squadrons were specially adapted to perform this role. Faster and agile, the Mosquito proved more effective. A typical mission consisted of three Mosquitos. After meeting the Lead Bomber formation at the initial point, the Mosquitos would then pull ahead of the formation by about two minutes and start dispensing their chaff.

A waist gunner from the 92nd Bomb Group poses in his position with his 50-cal. (12.7mm) M2 Browning machine gun, in December 1943. (NARA)

ARMAMENT

M2 Browning Machine Gun

The standard armament for both Eighth Air Force heavy bombers was the 50-cal. Browning M2 machine gun. The B-17G typically carried 12 guns with approximately 4,880 rounds. The B-24J carried ten machine guns with 3,900 rounds. Rate of fire for the M2 was 800 rounds per minute with an effective range of 1,200 yards.

Bombs

The General Purpose (GP) bombs used by the Eighth Air Force starting in September 1942 comprised five types: the M30 100lb, M31 300lb, M43 500lb, M44 1,000lb, and M34 2,000lb. The Eighth tried using their 1,000lb and 2,000lb bombs for attacks on German submarine pens, but they had little or no effect.

91st Bomb Group B-17Fs equipped with external bomb racks carry two 2,000lb bombs. During the war, Eighth Air Force bombers dropped a total of 20,246 2,000lb bombs. (Author's collection)

In December 1942, a report revealed that 30 percent of the bombs dropped failed to explode due to the freezing of the arming mechanism. As a result, fuses were only installed just before take-off.

Starting in 1943, new GP bombs were issued: the M57 250lb, M64 500lb, M65 1,000lb, and M66 2,000lb. These accounted for most of the bombs dropped in 1945.

Bomb Types	
Incendiary Bombs	In November 1942, the M50A1 41lb magnesium bomb was added to the arsenal. It was packed in 100lb clusters which had a tendency to open prematurely, disperse too widely, and cause damage to other planes in formation. In January 1944, the 500lb M17 cluster bomb was introduced, which had better ballistics.
Napalm Bombs	In the latter half of 1944, a refined petroleum jelly called Napalm became available. Known as Class-C fire bombs and with a capacity of 108 US gallons, these bombs were only used in a few missions.
Fragmentation Bombs	Used as antipersonnel bombs during ground force support attacks, the 20lb M41s were fitted in 120lb and 500lb clusters.
VB-1 Azon Bomb	A basic 1000lb bomb, but with a radio-controlled tail attachment which allowed it to be steered over a distance of 200ft to either side of the point of impact from a height of 20,000ft. A handful of missions were flown by the 458th Bomb Group in 1944 with limited success.
GB-1 Glide Bomb	The GB-1 was made from a M34 2,000lb bomb fixed to a 12ft-span glider unit attached to a B-17 underwing shackle. Using a gyrostabilizer-base autopilot that controlled azimuth, the bomb could be set to a specific course following release at a specific altitude and distance. On May 28, 1944, 113 bombs were dropped on the Eifeltor marshaling yard in Cologne. A total of 42 made impact but missed their target. They were not used again by the Eighth Air Force.
Disney Rocket Bomb	This bomb was designed to penetrate the thick concrete U-boat shelters. It was free-fall until a rocket motor fired at 5,000ft pushing the missile to speeds of 2,400ft per second. It was first used by the 92nd Bomb Group on February 10, 1945.

Norden bombsight

One of the reasons the Air Corps committed to daylight precision bombing was the gyro-stabilized Norden M-4 bombsight, developed in the mid-1930s, ironically for the US Navy. The Air Corps ordered the Norden for its new B-17s, and tests of the Norden/B-17 combination—under ideal weather and visibility conditions—showed that it greatly exceeded the accuracy of its predecessors and would allow "precision bombing" from high altitude. The press fawned on the

Norden, and to add to its mystique no photos were released and the details of how it worked remained top secret. However, the Norden was best when used by single aircraft that could maneuver to line up on the target independently. In combat, except for the few seconds of the bombing run, all phases of the bombing mission were dominated by considerations of defense, so the maneuvering necessary for the Norden to perform its best could not be met and the Norden bombsight, with its delicate adjustment, lost much of its value. The conditions that were best for both accuracy and protection from Flak would not provide sufficient defense against fighter attacks in combat, and even under good conditions more than half the bombs hit more than 1,000ft from the target. At one point, there was consideration of acquiring an inferior sight requiring less careful adjustment, a step which would seriously have compromised the ideal of precision which underlay the American bombardment theory.

FIGHTER TACTICS
P-47 Thunderbolt

There was no official edict on how formations should be flown when the Eighth Air Force commenced fighter operations in the ETO, so P-47 groups experimented to find the most desirable for control and deployment against an increasingly elusive enemy.

On April 17, 1943, 56th Fighter Group commanding officer Colonel "Hub" Zemke tried out a new formation, staggering the squadrons and flights so that the group was like a giant V when viewed in plan. Twelve days later, 112 P-47s of the 4th, 56th, and 78th Fighter groups flew a high-altitude Rodeo over the enemy coastline, sweeping overland from Ostend to Woensdrecht. The 56th Fighter Group, led by Major Dave Schilling, lost two Thunderbolts to enemy Fw 190s flying in pairs and firing short, well-aimed bursts, before diving away. A change in US tactics followed.

Hitherto, individual flights had gone out in close finger-fours, each shifting into string trail behind its leader at the enemy coast. This flight battle formation, advised by the RAF in Stateside training days, placed the rearmost pilot in a very vulnerable position. Squadron mates were usually unable to warn him of a surprise attack from the rear, and in such an event the enemy was ideally placed to pick off the remaining aeroplanes ahead in the line. To improve matters, Zemke staggered the two-aeroplane elements in a flight, and spread flights out in very loose formation to give better positioning for spotting attackers coming in from the rear. Pilots now had more flexibility for evasion too.

On May 18, when the three P-47 groups sortied along the Dutch coast once again, a dozen Bf 109Gs approached the 4th Fighter Group at 30,000ft after the Thunderbolts had turned for England. The German fighters came in astern and the P-47s broke around and dived on them. The Bf 109Gs dived away in accordance with Jagdwaffe standard procedure, but this was a suicidal move. The Thunderbolts turned into them with a vengeance, 1st Lieutenant Duane W. Beeson (the top ace in the 4th Fighter Group during the P-47 era) chasing Oberfeldwebel Heinz Wefes of 4./JG 54 until he baled out at 100ft for the first of his 17 victories. This was also the first Bf 109 to fall to a P-47.

The engagement on May 18 revealed the strong points of the Thunderbolt, which were exploited over and over again by USAAF pilots through to VE Day. It had quickly become obvious to Eighth Fighter Command that the P-47 was inferior to the Bf 109G and Fw 190A at altitudes up to 15,000ft, and that the German aircraft had

The US Army Air Force Training Aid Division produced numerous posters highlighting the different dos and don'ts of fighter-versus-fighter combat. Most of the pilots who were shot down during the war never saw the aircraft responsible for their demise. This poster was designed to address that problem. (Author's collection)

P-47D-15 42-75864 of Colonel Hubert "Hub" Zemke, 56th Fighter Group, March 1944

Zemke used this modified P-47D to obtain 2¼ aerial victories (and a probable) over German fighters on March 6, 1944. (Artwork by Chris Davey © Osprey Publishing)

notably better rates of climb. Indeed, according to Luftwaffe Flight Test Center pilot Hans-Werner Lerche, who extensively flew a captured P-47D-2 in late 1943, "the Thunderbolt was rather lame and sluggish near ground level, with a maximum speed of barely 310mph."

Above 15,000ft, the Thunderbolt's performance steadily improved to the point where, between 25,000ft and 30,000ft, it surpassed the Bf 109G and Fw 190A in all areas bar rate of climb and acceleration—the heavy P-47 was, after all, double the weight of either German fighter. Lerche concurred, stating, "I was astonished to note how lively the Thunderbolt became at higher altitudes. Thanks to its excellent exhaust-driven turbo-supercharger, this American fighter climbed to 36,000ft with ease." Under full power, the P-47 was faster than both enemy types above 15,000ft, and as much as 30mph quicker at 30,000ft. The Thunderbolt's performance at altitude, and ability to build up tremendous speeds when diving, ultimately proved to be its biggest assets in combat. USAAF bombers usually operated at heights in excess of 24,000ft, which was in the P-47's optimum performance zone.

Enemy fighters would attempt to get above the "heavies" and dive through their ranks in slashing attacks, and this suited the P-47 pilots, who would in turn try and get above the Fw 190s and Bf 109s and hunt them down as they dived on their targets.

Thanks to its weight advantage, the P-47 could soon close on a diving German fighter, even if the latter initially accelerated away from the pursuing American interceptor. Hans-Werner Lerche found that the performance of the Republic fighter when heading earthward was a revelation. "The strength of the Thunderbolt in a dive was particularly impressive. This was just as well, as it was no great dogfighter, particularly at heights below 15,000ft. It was excellent at higher altitudes, in diving attacks, and when flying with maximum boost. No wonder then that the P-47s were always the decisive factor as escort fighters for bomber attacks conducted at higher altitudes."

Although acknowledging its limitations, "Hub" Zemke was also fulsome in his praise of the P-47:

> A rugged beast with a sound radial engine to pull you along, it was heavy in firepower—enough to chew up an opponent at close range. It accelerated poorly and climbed not much better. But once high cruising speed was attained, the P-47 could stand up to the opposition. Strangely, the rate of roll and maneuverability were good at high speeds. At altitude, above 20,000ft, the P-47 was superior to the German fighters. In my book, you use your aircraft as advantageously as you can. In the dive, my God, the P-47 could overtake anything. Therefore, I made it policy in my group that we used the tactic of "dive and zoom." We stayed at high altitude, dived on the enemy, then zoomed back to high altitude before the next attack. To try to engage Bf 109s and Fw 190s in dogfights below 15,000ft could be suicidal—that was not playing the game our way.

Fighter groups would approach the enemy coastline at 30,000ft, which was well above the optimum altitude of the Fw 190A and Bf 109G. And although their presence was noted by the Gruppen scrambled to engage USAAF bombers at 20,000–25,000ft, they could often be ignored by the German pilots as they were rarely released to dive on them by overcautious commanders. Numerous seasoned Luftwaffe aces developed an open contempt for the P-47s during this period, dubbing them the "non-intervenors." Such an attitude would come back to haunt the Jagdflieger as the year progressed and Eighth Fighter Command grew more confident in its use of the Thunderbolt.

In early 1944, with the Eighth Air Force still very much up against it in respect to the losses its bombers were incurring at the

Doolittle's decision to free the escort fighters from close escort increased attrition against German fighters. This dramatic gun-camera footage is from the P-51B flown by Lieutenant-Colonel Glenn Duncan of the 353rd Fighter Group on the mission of February 22, 1944. After strafing a German airfield, Duncan caught this Fw 190 alone and unaware. Hits on the right-wing root caused the landing gear to drop; the aircraft crashed shortly after. Duncan was credited with 19½ kills during 1944. (NARA)

hands of a stubborn enemy as the "heavies" broadened their campaign against targets across Germany, the way in which Eighth Fighter Command was to be used to combat the Jagdwaffe significantly changed. "Hub" Zemke recalled:

General Ira Eaker (commander of the Eighth Air Force) had always told us that our first objective was to bring back the bombers and our second was to shoot down enemy aircraft. Now Lieutenant-General James Doolittle (who took over control of the Eighth from Eaker in January 1944) told us to pursue the enemy when and wherever we could—we were now permitted to follow him down, and no longer had to break off attacks. At lower altitudes the P-47 would have to be wary of getting into dogfights, but apparently our generals believed that there were now sufficient P-47s to warrant the risk of it keeping the pressure on the now hard-pressed Luftwaffe fighter arm. It also meant official recognition of what I had long advocated—getting way out ahead to bounce the enemy fighters before they had a chance to make their attacks on the bombers.

P-51 Mustang

When it came to implementing aerial tactics, the P-51's group leader was the "quarterback of the team." Eighth Fighter Command units invariably employed the standard three-squadron formation when escorting bombers over occupied Europe, with each squadron composed of a quartet of four-ship flights and two aircraft as mission spares. The down-sun squadron flew 2,000–3,000ft above the lead unit, while the up-sun squadron positioned itself about 1,000ft below the lead unit. Each squadron flew about 3,000ft horizontally apart from the lead unit.

When it came to offensive tactics, 17½-victory ace Captain John B. England, CO of the 362nd Fighter Squadron, 357th Fighter Group, opined that the most perfect bounce would be made from out of the sun, and from 3,000–5,000ft above the enemy:

A pilot making a bounce should always instinctively have the advantage in speed or altitude, since one can be converted into the other. Flights should fly close formation, relying on mutual support for protection. The enemy will think twice before he jumps 18 aeroplanes in good formation. This has been proven many times by our experience.

The best defensive maneuver for the P-51 against the common enemy fighter aeroplane is just a simple tight turn. I have never seen one of our fighters shot down in a tight turn, but I have seen our fighters shot down while trying to evade the enemy by diving to the deck, or pulling some fancy maneuvers. I say never be on the defensive list—if you are on the defensive, turn it into an offensive situation immediately. Always let the Hun know you're after him from the beginning.

Fellow ace Major John A. Storch (10½ kills), who was CO of the 357th Fighter Group's 364th Fighter Squadron, related at the time:

The basic defensive maneuver is to turn into the attacking enemy. Often this will automatically turn a defensive situation into an offensive one. If the German turns with you, the P-51 should be on the tail of the average enemy aeroplane in short order. If, as we have found to be more often the case, the German split-esses for the deck, without top cover, you can split-ess after him. He may out dive you on the way down and out maneuver you during this dive, but when you level out on the deck you will probably be able to catch him.

When attacked by superior numbers, if no cloud cover or help is available, about the only thing you can do is to keep turning into his attacks and take such shots as you can get, hoping to even things up. You should, under such circumstances, continue to watch all the time for an opportunity to make a break for home. However, it does not pay to straighten out on a course unless you are very sure you will be out of accurate firing range. My own opinion is that the best way to make the break is a shallow dive with everything full forward. If the enemy starts to overhaul you again and gets within accurate range, about the only thing to do is to turn again and force him to take a deflection shot at you.

When attacked I like to have my wingman stay close enough that he can take an aeroplane off my tail, and I can do the same for him. He is of no help, however, if he stays in so tight that we cannot maneuver, and are practically one target. The preceding and following statements are completely dependent upon circumstances, and no hard and fast rules can be set down.

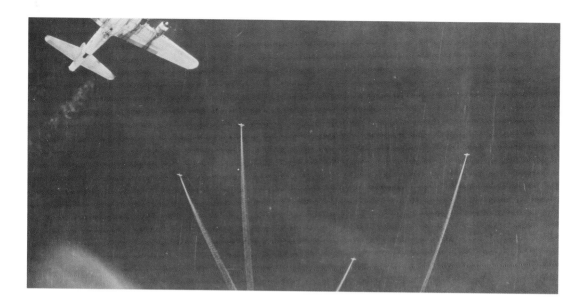

P-51D Mustangs provide top cover in a loose "finger-four" formation. (Author's collection)

When attacking an enemy aircraft, the leader should go in for the first shot while his wingman drops out and back far enough that he can watch the sky and clear his own, and his leader's, tail. If the leader overshoots or has to break off his attack, his wingman will be in position to start firing with the leader covering him. If you have to break off combat but want another shot later, break up and either turn to the right or left, but not in a turn of 360 degrees, as you probably will be unable to catch the enemy aircraft after you complete it.

P-38 Lightning

Lieutenant-Colonel Mark. E. Hubbard was the commanding officer of the 20th Fighter Group. During World War II, he was credited with shooting down 6½ German aircraft. He was awarded the Silver Star, Distinguished Flying Cross for his actions in both the Mediterranean and European theaters flying the P-38. What follows is a summary of his best advice for fighter pilots drawn from personal experience of combat.

Hubbard was a big believer in line-abreast formation, with flights spaced far enough apart for neutral aid. This spacing would vary from 800 to 1,500 yards depending on the aeroplane's maneuverability. He

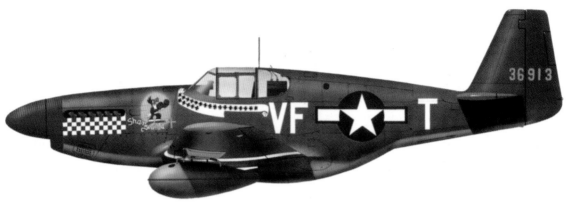

**P-51B-5 43-6913 of Captain Don Gentile,
336th Fighter Squadron, March 1944**
Gentile enjoyed great success in the few brief weeks that he flew the P-51 in action, claiming triple victory hauls on March 3 and 8 and April 8, 1944—the latter two whilst flying *Shangri-La*. (Artwork by Tom Tullis © Osprey Publishing)

also believed squadrons should be within good visual distance, meaning not more than two to three miles apart.

Control could be maintained with radio transmission if squadrons or units were within eyesight. For Hubbard, the group leader needed to have control in order to use his force to the best advantage when the situation was met. A well-defined plan, understood by each pilot to aid in performing the mission and maintaining control in the event radio transmission should fail, was also vital.

Hubbard also listed the below points as particularly important:

- "Know your aeroplane" in order to use its advantages against the enemy, and keep those advantages by knowing its disadvantages. To achieve this, keep training and be continuous.
- To win any fight, superiority in numbers is all-important.
- A wingman should always stay with his leader. Under no circumstances should there be fewer than two aeroplanes working together as one man cannot protect his own tail, and 90 percent of all fighters shot down never see the person who hit them.
- The minimum number of aircraft working together should be a flight of four.
- Each pilot should know what is expected of him in no uncertain terms.

**P-38J-10 42-67973 of Lieutenant Victor Wolski,
436th Fighter Squadron, May 1944**

This camouflaged P-38 was assigned to Wolski when the 436th arrived at Wattisham
in the spring of 1944. (Artwork by Chris Davey © Osprey Publishing)

- Instrument training is essential, both individually and as
  members of a flight. Emphasis should be placed on recovery
  from spirals, spins, and stalls, and smooth, straight, and level
  flying.

Lieutenant-Colonel Hubbard also described his model approach to
P-38 defensive flying when under attack from an enemy fighter:

1. The P-38J will out turn any enemy fighter in the air up to
   25,000ft, so we wait until he is about one-half to one mile in
   back of us and then turn into him. Flights on either side may be
   despatched to attack if time permits.
2. After the turn we generally can attack him. If he zooms up, we
   climb until he breaks down, when we attack. If we cannot out
   climb him we continue on our course (opened up, line abreast)
   and let him make another pass if he so desires. Eventually, he
   will break down and we attack.
3. We always approach on the up-sun side. Use cloud cover for
   defense only, which is damn seldom except with a cripple.
4. When the enemy attacks, we out turn him and continue on
   course always in line abreast opened up formation so we support
   each other. We hit the deck only as a last resort because then you
   are combating enemy fighters and light Flak—personally, I'll take
   the fighters as I can see them and fight them. Hitting the deck is
   a good manoeuvre in open unprotected country, but not in well-
   populated well-protected country such as *Festung Europa*. On
   the deck you never know when you'll bust right over some well-
   protected target or airdrome. I believe light Flak has accounted for

one-half of all missing fighters who hit the deck.

5. My wingman stays as close to me as possible while manoeuvring. When straight and level, he moves out to one side, line abreast, about one-half mile.

6. I would hit the deck when heavily outnumbered, or on one engine and under attack by enemy aircraft.

Hubbard's offensive P-38 tactics in a model encounter with an enemy aircraft were described as follows:

1. The wingman moves out to the side so we can protect each other's tail. He only attacks an enemy aircraft working on me if directed by me to attack another aircraft. Then I cover him. We do not attack the same aeroplane under any circumstances.

2. The enemy will try turning with us and then invariably half rolls. We spiral after him as we cannot follow him in a prolonged dive due to buffeting in the P-38, although we can initially out-dive him.

3. The force with the greatest altitude does the attacking. We attack any numbers when we have altitude. We zoom back up unless we are able to follow him when he half rolls or turns. We always try to get on his tail and get a minimum deflection shot. We always leave a portion of the force for top cover.

4. It is inadvisable to attack the enemy when he has top cover above us and superior numbers also. Unless we can attack the top cover first, we try to avoid combat. Generally, he attacks anyway, but we can't beat off his attack, then his top cover is generally gone, so it winds up into a free-for-all.

5. To avoid overshooting, dive below him and pull up after him to kill speed. Throw down combat flaps and retard throttles. We stay until buffeting starts.

6. Wingman should be out to the side at least one-quarter mile.

7. I try to fire in line dead astern, but will fire at any deflection if range is under 500 yards.

B-17s of the 390th Bomb Group leaving the burning Fw 190 factory at Marienburg on October 9, 1943. For the first time, the B-17s dropped 100lb jellied gasoline incendiary bombs on this mission. The Marienburg facility was responsible for nearly 50 percent of Fw 190 output at the time. The B-17s, flying at 11,000–13,000ft, dropped 60 percent of their bombs within 1,000ft of their intended point of impact, while 83 percent fell within 2,000ft. General Ira Eaker described the results as "a classic example of precision bombing." (Author's collection)

CHAPTER 6

THE EXPERIENCE OF BATTLE

Facing the Flak, Dueling the Fighters

The airmen of the Mighty Eighth were alerted the day or evening before that a mission was to be flown the following morning. Once a target had been selected, the lead crew officers were awakened—these being the men specially trained to lead the group formation. They were up before the rest of the crews and four hours before take-off to attend pre-briefings in the operations room. Lead navigators and bombardiers were informed of the target and details of their route. Lead pilots received the same information and studied the course fixed for the mission to ensure that everyone understood their task and objective.

In the course of these briefings, the rest of the men taking part in the day's operations were roused from bed, many having slept fitfully in anticipation of the dangers that lay ahead. If enlisted men and officers shared different quarters from the rest of the crew, the men of each bomber crew would usually live within a short distance of one another so that the whole could be summoned at once by the duty sergeant. It was not uncommon for crews to be awakened at two or three o'clock in the morning, with half an hour allowed for washing, shaving, and dressing, and a stop at the latrine before proceeding to the mess hall. There the cooks and kitchen staff, awakened an hour before the crews, would have food already prepared—fruit juice, cereal, toast, and coffee with either pancakes or powdered (and, very occasionally, fresh) eggs. Two hundred to 400 men could be fed at once, so enabling an entire combat group to be readied for their mission.

From the mess hall the men were conveyed by covered truck, each carrying two or three bomber crews, to the briefing rooms, which could seat approximately 200 men. Officers and enlisted men were sometimes briefed together, but in many cases they were informed of the details of their mission in separate rooms or buildings. A briefing room usually had a raised podium behind which, on the wall above, hung a large map of the area of operations.

A duty clerk would already have marked out the mission route, target, and fighter rendezvous points on the map with colored ribbons and pins. The briefing officer entered the room, walked down the aisle, mounted the dais, and drew back the curtain so all assembled

B-17 waist gunners pose for the camera. Early on, the guns were fed from ammo cans, which had to be replaced when they ran out. This was quickly changed to a belt-fed arrangement. (NARA)

were made aware of the objective simultaneously. If the raid required a deep penetration into enemy territory, the men's reaction of deep foreboding was usually palpable. Bud Klint, serving out of Molesworth, remembered the scene on August 17, 1943 when "every heart in the briefing room hit rock bottom when they pulled the cover off the mission map and revealed that black tape running direct from England to Schweinfurt," the site of a heavily defended ball-bearing plant in the heart of Germany. In the event, 231 B-17 crews were to remain in the air over enemy territory for almost four hours. Dale Rice, in the same aircraft, recalled how the officer opened the curtain and announced, "'This is it. This is the big one,' and gave a few more details. By the time it was finished and we realized how far we were going, I think we were all in a state of shock."

Ed Leighty, a B-17 waist gunner, remembers the trepidation he felt on the morning he and the other members of the crew were sent on the first daylight attack against Berlin, not surprisingly the most heavily defended city in the Reich:

> The intelligence officer was a big man; he looked as if he had lived a good life. He pulled back the curtain over the wall map, and there was the target marked out by a long wool string from England to Germany. "Men," he said pointing with his stick, "today you will bomb Berlin." I don't know about any men being there in the room, but I know there were a lot of frightened boys.

The briefing officer had the unenviable job of explaining the purpose and details of the mission in a concise and articulate manner, carefully interjecting humor where possible to relieve some of the tension from which the men inevitably suffered. The length of the briefing usually depended on the importance and relative danger of the mission.

After the ground control or operations officer finished his briefing, an intelligence officer explained the details of the target and the enemy's defenses, both on the ground and in the air. Crews would be informed of the intensity of antiaircraft fire they could expect to experience along the route to, and over, the target, as well as likely opposition to be offered by enemy fighters. Where available, photographs of the targets were projected on a screen. The staff weather officer then discussed predicted weather conditions that might affect the flight. Finally, the principal briefing officer opened the floor to questions before calling for all crewmen to synchronize their watches. The main briefing normally averaged about 40 minutes, after which the bombardiers and navigators moved to another room or rooms to make their own plans and preparations with the help of operations and intelligence staff. Specifically, navigators used maps to draw up their flight plans, notwithstanding the fact that a bomber group flew as a formation. Meanwhile, the bombardiers examined the available data concerning the target for the day, which they hoped would include photographs revealing prominent landmarks, natural or man-made, which could serve to guide the path of the aircraft and aid in bombing.

A flight of P-51B/D Mustangs of the 352nd Fighter Group, the "Blue Nose Bastards of Bodney," escort 458th Bomb Group Liberators across the English Channel, mid-1944. (Author's collection)

Gunners generally received their own briefing in a separate room, where details of the mission were discussed, with emphasis on the strength of fighter deployment and the locations of possible fighter interceptions. An operations officer also dealt with issues such as altitude, weather, the type of fighter escort available, and rendezvous points for the bombers. Afterwards, the gunners collected their flight rations, electric flying suits, and other clothing, harnesses and parachutes, oxygen masks, and inflatable life jackets.

Prior to take-off, the gunners checked their weapons and ammunition, which had been removed after the previous mission for maintenance and cleaning, before being returned to the aircraft on the morning of the next mission. Flak suits, other body armor, and steel helmets had also already been loaded beforehand either onto the bomber itself or into a tent that was erected on the ground for the waiting crew and their equipment. Meanwhile, the pilot and crew chief walked around the aircraft inspecting the tires, fuel vents, propellers, and other moveable parts to ensure that all was well. The pilot and any other members of the crew not yet dressed in their flying suits could then do so while the rest of the crew relaxed as best they could, often with a cigarette in hand.

Ten minutes before the pilots started the engines, each airman checked the other's parachutes and life preservers to ensure they were in working order. They then climbed aboard the bomber to take up their positions or "stations." The easiest point of access for a B-17 was via the rear fuselage door which led forward through the bomb bay. Those with the requisite fitness could haul themselves up through the nose-hatch door—a difficult task in heavy flying clothes. If entering a B-24 through the rear, crewmen employed a ladder through the floor hatch, or through the open bomb bay which sat low to the ground. Once inside, access forward to the flight deck was gained across the 10in.-wide catwalk across the bomb bay and through the waist. The navigator and bombardier entered through the nose wheel hatch.

A green flare signaled the time for engines to be started, which came 25 minutes before scheduled take-off. This gave sufficient time for the pilots to repeat the same checks that had been conducted by the ground crew several hours before. At the same time, the flight

**B-17G 42-39775 *Frenesi*, 333rd Bomb Squadron,
94th Bomb Group, January 1944**

This aircraft is finished in standard USAAF olive drab and gray. It sustained
considerable battle damage on a mission to Braunschweig on January 11, 1944.
(Artwork by Jim Laurier © Osprey Publishing)

engineer, who doubled as the top turret gunner, stood behind the
pilot and co-pilot to monitor the instrument panel and gauges. When
the time for taxiing arrived, the pilot gave a signal to the ground crew
to remove the wheel chocks. Sergeant George Hoyt, a B-17 radio
operator, recalled this phase of a mission thus:

> As we taxied out to become part of a long procession of B-17s waddling
> along the taxi strip, I stood up on an ammo box to let my head get above
> the radio room roof. I saw a long, ambling line of Forts proceeding like
> huge, drab prehistoric birds that made screeching cries as the brakes were
> constantly applied to keep them on the taxi strip. It was an otherworldly
> scene in the dim light just at sunrise.

The pilot had been briefed on the order of taxiing and he carefully
watched to ensure that the order of take-off was maintained according
to the flight plan, which in turn dictated the formation of the bomber
group into its usual three positions—lead, high, and low. To ensure
his correct position in the line, a pilot usually kept an eye on the call-
letter painted on the tail of the aircraft in front.

When a green light was flashed from the flying control van parked
off the head of the runway, the pilot of the lead plane released his
brakes and the long process of bringing the formation into the air
began, each co-pilot advancing all throttles for maximum power. A

Engine start-up. This garishly painted 491st Bomb Group B-24 formation assembly ship readies for another mission in 1945. Equipped with signal lighting and a quantity of flares, each aircraft was painted with a group-specific, high-contrast paint scheme of either polka dots or stripes. (Author's collection)

B-17 or B-24, weighing 65,000lb, generally lifted off after traveling approximately 3,000ft, by which time it would be moving at about 110–120mph, with aircraft ascending at 30- to 45-second intervals. During the ascent, turret gunners—positioned in the bomber's underside—sat in the radio room in case of a crash, which would, of course, place them in greater jeopardy than anyone else aboard. To avoid spending more time than absolutely necessary in his cramped station, the ball gunner would not establish himself in his post until after the aircraft had reached an elevation of several thousand feet. Eventually, all the bombers—apart from those obliged to abort owing to a malfunction during take-off—would reach the agreed assembly point, establish their formation, and proceed to the target.

Once an aircraft reached a height of 10,000ft, the navigator or co-pilot spoke over the interphone system to the remainder of the crew, advising them to switch on their oxygen supply. Each man then adjusted his mask and checked his oxygen-flow regulator. To check that every member of the crew was receiving oxygen, the bombardier, or sometimes the pilot, periodically spoke to each man to ensure that all was well. This procedure could save a man's life, for an insufficient supply of oxygen would lead to unconsciousness and death after about 20 minutes. Anoxia occurred only gradually, with a man starved of oxygen unaware of the fact as he grew successively more drowsy.

ENEMY COAST AHEAD

By the time the bomber group entered hostile airspace, its aircraft had normally reached an altitude of over 20,000ft, roughly between 24,000 and 27,000ft for B-17s and 20,000 and 24,000ft for B-24s, the latter bombers being more difficult to control at the higher altitudes. By this time, any aircraft that had experienced technical difficulties would have aborted the mission and returned to base. In addition, the bombardier instructed the gunners to test-fire their weapons—into the sea if over the Channel for those aircraft operating out of England, or over the Mediterranean or Pacific, if operating in those theaters. The alternative, of course, was simply to fire into the open sky, taking care not to hit other aircraft in the formation.

Necessary though their heavy clothing was, it created problems for men wishing to relieve themselves during such stages of the mission. Sometimes they could make use of a little rubber funnel attached to a hose that led outside the aircraft. Notwithstanding this

B-17 Navigator's position. Secondary duties for a navigator included manning one of the two machine guns located just forward of his position. (NARA)

innovation, with a fleece-lined suit, parachute harness, and Flak suit, long underwear, wool trousers, and a heated suit, answering the call of nature remained extremely difficult.

Prior to reaching an altitude at which it was necessary for men to don their oxygen masks, the bombardier went to the bomb bay and removed the safety pins from the ordnance. This task was performed at a relatively low altitude, for at a greater elevation the pins could freeze, thus preventing anyone from arming the bombs. At about the same time, the crew plugged in and switched on their heated flying suits, if the mission required them. The desired temperature was controlled by a rheostat.

Wireless telegraphy could transmit Morse signals up to 600 miles at combat altitude and radio telephones could be used up to 150 miles for bomber-to-bomber communication. Other methods were used to maintain contact with base when flying over friendly territory. Except in rare circumstances, radio silence was strictly maintained over enemy territory to prevent detection. Meanwhile, navigators used a variety of methods to reach the target—dead reckoning being the most popular— all worked out before the mission began. In order to deceive the enemy as to the objective, bombers rarely followed a straight course to the target, adopting instead a series of changes of course.

As a bomber entered enemy territory, tension aboard the aircraft naturally rose. "The element of fear began to grow within me as we continued onward," Bob Gillman recalled, "and I could see the whole crew beginning to tense up ... I quickly reasoned, as I would do many times again, that nothing could be changed. There were no choices here but to go on." Calm as the men may have seemed, in reality many were extremely anxious. Ben Smith admitted later:

> I used to lie awake in bed dreading the time when I would have to lay it on the line or forever be lost in the infamy of disgrace (I learned later that I was not the only one). This was so real to me. Outwardly, I was lighthearted and jovial, well-liked by my friends. They thought I was a pretty cool customer, but inside I was sick, sick, sick! My bravado was sort of a rallying point, though phony as a three-dollar bill. I wore a "hot pilot's" cap, smoked big black cigars, and drank boilermakers. The only one who wasn't fooled was me.

Such tension was natural, for at some point during the mission a bomber group was certain to encounter opposition from enemy fighters. While bombers naturally made use of their machine guns to ward off their much more maneuverable opponents, the best form of defense was to have a fighter escort. Initially, as no fighter could escort bombers the entire length of their mission, fighter cover was only provided for as long as the escort could remain in the air with sufficient fuel to enable them to fight and to return safely to base. Eventually, the Americans designed fighters that could escort bombers well above 20,000ft and for missions sent deep into German territory. No single innovation contributed more to the preservation of bomber crews than the development of long-range fighter aircraft.

Frank Morrison, a B-17 navigator, explained the effectiveness of what bomber crews called "little friends" in his description of the harrowing moments when his stricken aircraft nearly failed to make it home:

> We took a series of Flak hits over the target at 26,000ft, and with two engines out and a broken oxygen line, we could not take evasive action to escape the extremely heavy ground fire. We began to gradually lose altitude, and we called for a fighter escort. Almost at once those beautiful P-51s appeared and stayed right on our wing tips as we limped for the coast. The Me 109s just loved to get a wounded B-17 alone, but they surely didn't want to tangle with a couple of P-51s. As we reached the Channel, we were down to near 1,000ft, and the pilot gave the order to jettison all expendable cargo. That seemed to be just enough to let us land at the first fighter base on the English shore.

12 O'CLOCK HIGH

Before the advent of the long-range fighter, Eighth Air Force bombers needed rear-facing firepower to confront enemies attacking from behind, as well as armor plating to protect personnel and the essential instruments that kept a bomber in the air.

In opposing attacking fighters, gunners generally called out the approaches of such aircraft over the interphone, using the positions

A direct hit by a heavy Flak shell was almost always fatal, although some aircraft such as B-17G 42-98004 of the 508th Bomb Squadron, 351st Bomb Group had a lucky escape. During a raid on Cologne on September 27, 1944, an 88mm shell entered the fuselage near the rear entrance to the radio room and exploded, blasting away the ball turret with the gunner, Sergeant Kenneth Divil, still inside—he was killed. Special radio operator Sergeant John Kurtz, a German-speaker who was monitoring enemy transmissions for the Y Service, fell through the hole in the aircraft's fuselage but survived as a POW. The aircraft made it back to the 351st Bomb Group's base at Polebrook, Northamptonshire, where its pilot, Captain Jerome Geiger, was photographed surveying the damage. (Author's collection)

of the clock to identify the enemy's position, with "high," "low," or "level" to indicate his relative altitude. Thus, "Bandit at one o'clock!" might be blurted out over the interphone, or, "Six fighters at three o'clock!" By this method, other gunners, unable to see the enemy from their particular stations, could anticipate his approach from a particular direction and thus be prepared to fire when the fighter appeared. Bombers depended almost entirely on the massed defensive fire of their machine guns to ward off the enemy, for the only evasive maneuver was to move up and down; any other radical movement might lead to collision with other bombers. In any event, many airmen believed maintaining a steady course was the best option, for it provided the gunners with the best chance of hitting their targets.

Sergeant Richard Grimm, a 19-year-old radioman from Pittsburgh, described the attack of an Fw 190:

> He was coming in at 5 o'clock high, and he saw that there was no firing from the tail. I know because he dropped his flaps and took a long slow pursuit curve at us. He was taking his time and was going to come right in and get us. I gave him two short bursts at practically zero deflection and hit him with both of them. I could see things fly off, but he kept coming. I kept the trigger down, and he blew all to hell, like dust in the air. I wondered, did I hit his fuel and 20mm shells?

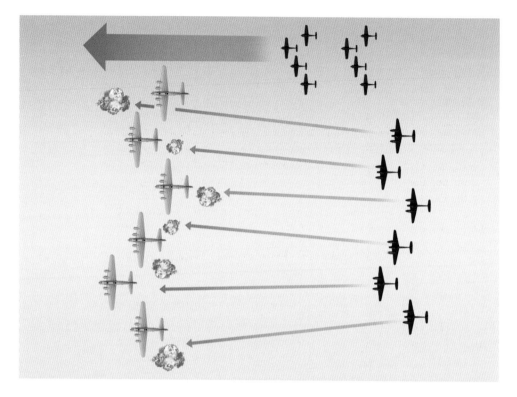

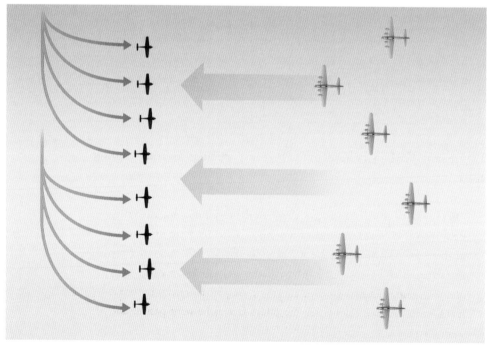

Luftwaffe Fighter Mass Attack (opposite)

In the fall of 1943, the Germans began to equip their Bf 110 and Me 410 *Zerstörers* ("Destroyers," heavy fighters) with the Wfr. Gr. 21 aerial rocket to break up the American bomber formations, and with the development and deployment of these weapons the Luftwaffe developed a method of coordinating the firepower of the rocket-armed fighters with their classic head-on "12 o'clock high" attack. A formation of *Zerstörers* would be joined by a formation of single-seat fighters that would position themselves above and fly parallel to the *Zerstörers*. As the *Zerstörers* approached the bomber formation from behind, the single-seat fighter formation would accelerate and climb to get in front of the bomber formation. Once they were well in front of the bomber formation, they turned toward the bombers and the *Zerstörers* would fire their rockets into the formation. (Artwork by Adam Tooby © Osprey Publishing)

John Doherty described a similar scene on the same mission:

> They came right through the middle of the formation, trying to peel us out, one or two of them, and the others would be circling to pick out someone who didn't get right back into formation real quick; I was in the waist and they came in so close I could actually see the faces of the German pilots, right outside the wingtip, going through. You could see them with their goggles on. They had their tops back and their scarves were flying, right in their face. It was lots of shooting, lots of shooting.

Lieutenant Carl Fyler remembered one particular German fighter thus:

> On my right I could see a row of German fighters lining up. Then they flew out ahead of us, and turned around to attack us head on … One of them came right at me. He rolled right side up and came over my right wing, still firing. S/Sgt. [staff sergeant] Bill Addison, my top turret gunner, swung his two guns to the right and fired practically "point blank." He got him! I could see the pilot's face as he went past us and went down.

Many bombers, however, being large and ponderous, often fell victim to German fighter attack. A 19-year-old radioman of the B-17 *Iza Vailable* recalled:

> Fortresses were falling everywhere. As they dropped out of the protective formations, enemy fighters roared in for the kills. Parachutes began peppering the sky as American airmen jumped from burning B-17s. At least they stood a chance of surviving in German POW camps. What sickened me to the point of tears were the Fortresses that were exploding in midair with no hope of their crews' escape.

RECEIVING FLAK

On approaching the target area, a bomber group could expect to receive antiaircraft fire directed from the ground and known to American crews as "Flak." Sometimes the Germans calculated the elevation of an incoming raid accurately enough to send up such an intense barrage in the path of the bombers that the exploding shells gave the impression of storm clouds. Bob Gillman remembered how 20 miles from his target:

> We could clearly see some weather ahead over the target [Ploesti, in Romania], as we could see dark clouds forming. This was surely strange, since the weather had been so clear ... As we got closer, we could begin to see that something was very strange about the cloud formations. They seemed to be constantly moving ... Then it hit me! *My God, it wasn't clouds at all—but barrage Flak!*

The approaching formation was easy prey for the Germans, who had used radar to determine the bombers' altitude. Flak was particularly dreaded because unlike fire issued by enemy aircraft, it was impossible to tell if a hit was about to occur, nor could one reply to antiaircraft fire by firing back.

It was critical that the pilot, above all, remained calm for, if he panicked, he was likely to cause the death of the entire crew. Philip Ardery, a B-24 squadron commander, recalled how:

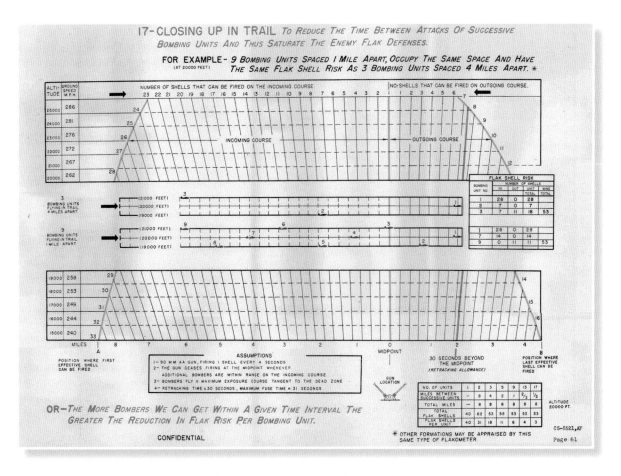

When the Flak started breaking right against my airplane, or when I saw the enemy fighters practically flying through our waist windows, I could feel my pulse rise. Particularly, if I saw one of our ships filled with friends of mine sprout flames for a few seconds and then blow up—which wasn't uncommon—the icy fingers I hated would reach right around my heart. I would shut my eyes for a brief instant, pray for a little nerve, and then say to myself, "R-e-l-a-x, you jerk!" My temples would pound, but I would keep my hands flexible and easy of motion and feel.

Once it was clear that a bomber was fatally hit, the crew had no option but to bale out (attempts to crash-land rarely succeeded), the pilot being the last to go. Roy Kennett, a B-24 radio operator, recalled his formation being attacked by a large formation of Fw 190s and the necessity of ditching:

An example of the "Flak analysis" conducted by the USAAF. (Author's collection)

All of a sudden, all hell broke loose. When we got hit, a fire broke out in the airplane, and it spread into the bomb bay ... The fire was just tremendous ... and there was no chance of getting out ... Gasoline was pouring down into the bomb bay and was feeding the fire, so I looked upwards toward the flight deck ... the co-pilot was standing there motioning for me to get out ... [I] grabbed my parachute and snapped it on ... Then I turned around on the catwalk and rolled out of the bomb bay.

BALING OUT

Even if a flyer managed to escape from a crippled bomber, it was hardly the end of the story. Dean Whitaker, a B-17 navigator, had to bale out over enemy territory, with the expected consequences:

As soon as I hit the slipstream going by at 160 knots, the Flak suit ripped off. I was free now to put the rest of my chute on but the only problem was that due to the lack of oxygen and the force of the wind I could not get the other side of the chute fastened ... As soon as I entered a layer of low stratus clouds, I knew it was now or never time to pull the rip cord. Being half-dazed by the lack of oxygen, it seemed as if I was floating through the air without a worry in the world. This abruptly was broken by the sound of rifle fire and bullets zinging by me. Looking down, I could see a couple of Germans shooting at me ... Before I hit the ground, a soldier came running ... He stopped the civilians from shooting me. Hitting the ground hard dazed me for a few minutes, but when I looked up the German soldier was standing over me with his rifle pointing at me ...

A stricken bomber will eventually begin its descent in a spin, and the centrifugal force sometimes trapped the crew inside unless the slipstream forced them out, as occurred to B-24 radio operator Roy Kennett following his baleout:

Now, the sound of being pulled out into the slipstream—you'd almost have to hear it, and a person telling you probably can't describe it either. The best way I can think of to describe what happens when you first jump out of an airplane is this: If you're traveling down the road in an automobile and you throw a piece of paper out the window, you notice how it flutters and turns and does all kinds of whirligigs, and then all of a sudden it just calms down and very gently floats down to the ground. Well, the initial reaction to a jump is very much the same. When I rolled off that catwalk and into the slipstream, it just turned me every which way but loose for a few minutes. Then it sort of comes down to your normal falling speed—around 120 miles per hour. But you have no sensation of falling, because you have no reference point. If you fall off a ladder, you can see the house go by. When you're five miles up in the air, you're not passing anything (although there were pieces of airplanes falling down all around you). It isn't noisy; you don't hear anything but the wind whistling next to your ears. I know when I first came back, I told my father I had glided for over four miles before I pulled the ripcord.

Kennett was fortunate, for sometimes baling out was impossible, as when the aircraft went into a tailspin. Gunner Bill Fleming recalled how, when flying over Hamburg at 28,000ft, his plane was hit by unidentified enemy fire:

> We went into a diving spin and the pilot rang the bale-out alarm but nobody could jump out because the centrifugal force was holding us. The experience is impossible to describe. Once I couldn't move, I knew there was no way we could come out of that dive and I was going to die. The fear I felt was unbelievable. As we came down, somehow, even the pilot couldn't say later how he did it, he pulled that plane out of the dive. We started at 28,000ft and leveled off only at 6,000.

Most of the time a stricken bomber plummeted to earth, taking its ten-man crew with it. Lieutenant Carl Fyler, the pilot of a B-17 called *Thumper Again*, witnessed the destruction of another bomber in his formation:

> Lt. Crockett's ship directly in front of us took a direct hit in the cockpit. Chunks of flesh came back at us, across our windshield. My co-pilot became ill. Crockett's ship seemed to come to a complete stop. Since I was directly behind him, with wingmen on both sides, I could not turn

5th Emergency Rescue Squadron P-47D serial no. 42-8554 5F-W undergoing engine overhaul outside the unit's blister hangar. (littlefriends.co.uk)

away to avoid a collision. I cut the throttles, and "fish-tailed" the bird, praying I'd miss the stricken ship. Somehow, it seemed to float over my right wing and was gone.

AIR SEA RESCUE

If a bomber or fighter was fortunate enough to ditch in the sea, Air Sea Rescue (ASR) procedures were launched to assist. Following the Battle of Britain, the RAF developed and perfected a very good ASR system to pick up downed fighter and bomber crews in the English Channel and North Sea. An elaborate communications system was set up to detect distress calls and to pinpoint their position. Aircraft like the Supermarine Walrus and motor rescue launches would then locate the downed crew and attempt a rescue.

When the Eighth Air Force began operations in England, they had no such system and when they began losing crews in the cold waters of the Channel, they formed their own ASR operation. These operations were integrated with the RAF's already established ASR network and had access to its Warwick and Hudson aircraft with air droppable lifeboats.

In the lead-up to D-Day, the RAF and Eighth Air Force agreed that the 65th Fighter Wing would take responsibility for air-sea-rescue for the Eighth. The 5th Emergency Rescue Squadron was formed using war-weary P-47s. These aircraft were equipped with air droppable dinghies and marking flares. With a drop tank, the P-47 had 150 gallons of extra fuel that allowed for five hours flying time, which meant it could go from England to the Dutch Islands, conduct a two-hour search, and return safely.

When a bombing raid was launched, two ASR P-47s would take off and track the outbound bombers as they crossed the Channel or North Sea. This would be repeated on the return trip from the target. When a distress call came in, they would be guided to the last known location of the ditched aircraft. There they would circle, drop marking flares and dinghies if needed, and keep watch until the rescue boat arrived. Later, Catalina PBY flying boats were added to squadron.

In total, 938 men were rescued with the help of the 5th Emergency Rescue Squadron.

Downed flyers particularly dreaded landing in the Channel in the winter, when the water was especially cold. Still, they had inflatable boats with "Gibson Girl" emergency radios, which were operated by a crank. Moreover, the Royal Navy operated high-speed motor launches out of Harwich and Great Yarmouth to rescue downed airmen, both RAF and USAAF personnel. One such launch rescued the crew of *The Old Squaw*, which ditched after losing fuel when hit by enemy fighters during a raid on Stuttgart in September 1943. After debating whether or not to try to land in Switzerland, where international law would have required them to be interned for the remainder of the war, the crew took a vote and decided to make for the English coast, only to run out of fuel just short of land. Elmer Brown later described the incident:

> About halfway across France I recommended jettisoning excess equipment to reduce the weight and aid us on gas consumption. Soon afterwards we started throwing things out. We kept just enough ammunition to ward off fighter attacks, which, thank goodness, we didn't get ... We were still throwing clothing, extra ammunition, and spare radio equipment overboard when No.3 engine exhausted its supply of fuel. For our own

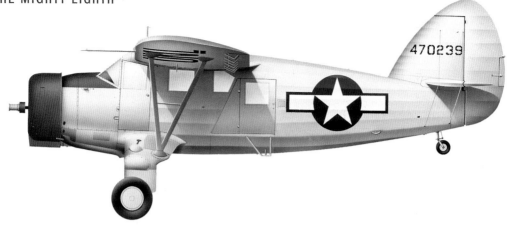

UC-64A Norseman 44-70239, 56th Fighter Group HQ, April 1945

A popular Canadian-built liaison type, some 60 UC-64As were shipped to the UK in 1944. Norseman 44-70239 served with the Air Sea Rescue Squadron, before being transferred to the 56th Fighter Group HQ. (Artwork by Chris Davey © Osprey Publishing)

protection, we had to stay with the rest of the formation as long as we could. That became no longer possible when we lost our second engine, still over France. Luckily, there were no enemy fighters in the vicinity, but even so, an awfully empty feeling crept over me as we began to drop behind and below the other ships.

Once a fighter escort appeared, the bomber no longer had any need for its ammunition, and jettisoned that, too. By the time it left the French coast, *The Old Squaw* was down to 14,000ft, with the crew discarding its machine guns and about 7,500 rounds of ammunition. Just before the fuel supply was exhausted, the crew spotted a surface vessel, nationality unknown. Brown continued:

The last engine quit and we put the ship into a glide, trying to get as near to the boat as we could … Just before hitting, the pilot feathered the No.4 engine, and we all sat tight, and I for one said a little prayer … Out of my window I saw the choppy and rough sea coming up towards us, closer and closer, and I prayed fervently as I continued to beat out those SOS signals.

The pilot hit the ditching alarm buzzer, the tail hit the top of a wave at 80mph, while the ball turret hit another. The aircraft then settled into the water, in the course of which the Plexiglas nose was shattered, the leading edge of the wing was torn off, and the propellers were bent. Within a few seconds, the men were already in water up to their knees, though miraculously they were all unhurt. Within 45 seconds, the crew were out of the bomber and onto the wings and fuselage, by which time the water was waist deep. Following procedure, the crew inflated their "Mae Wests" and deployed the rubber dinghy amid 4–5ft swells. Another member of the crew described the aircraft's final moments: *The Old Squaw* stayed afloat about five minutes, then reluctantly gave up the ghost. Our last sight of her was with the tail straight up in the air and then, suddenly, she was gone."

Air Sea Rescues, January 1943–April 1945	
B-17 Crews	
Number of men ditched or baled out over water:	3,336
Number of men rescued:	1,266
Percentage rescued:	37.9
B-24 Crews	
Number of men ditched or baled out over water:	1,025
Number of men rescued:	272
Percentage rescued:	26.5
P-47 Pilots	
Number reported ditched or baled out over water:	69
Number rescued;	27
Percentage rescued:	39.1
P-38 Pilots	
Number reported ditched or baled out over water:	27
Number rescued:	12
Percentage rescued:	44.4
P-51 Pilots	
Number reported ditched or baled out over water:	131
Number rescued:	56
Percentage rescued:	42.7

RETURNING HOME

Once a bomber formation had released its bombs over the target area, the aircraft turned around and proceeded to a pre-determined rallying point, selected so as to be out of range of antiaircraft batteries. There the whole formation could re-form and return to base with its aircraft—their numbers thinned by enemy action—flying in their

OVERLEAF *The Changing Size and Character of Heavy Bomber Operations.* This graphic provides a concise overview of the achievements of Eighth Air Force's bomber operations from August 1942 until June 1944. (Author's collection)

BOMBER AND ESCORT SORTIES, BOMBER EXPOSURE HOURS,
ESCORT EFFECTIVE HOURS, INSTANCES OF BOMBER COMBAT.

KEY AND STATISTICS

PERIOD	BOMBER						ESCORT				
	NO. OF SORTIES	AVER. HRS. PER SORTIE			TOTAL EXPOSURE HOURS	N°. INSTANCES OF COMBAT	NO. OF SORTIES	AVER. HRS. PER SORTIE			TOTAL EFFECTIVE HOURS
		OPERATIONAL	UNEXPOSED	EXPOSED				OPERATIONAL	INEFFECTIVE	EFFECTIVE	
AUG.–DEC.1942	977	4.37	1.75	2.62	2557	447	4938	1.5	1.0	.5	2469
JAN.–APR.1943	1722	4.62	1.73	2.89	4981	926	2254	1.5	1.0	.5	1127
MAY–AUG.1943	7226	5.34	2.5	2.84	20553	3547	9005	1.82	1.0	.82	7416
SEPT–DEC.1943	13401	6.65	3.0	3.65	48880	3558	16655	2.69	1.0	1.69	28180
JAN.–FEB.1944	14288	6.91	3.0	3.91	55834	2791	17176	3.12	1.0	2.12	36465
MAR.–APR.1944	22153	7.25	3.0	4.25	94196	2251	26443	3.64	1.0	2.64	69730
MAY–JUNE.1944	42404	6.75	3.0	3.75	159023	1486	(OMITTED)	(OMITTED)	(OMITTED)	(OMITTED)	(OMITTED)

* ESTIMATED   * ESTIMATED TIME TO AND FROM POINT OF INITIAL EXPOSURE TO FIGHTER ATTACKS.   * * ALLOWED CLAIMS PLUS ESTIMATED COMBATS OF LOST BOMBERS.

AUG–DEC 1942   (5 MONTHS)
CHARACTER OF MISSIONS

Shallow penetrations in France, Holland and Belgium.

Chiefly to sub-bases, airdromes, R. R. yards.

SIZE AND COST   26 Day Operations

Max. force – 88 sorties – 9 Oct.
Aver. Force – 38 sorties

Max. loss as % of attacks
20%, 3 A/C, LORIENT, 21 Oct.

Aver. loss as % of attacks: 4.0%

No losses on first 9 missions.

FORMATION AND ESCORT

Flew in boxes of 6 to 25 A/C widely spaced; boxes sometimes tight, but more often scattered, especially on withdrawal. At first bombed by elements, but for better defense against fighters, increased bombing unit to 6 A/C, then to 18 A/C.

High ratio RAF escort, but usually not close and usually not entire route. Sometimes none.

ENEMY OPPOSITION

Upwards of 100 E/A employed, often broke through escort; attacks on bombers sporadic, long range, 1 E/A at a time; attack from nose became frequent in December.

Combats reached about 100 on each of 3 missions.

Evasive action used effectively.

JAN–APR 1943   (4 MONTHS)
CHARACTER OF MISSIONS

Deeper penetrations in France; nearby in Germany.

Chiefly to sub-bases, shipping installations, R. R. yards and shops.

32% of attacks involved German targets.
1st attack on Germany: WILHELMSHAVEN, 27 January.

SIZE AND COST   25 Day Operations

Max. force – 111 sorties, 27 Apr.
Aver. force – 68 sorties

Max. loss as % of attacks:
15%, 16 A/C, BREMEN, 27 April.

Aver. loss as % of attacks: 5.5%
German targets   – 7.8%
Non-German Targets – 4.5%

FORMATION AND ESCORT

Flew in boxes of 12 to 24 A/C widely spaced. Some groups flew tight formation, but in general boxes were loose, particularly on withdrawal.

The different groups experimented with various fighter defensive and flak defensive formations. Individual evasive action was encouraged.

Usually had moderate RAF escort, but 1st 6 operations to German targets had no escort.

ENEMY OPPOSITION

Heaviest E/A opposition at BREMEN, WILHELMSHAVEN, VEGESACK, from 100-150 E/A with 2-3 E/A attacking simultaneously.

German-based E/A cautious at first, but by April were pushing attacks in to close range.

HIGHLIGHTS

First air-to-air bombing..... February
First parachute mines........ February
First airborne rockets....... April

MAY–AUG 1943   (4 MONTHS)
CHARACTER OF MISSIONS

Operations extended to Northeast, Central, and South German targets, and Norway; also shuttle operation to Africa.

Chiefly to sub-bases, airdromes, aircraft factories, and miscellaneous industrial targets.

49% of attacks involved German targets.

SIZE AND COST   36 Day Operations

Max. force – 361 sorties, 17 Aug.
Aver. force – 280 sorties.

Max. loss as % of attacks:
37%, 22 A/C, KIEL.............. 13 June
19%, 60 A/C, REGENSBURG,
        SCHWEINFURT..... 17 Aug.

Aver. loss as % of attacks: 6.4%
German Targets   –10.1%
Non-German Targets – 2.9%

FORMATION AND ESCORT

Formations of up to 10 boxes of 18-21 each; attempts to tighten box for better defense from E/A were fairly successful.

2 or 3 boxes joined into Combat Wings, with 1 minute between wings for position defense; but often loose and widely spaced.

P-47s in VIII F.C. start escorting; added 75 gal. belly tank in August; range increased from 170 miles to 235 miles.

ENEMY OPPOSITION

Maximum number E/A in combat: 17 Aug, 260 single-engined, 80 twin-engined.

Stragglers became major problem; almost half of lost A/C were first stragglers.

Enemy developing new tactics to use against 18-21 A/C box.

On deep penetrations, main attacks were launched only after escort turned back.

10-12 E/A abreast spray combat box with 20 mm. shells and rockets trying to scatter bombers.

3-4 E/A abreast attack single bomber simultaneously.

Vertical attacks from above.

Most attacks driven in to close range.

Extensive use of air-to-air bombing; believe 2 A/C lost to this cause in 6 months.

HIGHLIGHTS

First large bore, time-fuzed cannon shells ....June

---

SEPT–DEC 19
CHARACTER OF MIS

Depth of avera

Chiefly to a
airdromes,
industrial

72% of attacks
48% of attacks

October had 1 r
Germany (including
Sept. had a hig
targets.

No German targe
after 14 October;
tacked were bomber

SIZE AND COST

Max. force –
Aver. force –

Max. loss as % of
26%, 60 A/C,
17%, 45 A/C,

Ave. loss as % of
German Visual
German Blind
Non-German Vi

FORMATION AND ESC

Fairly tight bo
flew as a loose co
bat wings widely s
by combat wings.

Traffic at targ
P-47 range incr
in September.
P-38s with belly
bombers in October
P-51s with wing
bombers in December

ENEMY OPPOSITION

Maximum number M
single-engined, 90
al E/A airborne, bu

Escort found nee
targets deep in Cer
Enemy typically had
fighters just bey
intercepted escort.

Bombers face sim
single bomber by 10
rections; and head
waves of 18-20 E/A.

More air to air
ted to airborne roc
tive against bomber
go the entire route

HIGHLIGHTS

First blind bomb
First Crossbow t
B-17Gs, B-24Hs a
volume.
CARPET first used
WINDOW first used
First Crossbow a

BOMBER EXPOSURE HOURS

SORTIES   HOURS   BOMBER COMBATS   SORTIES   HOURS   BOMBER COMBATS   SORTIES   HOURS   BOMBER COMBATS   SORTIES

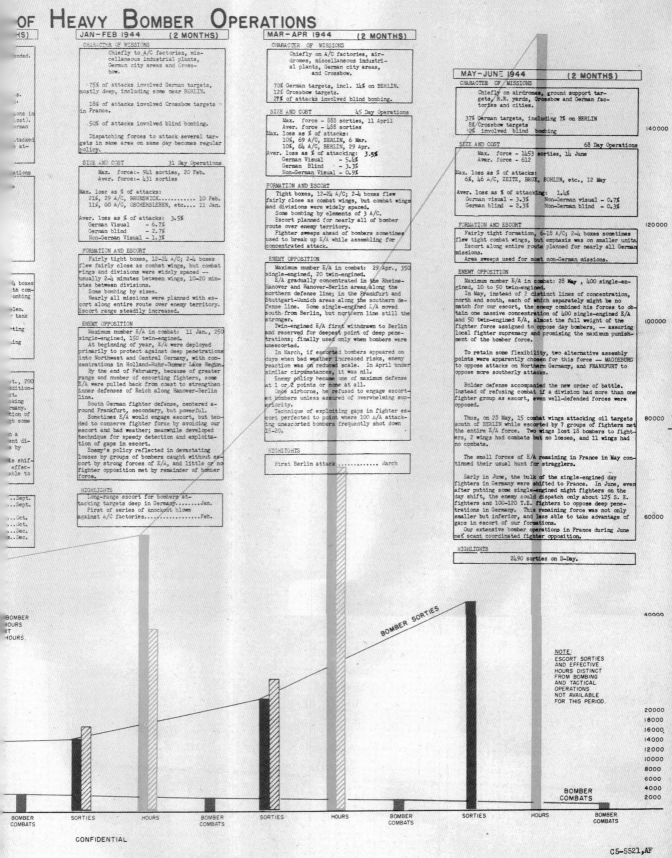

JAN-FEB 1944 (2 MONTHS)

CHARACTER OF MISSIONS

Chiefly to A/C factories, miscellaneous industrial plants, German city areas and Crossbow.

75% of attacks involved German targets, mostly deep, including some near BERLIN.

18% of attacks involved Crossbow targets in France.

50% of attacks involved blind bombing.

Dispatching forces to attack several targets in same area on same day becomes regular policy.

SIZE AND COST   31 Day Operations

Max. force:- 941 sorties, 20 Feb.
Aver. force:- 431 sorties

Max. loss as % of attacks:
21%, 29 A/C, BRUNSWICK........... 10 Feb.
11%, 60 A/C, OSCHERSLEBEN, etc... 11 Jan.

Aver. loss as % of attacks: 3.5%
German Visual   - 6.7%
German blind   - 2.7%
Non-German Visual - 1.3%

FORMATION AND ESCORT

Fairly tight boxes, 12-24 A/C; 2-4 boxes flew fairly close as combat wings, but combat wings and divisions were widely spaced -- usually 2-4 minutes between wings, 10-20 minutes between divisions.

Some bombing by sixes.

Nearly all missions were planned with escort along entire route over enemy territory. Escort range steadily increased.

ENEMY OPPOSITION

Maximum number E/A in combat: 11 Jan., 250 single-engined, 150 twin-engined.

At beginning of year, E/A were deployed primarily to protect against deep penetrations into Northwest and Central Germany, with concentrations in Holland-Ruhr-Dummer Lake Region.

By the end of February, because of greater range and number of escorting fighters, some E/A were pulled back from coast to strengthen inner defenses of Reich along Hanover-Berlin line.

South German fighter defense, centered around Frankfurt, secondary, but powerful.

Sometimes E/A would engage escort, but tended to conserve fighter force by avoiding our escort and bad weather; meanwhile developed technique for speedy detection and exploitation of gaps in escort.

Enemy's policy reflected in devastating losses by groups of bombers caught without escort by strong forces of E/A, and little or no fighter opposition met by remainder of bomber force.

HIGHLIGHTS

Long-range escort for bombers attacking targets deep in Germany....Jan.
First of series of knockout blows against A/C factories.............Feb.

MAR-APR 1944 (2 MONTHS)

CHARACTER OF MISSIONS

Chiefly on A/C factories, airdromes, miscellaneous industrial plants, German city areas, and Crossbow.

70% German targets, incl. 14% on BERLIN.
12% Crossbow targets.
27% of attacks involved blind bombing.

SIZE AND COST   45 Day Operations

Max. force - 883 sorties, 11 April
Aver. force - 488 sorties

Max. loss as % of attacks:
10%, 69 A/C, BERLIN, 6 Mar.
10%, 64 A/C, BERLIN, 29 Apr.

Aver. loss as % of attacking: 3.5%
German Visual - 5.4%
German Blind   - 3.3%
Non-German Visual - 0.9%

FORMATION AND ESCORT

Tight boxes, 12-24 A/C; 2-4 boxes flew fairly close as combat wings, but combat wings and divisions were widely spaced.

Some bombing by elements of 3 A/C.

Escort planned for nearly all of bomber route over enemy territory.

Fighter sweeps ahead of bombers sometimes used to break up E/A while assembling for concentrated attack.

ENEMY OPPOSITION

Maximum number E/A in combat: 29 Apr., 350 single-engined, 20 twin-engined.

E/A gradually concentrated in the Rheine-Hanover and Hanover-Berlin areas along the northern defense line; in the Frankfurt and Stuttgart-Munich areas along the southern defense line. Some single-engined E/A moved south from Berlin, but northern line still the stronger.

Twin-engined E/A first withdrawn to Berlin and reserved for deepest point of deep penetrations; finally used only when bombers were unescorted.

In March, if escorted bombers appeared on days when bad weather increased risks, enemy reaction was on reduced scale. In April under similar circumstances, it was nil.

Enemy policy became one of maximum defense at 1 or 2 points or none at all.

Once airborne, he refused to engage escorted bombers unless assured of overwhelming superiority.

Technique of exploiting gaps in fighter escort perfected to point where 100 E/A attacking unescorted bombers frequently shot down 15-20.

HIGHLIGHTS

First Berlin attack .... March

MAY-JUNE 1944 (2 MONTHS)

CHARACTER OF MISSIONS

Chiefly on airdromes, ground support targets, R.R. yards, Crossbow and German factories and cities.

37% German targets, including 7% on BERLIN
8% Crossbow targets
32% involved blind bombing

SIZE AND COST   68 Day Operations

Max. force - 1453 sorties, 14 June
Aver. force - 612

Max. loss as % of attacks:
6%, 46 A/C, ZEITZ, BRUX, BOHLEN, etc., 12 May

Aver. loss as % of attacking: 1.4%
German visual - 3.3%   Non-German visual - 0.7%
German blind - 2.3%   Non-German blind - 0.3%

FORMATION AND ESCORT

Fairly tight formation, 6-18 A/C; 2-4 boxes sometimes flew tight combat wings, but emphasis was on smaller units.

Escort along entire route planned for nearly all German missions.

Area sweeps used for most non-German missions.

ENEMY OPPOSITION

Maximum number E/A in combat: 28 May, 400 single-engined, 10 to 50 twin-engined.

In May, instead of 2 distinct lines of concentration, north and south, each of which separately might be no match for our escort, the enemy combined his forces to obtain one massive concentration of 400 single-engined E/A and 50 twin-engined E/A, almost the full weight of the fighter force assigned to oppose day bombers, — assuring local fighter supremacy and promising the maximum punishment of the bomber force.

To retain some flexibility, two alternative assembly points were apparently chosen for this force — MAGDEBURG to oppose attacks on Northern Germany, and FRANKFURT to oppose more southerly attacks.

Bolder defense accompanied the new order of battle. Instead of refusing combat if a division had more than one entire E/A force as escort, even well-defended forces were opposed.

Thus, on 28 May, 15 combat wings attacking oil targets south of BERLIN while escorted by 7 groups of fighters met the entire E/A force. Two wings lost 18 bombers to fighters, 2 wings had combats but no losses, and 11 wings had no combats.

The small forces of E/A remaining in France in May continued their usual hunt for stragglers.

Early in June, the bulk of the single-engined day fighters in Germany were shifted to France. In June, even after putting some single-engined night fighters on the day shift, the enemy could dispatch only about 125 S.E. fighters and 100-120 T.E. fighters to oppose deep penetrations in Germany. This remaining force was not only smaller but inferior, and less able to take advantage of gaps in escort of our formations.

Our extensive bomber operations in France during June met scant coordinated fighter opposition.

HIGHLIGHTS

2490 sorties on D-Day.

NOTE:
ESCORT SORTIES AND EFFECTIVE HOURS DISTINCT FROM BOMBING AND TACTICAL OPERATIONS NOT AVAILABLE FOR THIS PERIOD.

BOMBER SORTIES

BOMBER COMBATS

BOMBER COMBATS   SORTIES   HOURS   BOMBER COMBATS   SORTIES   HOURS   BOMBER COMBATS   SORTIES   HOURS   BOMBER COMBATS

40000
20000
18000
16000
14000
12000
10000
8000
6000
4000
2000

B-24s of the 93rd Bomb Group on the way to hit front-line targets at Ahrweiler, Germany, December 24, 1944, during the Battle of the Bulge. The lead aircraft is a pathfinder, equipped with H2X radar in place of the ball turret. (Author's collection)

original positions or filling the gaps left behind by those shot down. Without its bomb load and having expended much of its fuel, a bomber now increased speed to up to 180mph. After leaving the enemy coast, radio communication could be resumed, and within 100 miles of the English coast any damaged aircraft which urgently needed to land could communicate its state of distress and seek to touch down at the nearest airfield.

Once bombers descended to beneath 10,000ft, the crew ceased to rely on their oxygen masks and could smoke if they wished. By the time a bomber reached the coast of England, it was likely to have descended to only a few thousand feet. The home station was contacted and the estimated time of arrival reported. The base operations officer then proceeded to the tower to oversee the landing, while other officers alerted ground crews, ambulances, and fire tenders of the bombers' imminent arrival. Any aircraft bearing casualties on board or itself stricken with severe damage was given priority to land. Others landed according to their position in the group, with ten to 20-second intervals separating touchdown for each bomber, which then cleared the runway for the aircraft immediately behind.

Those bombers with wounded turned off the runway as soon as they could, stopping near a hardstand where an ambulance would be waiting. Other aircraft taxied to their usual ground positions and the crews disembarked with their personal equipment. Flying suits were usually removed and carried away in trucks, together with the guns, which would be taken away, inspected, and cleaned. Flight engineers and pilots reported any damage and mechanical problems, and both the air and ground crews inspected the aircraft for damage before the former were taken back by truck for debriefing. A typical damage report, issued by an officer of the B-17 *Lady Luck*, ran thus: "20mm [shell] exploded in bomb bay damaging several bombs. Vacuum system and four oxygen bottles smashed by another 20mm shell. Flak holes in right wing." Some bombers returned to base literally perforated from antiaircraft fire. In August 1943, on returning from a raid on Watten, in northern France, Sergeant Eddie Deerfield counted more than 200 Flak holes in *Iza Vailable*.

RELIEF AND DEBRIEF

With the bombers safely on the ground and their engines off, the vast array of equipment which they carried was handed in—escape kits, life preservers, parachutes, flying suits, oxygen masks, and so on—and the men made short shrift of the food, usually donuts or sandwiches, provided by Red Cross workers. After taking refreshments, the crews were interrogated by an officer who questioned them on the targets, Flak, and fighter opposition, the number of fighters claimed to have been shot down, the number of friendly aircraft downed, the state of the weather, and other information. Navigators and bombardiers issued separate reports, with the former submitting their logs and the latter completing forms relevant to their role in the mission. Debriefing could take over an hour before crews were allowed to return to their quarters either for a shower and much-deserved sleep or to the mess hall for a more substantial meal. Most flyers preferred to go straight to bed, well aware that, if the need was urgent, they could be called upon to fly another mission as early as the following day.

While the air crews slept, the work of the men on the ground continued. The bombers had to be repaired where necessary, with holes caused by shrapnel, bullets, and Flak mended by repair teams who riveted patches to the aircraft skin. Meanwhile, an assessment was quickly made as to which bombers were serviceable for the next mission and which required substantial repair. Some aircraft enjoyed remarkable service records, proving the resiliency of bomber aircraft. The 427th Squadron's *Sweet Rosie O'Grady* was a veteran of 143 missions, having been flown by numerous different crews. Some aircraft survived only a few missions before being shot down, or were so heavily damaged that their parts were cannibalized to keep other aircraft operational. Finally, fuel tanks and oxygen were replenished for those aircraft deemed fit for immediate service; the machine guns were prepared for the next mission; the photographs from the strike cameras developed and the data analysed. Detailed reports were drawn up on the effectiveness of the mission; friendly losses and claims of enemy fighter kills were assessed; Missing in Action forms were completed; and the location and strength of antiaircraft fire logged for the benefit of future missions sent against the same target. All the foregoing data would remain of interest to intelligence officers and others long after the crews themselves consigned the mission to the past and prepared for their next.

CASUALTIES

Losses among bomber crews were the heaviest of those in any arm of service during World War II. A flyer returning from a mission knew almost immediately—unless he nursed the usually vain hope that more aircraft would return late—who had been lost and who had made it safely back. As Ben Smith put it, "The empty beds in the huts were silent witnesses to that fact." Some men managed to survive all 25 required missions, after which they could re-enlist or receive an honorable discharge and return home. Others were unfortunate enough to be killed on the first one, like radioman Charley Gunn, for whom a cablegram was waiting back at his base informing him of the birth of his son.

Some men eventually became inured to news of the death of their comrades, but others were deeply affected. Philip Ardery noted:

> When a group lost heavily on one or two raids, there was a natural strain on the morale of the remaining combat crews. It was hard for the boys coming back to go to quarters that were practically vacant—quarters that had been full a few hours before. It wore on their nerves to go to the club and find the place more filled with the ghosts of those who had gone than the presence of the few who remained.

Death of a B-17. This gun-camera image from a Bf 110G-2 from June 1944 shows the approach from the rear from a range of about 600m. (Author's collection)

Those who survived 25 missions usually seized the opportunity to return home rather than take their chances against Flak and fighters, though they sometimes felt a sense of guilt that friends with fewer missions behind them would be obliged to carry on without them. Bob Gillman remembered the excitement he felt when the moment finally arrived:

> I am in a state of euphoria, since this is my last mission, and each of the crew have been joking about how nice it would be if I would volunteer to fly additional missions until they are finished too. Fat chance! I feel as though an enormous weight has just been lifted from my back, and it's really hard to believe that I will not be flying any more combat missions. What a thrill to bring the formation over the field for the last time, peeling off in turn and landing.

COMBAT FOCUS: 303RD BOMB GROUP "HELL'S ANGELS"

The 303rd Bomb Group was in the vanguard of the daylight bombing campaign through to VE Day. Along the way it enjoyed a number of "firsts"—one of its B-17s was the first bomber to complete 25 missions (June 1943); it was the first bomb group to complete 300 missions from the UK; and it eventually flew more missions than any other B-17 group in the "Mighty Eighth." Awarded a Distinguished Unit Citation in January 1944, the 303rd also had two of its crewmen presented with the Medal of Honor, America's ultimate military decoration.

In Eighth Air Force history, four B-17 groups—the 91st, 303rd, 305th, and 306th—are known as the "pioneers" because, while other units flew missions earlier, these were the first whose assignment to the Eighth was permanent. They were the ones who faced the enormous job of translating prewar strategic bombing theory into war-winning reality. As one of the pioneer groups, the 303rd was part of the effort from the daylight campaign's very beginnings to its very end. The "Hell's Angels" accomplishments throughout easily make it one of the elite formations in one of the most respected military organizations in history.

The 303rd was activated on February 3, 1942, at Pendleton Field, Oregon, with a small nucleus of personnel under the command of Lieutenant-Colonel Ford Lauer. On the 13th, the group was transferred to Gowen Field near Boise, Idaho, where it began to receive men and equipment from other units to make up its first three Bomb squadrons, the 358th, 359th, and 360th Bomb squadrons. On July 13, commanding officer Colonel James took command of the 303rd Bomb Group.

B-17F-25-BO 41-24577 *Hell's Angels* of the 358th Bomb Squadron. A 303rd original, *Hell's Angels* not only inspired the 303rd's name, but was also the first Eighth Air Force B-17 to complete 25 missions, 23 with Captain Irl L. Baldwin's crew. This occurred on May 13, 1943, six days before *Memphis Belle* reached the 25-mission mark. *Hell's Angels* finished 48 missions without injury to any crewman. Its reputation as one of the most famous Eighth Air Force B-17s endures to this day. (Public Domain)

Considering that a number of early units, the 97th and 301st Bomb groups among them, were transferred to the Twelfth Air Force in November 1942 to support Operation *Torch*, the Allied invasion of North Africa, it is not surprising that the Eighth was effectively "starting over" when the 303rd and 305th Bomb groups arrived in England in late 1942. On the eve of the 303rd's first mission, November 16, 1942, the Eighth had just the four "pioneer" B-17 groups (the 92nd Bomb Group had been given the mission of training replacement crews) and two B-24 groups, the 44th and 93rd, to continue the bombing offensive. These were the only heavy bomber groups the Eighth would have for the next six months when new units, and significant numbers of replacement crews, began to join the daylight campaign in May 1943.

A Rocky Start

High excitement prevailed on the morning of November 17, 1942 when Colonel Wallace announced at briefing that the 303rd, along with four other groups, would be attacking St Nazaire. After 288 days of training, virtually everyone at Molesworth was ready to do his part. To use a catchphrase popular at the time, "This was it!" It was a dramatic moment when Wallace announced the crews and aircraft that would be flying. He described the primary target in St Nazaire, the secondary target, a U-boat pen near Lorient, and mentioned Brest as the target of last resort.

The sense of anticlimax and frustration can be imagined when the 303rd finally reached the target area, only to find it obscured by cloud. There was no alternative but to take the bombs back to base.

Wallace would lead the next mission himself the following day, and this time the group would bomb St Nazaire. But post-mission reactions were not what might have been expected. Orders had been received for the group to bomb La Pallice, home of further U-boat pens, but due to a mix-up, new orders changing the target were not delivered to the right people until after the aircrew briefing. Wing headquarters was contacted and the 303rd received permission to attack La Pallice. The group dispatched 21 aircraft, the first taking off at 1025hrs, and there were only two aborts. Faulty navigation,

**Eighth Air Force's First "Deep Penetration"
Bombing Mission** (previous pages)

Shown here on January 11, 1944, just inside the Dutch coast, is *8 Ball Mk II* flown by Lieutenant-Colonel William Calhoun, lead pilot and CO of the 359th Bomb Squadron of the 303rd "Hell's Angels" Bomb Group. The entire Eighth Air Force was on the first "deep penetration" bombing mission against German industrial targets since the second Schweinfurt raid on October 14, 1943. The bombers are under attack from Fw 190s, who attacked straight through the formation from all angles. As lead group, the 303rd faced the brunt of the Luftwaffe attacks, losing 11 of 40 B-17s.

The other aircraft shown here is early H2X radar-equipped B-17F 42-3491 from the 812th Bomb Squadron, 482nd PFF Bomb Group, which was eventually lost over Berlin on March 6, 1944. The Fw 190 passing between the two bombers is shown in period markings of Jagdgeschwader 1 which, according to combat reports, fought a series of running battles with the 303rd Bomb Group during the course of the January 11, 1944 mission. (Artwork by Mark Postlethwaite © Osprey Publishing)

however, caused the group to veer over 100 miles off course. The 303rd followed another group to what was thought to be the target area and dropped its bombs from 19,400ft in the face of "intensely heavy" but inaccurate Flak. Many hits in the dock area were observed in exchange for light damage to several group aircraft and three slightly wounded men.

When the group returned to Molesworth, an incredulous Wallace was told that the wrong city had been bombed, and it reportedly took "a considerable amount of time" for him to accept the mistake. Clearly, the group had improvements to make in pre-mission procedures and aerial navigation if future raids were to go according to plan. "Our officers didn't have much experience reading the old RAF maps we were given," according to Louis "Mel" Schulstad, who was first pilot of the 360th Bomb Squadron's 41-24567 *Beats Me*.

1943 would be a year of supreme challenges for the 303rd and the Eighth as American airmen continued to struggle with the deadly challenge of accurate bombing and getting home alive.

On January 3, the 303rd led a mission against "Flak city" (St Nazaire). The group dispatched 17 aircraft and had three aborts. In a crystal clear but freezing cold sky, the 14 B-17s flew over the target into a hell of black Flak bursts and fighters. A record total of four 303rd aircraft, one from each squadron, was lost. It was clear that the 303rd and Eighth Air Force still had much to learn about high-altitude bombing.

On May 13, the 303rd achieved operational perfection in all areas, albeit under ideal conditions. Ground crews got 21 aircraft ready for the raid and there were no aborts. The group received outstanding fighter cover from a combination of Spitfires and P-47s, and there was no damage from enemy fighters or the light Flak that was encountered. The target, the Potez aircraft factory at Meaulte, was virtually annihilated on the bomb run. All group B-17s returned to Molesworth without a single personnel casualty.

25 Missions

The remainder of May provided an opportunity for the new groups to be "blooded" in a series of missions against both the French submarine pen cities and U-boat yards along the north German coast. This also gave the 303rd the opportunity, in the face of competition from the other "pioneer" groups, to achieve another milestone in the air war. It passed virtually unnoticed by the press, although it was always important to the bomber crews, and already a subject of deep concern to the American public. It would acquire even greater significance on the home front as casualties mounted during the coming air offensives. The milestone was, of course, completion by a bomber crew of the 25 missions that would enable crewmen to rotate back to the USA for less dangerous duties. The American public, not to mention the airmen themselves, needed reassurance that a heavy bomber crew had a real chance of completing a 25-mission tour, and that their sacrifices were justified.

Captain Irl Baldwin and the crew of *Hell's Angels* were the first to prove it could be done, but not before the 303rd suffered some additional, and particularly demoralizing, losses. USAAF brass were acutely in need of a neatly packaged "war story," complete with "the girl back home" waiting for her man to return, so the crew of the 91st Bomb Group's *Memphis Belle* would be recognized as "the first combat

This replenishing diagram shows the main fuel and oil tanks of the B-17G. Maximum fuel load was 2,800 gallons. A fully loaded Fortress drank fuel at a prodigious rate, over 400 gallons an hour climbing to altitude, and 200 gallons an hour cruising to the target. (Author's collection)

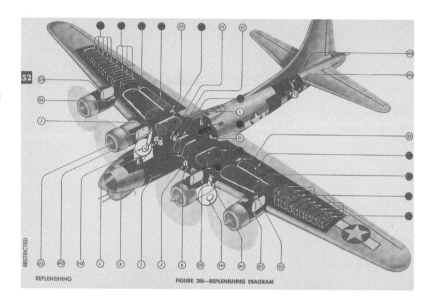

FIGURE 286—REPLENISHING DIAGRAM

crew to complete their required combat missions *and return to the United States*" (emphasis added). William Wyler's 1943 documentary film *The Memphis Belle: A Story of a Flying Fortress* certainly played a role in their decision.

Medal of Honor: Lieutenant Jack W. Mathis

The target on March 18, 1943, was a U-boat yard at Vegesack. The 303rd was lead group at the head of 76 B-17s and 27 B-24s. For the first time, the B-17s were using AFCE in combat. AFCE allowed the bombardier to fly the aircraft on the bomb run by adjusting knobs on the Norden bombsight. Perhaps because of this, bombing was by squadron. The 359th was the high squadron, and leading it was Captain Harold Stouse's crew, one of the group's originals, in their regular ship 41-24561 *The Duchess*. The bombardier was 22-year-old Lieutenant Jack W. Mathis of San Angelo, Texas. He had enlisted a year before Pearl Harbor and joined the 303rd at Alamogordo.

As lead group, the 303rd suffered the bulk of fighter attacks, which started near Heligoland. But the gravest danger was Flak on the bomb run, which was described as "intense, heavy, black, concentrated and accurate." Mathis was crouched over his bombsight, eye pressed against the rubber eyepiece. Less than a minute from the bomb release point there was a large Flak explosion against the starboard nose of *The Duchess*. Mathis and the navigator, 1st Lieutenant Jesse Elliott, were hurled back 9ft against the aft bulkhead of their nose compartment. Elliott was slightly wounded and dazed, but Mathis received mortal wounds to his right side and abdomen, and his right arm was nearly severed below the elbow. Nonetheless, he managed to crawl back to the bombsight, uttering the word "bombs" just as he released. The word "away" was completed for him by Elliott, signaling Stouse to resume control of the aircraft.

Fighters resumed their attacks after the bomb run. Stouse told the top-turret gunner, Technical Sergeant Eldon Audiss, "As soon as these damn fighters leave, I wish you would go down and check on Jack. I think he's in trouble." The sight which greeted Audiss was grim. Elliott was sitting in shock at his navigation table and Mathis was slumped over the bombsight, his chest harness entangled in the bombsight's gears as the analogue mechanism continued to grind away. Audiss cut Mathis loose from the sight, only to discover that the bombardier was dead.

The group's bombing had been highly accurate, damaging seven U-boats and putting the shipyard out of operation for months. Slightly less than three months later, on July 12, Jack Mathis was awarded a posthumous Medal of Honor to become the Eighth's first recipient. Mathis was far from being the only casualty on this raid, however.

Medal of Honor: Staff Sergeant Forrest K. Vosler

The next mission, on December 20, was not so easy. One of 21 303rd crews taking part was Lieutenant John Henderson's of the 358th in *Jersey Bounce Jr.* The Luftwaffe was up in force and the Flak was bursting in 16-shell clusters. It set the No. 1 engine of *Jersey Bounce Jr.* on fire and Henderson dived out of formation to try to extinguish it. Fighters moved in to pick off the straggler, but Henderson's crew put up a furious defense, during which tail-gunner Sgt George Buske was badly wounded and the No. 4 engine knocked out. Staff Sergeant Forrest K. Vosler, 19, was also wounded by shrapnel but manned the radio-room gun to fight off a twin-engined fighter attacking the

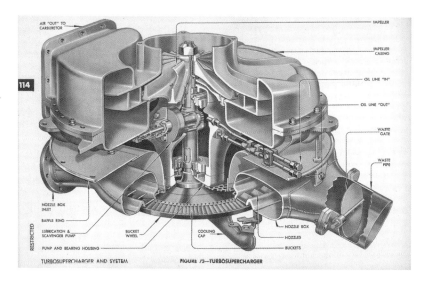

This cutaway drawing shows the inner workings of the exhaust-driven turbo-supercharger that equipped both the B-17s and B-24s of the Eighth Air Force. (Author's collection)

unprotected tail. In an almost face-to-face confrontation with the German pilot, Vosler scored some hits, driving the fighter off. Moments later, Vosler was peppered from head to toe with 20mm shrapnel which wounded both eyes, gravely impairing his vision.

As the B-17 headed back over the North Sea, Vosler was able to set up the aircraft's radio to broadcast an SOS, despite being half-blind and delirious from his wounds. Rescue ships and aircraft were on the scene when *Jersey Bounce Jr.* ditched. While the crew was evacuating the radio-room, Vosler then saved Buske's life. He grabbed the badly injured tail-gunner before Buske slid into the water from the wing's trailing edge, and called his crewmates to help pull him back. His vision permanently impaired, Vosler was awarded the Medal of Honor for conduct clearly above and beyond the call of duty.

The Last Mission

After April 25, 1945, the Eighth flew no more missions because the bomber generals had decided they had run out of targets. But there was still that 364th mission to get in against the Skoda Armament Works in Pilsen, Czechoslovakia. The group made it a maximum effort, putting up 42 aircraft, all of which reached the target, but since the huge factory complex could not be seen through six-tenths cloud on the first bomb run, a second was made. The Flak was terrible, wounding

P-47D-5 42-8461 of Lieutenant Robert Johnson, 61st Fighter Squadron, February 1944

Robert S. Johnson's third assigned aircraft, *Lucky*, was used to score his third, fourth, fifth, and sixth victories before being lost in the North Sea on March 22, 1944. (Artwork by Tom Tullis © Osprey Publishing)

five men and causing two aircraft to divert. Major damage was inflicted on 24 and minor damage on 15 group B-17s which returned to Molesworth. But the bombing had been effective—practically every bomb landed in the target area, and a large explosion was seen.

Just after bomb release, Flak hit a 427th B-17 flown by Lieutenant Warren Mauger's crew. It fell out of formation and went almost straight down with the No. 3 engine in flames. Mauger righted the aircraft to enable the crew to bale out and was heading for the nose hatch when the B-17 blew up. Four of Mauger's crew became POWs but three were killed. Miraculously, Mauger survived the explosion, opening his parachute despite burns to hands and face. He landed in soft earth, and with the help of friendly farmers evaded the enemy for ten days until he reached American troops.

The moment he did so was the time when the long, hard war so ably fought by the "Hell's Angels," the "champions of the European theater" was ended at last.

FIGHTER MISSION

For the fighter pilots of the Eighth Air Force, it was a different kind of war. They were the hunters. Their job was to seek out and destroy the enemy. Unlike the bomber crews who had to fly in formation and take whatever the Germans could throw at them, the fighter pilots could twist and turn and use their speed and agility to press home their attack or avoid destruction.

Pilot Officer Jim Goodson, who flew with No. 416 Squadron in 1942, said of the Spitfire:

> The first time I got onto the tail of an enemy aeroplane in a Spitfire, I missed him. It wasn't because I opened fire before I was in range, or anything like that. I should have blown him to bits, but the firing button was on top of the control column, and the Spitfire was so sensitive that, when I pressed the trigger, the nose pitched down and I missed the target. When you got used to the Spit you became part of it. You didn't aim your guns—you aimed yourself.

A Spitfire Mk VB serial no. BM635 of the 309th Fighter Squadron, 31st Fighter Group, September 1942. (Author's collection)

The European Theater of Operations had an awesome reputation which preceded it throughout the war. The Germans were the most formidable of foes and triple ace Colonel Clarence "Bud" Anderson aptly summed up how it felt to prepare for that first mission:

My pulse was playing a Gene Krupa solo as I walked to my plane that morning and climbed into the cockpit. Once you were strapped in and sitting there, so very alone, waiting to fire up and taxy away and take-off in line, the minutes were soldiers crawling on their bellies in mud. I never was one to dwell on bad possibilities and would generally use this time to focus on the mission, thinking about what lay ahead, and preparing the way an athlete prepares for a game. But on February 8, 1944, I was a little less sophisticated about that sort of thing. I had logged 893 flying hours already, better than an hour and 20 minutes a day for two years. But only 30 hours and 45 minutes of that was in P-51s. I knew I had lots to learn. And what I was thinking about before prodding the Merlin to life was not getting lost, not screwing up. I was more afraid of screwing up than of dying.

The 56th Fighter Group's 1st Lieutenant Robert S. Johnson was wingman on August 19, 1943, for Captain Jerry Johnson, who had claimed two Bf 109s destroyed 48 hours earlier, and who would ultimately down eight "Gustavs" (he was also the 56th Fighter Group's first ace):

I hit the throttle, giving the P-47 her head. The moment the second Me 109 spotted me coming in, he snapped over in a sharp turn and fled to the north. Jerry was only 90 degrees to him as I swung onto his tail. I closed in rapidly to 150 yards and prepared to fire. Suddenly Jerry kicked rudder and sent a burst into the Me 109. A good boy in that Messerschmitt—he pulled into a terrific turn and kicked his plane into a spin. I rolled and dove, waiting for the Me 109 to make his first full turn. I knew just where he'd be for his second turn, and I opened fire at this spot.

Sure enough! The Messerschmitt spun right into my stream of bullets. Immediately he kicked out of the spin and dove vertically. Oh no you don't! I rolled the Jug, and from 27,000ft raced after the fleeing Me 109. The Messerschmitt seemed to crawl as the Thunderbolt fell out of the sky. I lined up directly behind the sleek fighter and squeezed the trigger. Eight heavy guns converged their fire. My second kill vanished in a blinding explosion that tore the fighter into shreds.

COMBAT FOCUS: 4TH FIGHTER GROUP "DEBDEN EAGLES"

The longest-serving US fighter unit in World War II, the 4th Fighter Group scored more victories (550 and 461 ground) than any other Eighth Air Force units, and it was the first to engage the Luftwaffe over both Paris and Berlin. Formed around a nucleus of pilots already seasoned by their experience as volunteers in the RAF's "Eagle" squadrons, the 4th Fighter Group was established at Debden, in Essex, in late September 1942. Initially flying Spitfires until April 1943, the group then transitioned to the P-47 Thunderbolt, before receiving P-51 Mustangs in February 1944. The 4th Fighter Group's combat record was unmatched in the ETO, and it boasted more than 70 aces by the war's end.

The 4th Fighter Group was born on order of Eighth Fighter Command on September 12, 1942, at Bushey Hall, in Hertfordshire. The group's real purpose was to absorb the men of the RAF's "Eagle" squadrons (Nos 71, 121, and 133 squadrons), which would become the 334th, 335th, and 336th Fighter squadrons of the USAAF. Colonel Edward Anderson was named its first commanding officer.

The group flew its first major mission—escorting bombers to the Calais/Dunkirk area—on October 2. The 334th and 335th Fighter squadrons engaged enemy fighters at 24,000ft, and Fw 190s fell to Captain Oscar Coen and lieutenants Gene Fetrow and Stanley Anderson. Wing Commander Duke-Woolley and Lieutenant Jim Clark shared in the destruction of another Fw 190.

On November 22, Major Daley's tour of duty was complete and command of the 335th Fighter Squadron passed to the vastly experienced Captain Don Blakeslee. The hard-charging Blakeslee was already something of a legend, having seen combat with the RCAF since mid-1941.

From early January 1943 onwards, the battle-weary Spitfire VBs assigned to the 4th Fighter Group would soon be replaced by another aircraft on the Debden flightline—the Republic P-47C Thunderbolt. The largest single-seat, piston-engined American fighter to see combat, the immense P-47 was more than twice the

The unofficial group badge of the 4th Fighter Group. The outfit officially had no group or squadron badges during World War II. (Artwork by Chris Davey © Osprey Publishing)

Spitfire VB BL255 of 1st Lieutenant Don Gentile, 336th Fighter Squadron, October 1942

Gentile's *Buckeye-Don* wore two kill markings above the boxing eagle, denoting the Ju 88 and Fw 190 he claimed north of Dieppe during the ill-fated August 19, 1942 raid. (Artwork by Chris Davey © Osprey Publishing)

weight of the Spitfire. Pilots, especially the old hands who had flown with the "Eagle" squadrons, were dubious about the Thunderbolt. "Goody" Goodson recalled discussing the machine with a horrified Don Blakeslee. Goodson said that the Thunderbolt would catch anything in a dive, to which Blakeslee shot back, "It damn well ought to be able to dive—it sure as hell can't climb!"

On March 16, the 335th Fighter Squadron officially spent its final day flying Spitfires. Men from the unit who had been temporarily assigned to the 336th Fighter Squadron to learn how to fly the Thunderbolt returned to the 335th to teach their fellow pilots about the idiosyncrasies of the P-47. A week later, the first Republic fighters were issued to the 335th.

New Command

On New Year's Day 1944, Lieutenant-Colonel Don Blakeslee took over as commander of the 4th Fighter Group from Colonel Chesley Peterson. "The 4th Fighter Group is going to be the top fighter group in the Eighth Air Force," Blakeslee announced. "We are here to fight. To those who don't believe me, I would suggest transferring to another group. I'm going to fly the arse off each one of you. Those who keep up with me, good. Those who don't, I don't want them anyway."

On January 7, the group provided withdrawal support for bombers returning from Ludwigshafen, and the hard-flying Blakeslee was nearly undone by his aggressiveness. Near Hesdin, about a dozen Fw 190s

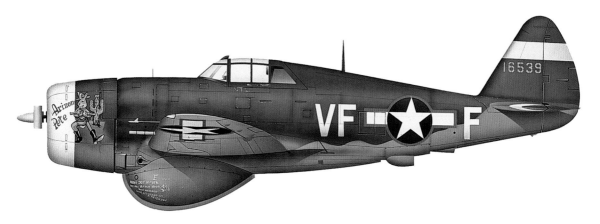

P-47C-5 41-6539 of 2nd Lieutenant Kenneth Peterson, 336th Fighter Squadron, June 1943

Peterson's Thunderbolt *Arizona Pete* referenced his hometown of Mesa, Arizona.
He flew this aircraft until it was damaged in a crash on June 28, 1943. (Artwork by
Chris Davey © Osprey Publishing)

attacked straggling B-17s from out of the sun. Blakeslee tried to bounce the enemy aeroplanes, but when he was cut off by some RAF Spitfires, he joined Captain Goodson's Red Section. "I had climbed up 12,000–14,000ft when I saw more Fw 190s attacking straggling 'Forts'," said Blakeslee. "I dived on these, being covered by Captain Goodson's section, and chased one enemy aircraft down to between 2,000–3,000ft."

Goodson, with wingman 1st Lieutenant Robert Wehrman in tow, followed Blakeslee line astern "to the best of my ability," he said, although he admitted it was "a rough ride." "Other 190s attempted to attack," he continued, "but usually broke away down through the clouds when I turned into them."

Suddenly, Blakeslee was jumped by three Fw 190s. One made a "determined attack, firing at Lieutenant-Colonel Blakeslee even after I started firing at him," recalled Goodson. "When I started getting strikes on him, he broke hard to port, but even though he pulled streamers from his wingtips, I was able to pull my sights through him. He suddenly did two-and-a-half flick rolls and then split-S'ed vertically through some light scud cloud. I followed in a steep wingover, and had to pull out hard to miss some trees as the cloud was lower than I had realized. As I did so, I caught sight of an explosion. Since the 190 had gone through vertically, I feel sure he could not have pulled out even if he had not been damaged."

Goodson soon joined up with Blakeslee again. "Before I could get close enough to prevent it, a 190 came in on Lieutenant-Colonel Blakeslee and commenced firing at short range," said Goodson. The German scored hits—71 by the count of Blakeslee's ground crew! Goodson got on his tail and fired, "and was relieved to see strikes all over him, and see him peel away and crash in flames on the ground, which was quite close." He had saved his CO, and "made ace."

On February 14, the first three P-51Bs issued to the group (one per squadron) arrived at Debden. Blakeslee immediately made it clear that he expected all pilots to check out in the new fighter between flying combat missions. There would be no downtime to permit units to transition pilots en masse. On February 25, 1944, 31 Mustangs flew into Debden.

Accidents, often due to mechanical failure, were synonymous with early Mustang operations in the ETO, as the P-51B was initially blighted by teething problems with its engine, propeller, wing tanks, cooling system, guns, and radio. Despite these maladies, the aircraft had double the range of the P-47D, and was far more agile in combat. One of its early proponents was ranking 336th Fighter Squadron ace Captain Don Gentile, who stated at the time that the Mustang "could go in the front door of the enemy's home and blow down the back door and beat up all the furniture in between."

Berlin

On March 3, 1944, Lieutenant-Colonel Blakeslee led a Target Support mission to Berlin—the 4th Fighter Group's first trip to the German capital. Flights from the 335th and 336th Fighter squadrons broke off from the main body to fend off enemy fighters, with nine Mustangs from the latter unit engaging no fewer than 60 Fw 190s and Bf 110s near Wittenburg. Pilots claimed five German aircraft destroyed.

On March 4, the group returned to Berlin. Just before the bombers reached the initial point, 20 Bf 109s and Fw 190s swarmed into attack, eight from head-on in two sections, with the others as top cover. After the first eight had flown through the bomber formation, the top cover dove on the 4th. 2nd Lieutenant Hugh Ward of the 335th Fighter Squadron gave chase to a Bf 109 in a dive:

**P-51B-5 43-6437 of Colonel Don Blakeslee,
4th Fighter Group, March 1944**

Eschewing nose art on all his mounts, the 4th Fighter Group's CO Blakeslee flew this aircraft during the first Berlin missions. (Artwork by Chris Davey © Osprey Publishing)

I opened fire as he started a slow turn to the left. I observed strikes on his wing root. He realized the situation and flicked over, and he dove straight down with me on his tail. I gave him a three-second burst with good strikes. He continued straight down, heading for heavy clouds as I began to overrun him. I pulled back on the throttle and gave him another blast. I got a heavy concentration of strikes all over his cockpit and engine covering. I kept firing as the Me 109 started to come apart. I attempted to back off but was too late.

A large section of the enemy aircraft smashed my canopy and windscreen, and it must have sheared off most of my tail section. My aeroplane began to snap viciously, end-over-end, and my right wing snapped off. I was stunned momentarily, but I managed to jettison my canopy. I pulled my harness release, which threw me out of the cockpit. I delayed opening my 'chute because of the speed, and I fell through the cloud layer. I opened my 'chute just in time. I landed in the suburbs of Berlin and I was captured by civilians.

Last Kill

On April 25, 1945, Colonel Stewart led a fighter sweep to the Linz-Prague area, where 1st Lieutenant William Hoelscher of the 334th Fighter Squadron spotted an Me 262 and dove to attack. He scored strikes all over the jet but, while chasing it, he too was hit by a 40mm round over Prague/Ruzyne airfield that tore the left elevator off his

P-51D and he had to bale out. Hoelscher landed amidst a group of Czech partisans, who hid him from the Germans. He hitched rides on motorcycles, Jeeps, and aeroplanes, and eventually made it back to Debden on May 12. Although Hoelscher's Me 262 was officially credited him as a probable kill, the 4th Fighter Group recognized it as its last victory of World War II. He had certainly been the group's last loss of the war!

On May 8, flights were suspended, the ammunition was removed from the Mustangs' wings and free beer started flowing at Debden at 1500hrs. The war was over. Hoelscher's Me 262 kill brought the group's final score to 1,011 aircraft destroyed in the air and on the ground—Eighth Fighter Command subsequently reappraised all claims and credited the 4th Fighter Group with 1,058½ victories.

COMBAT FOCUS: 56TH FIGHTER GROUP

One of the first Thunderbolt groups to see action in the ETO with the US Army Air Forces, the 56th Fighter Group was also the only fighter outfit with the Eighth Air Force to remain equipped with the mighty P-47 until war's end. Led by the inspirational "Hub" Zemke, this group was responsible for devising many of the bomber escort tactics employed by Eighth Fighter Command between 1943 and 1945. By VE Day, the 56th had shot down 100 more enemy aircraft than any other group in the Eighth Air Force, its pilots being credited with 677 kills during 447 missions.

Arrival

The USAAF had decided to establish two P-47-equipped fighter groups in the UK to support its daylight bomber operations, and the 56th would be one of these. The other was already in England and would convert from Spitfires. The 56th Fighter Group's Atlantic crossing proved to be both swift and uneventful, and the group disembarked at Gourock, in the Clyde estuary, on January 12, 1943—just six days after leaving Camp Kilmer. The men then completed their posting to the ETO with a slow train journey to King's Cliffe, in England's East Midlands. Here, Headquarters and the 61st and 62nd Fighter

Lieutenant Albert A. Knafelz's 62nd Fighter Squadron, 56th Fighter Group P-47D 42-26298 LM-A *Stalag Luft III*. Nose art was ubiquitous throughout the Eighth Air Force on both fighters and bombers. (littlefriends.co.uk)

squadrons were settled in on the nearby local airfield, while the 63rd was trucked the short distance to RAF Wittering.

Operational initiation came on April 8, when Colonel Zemke, Major David Schilling, and captains John McClure and Eugene O'Neill in aircraft of the 62nd Fighter Squadron joined a combined formation of 4th and 78th Fighter Group P-47s for a high-altitude sweep of the Pas de Calais area of the French coast.

First Kills

The Rodeo flown on June 12 resulted in the first credit for an enemy aircraft destroyed by the group. While over Belgium, and with the advantage of being up sun, the 62nd Fighter Squadron found itself in the position to make diving attacks on a *Staffel* of Fw 190s seen several thousand feet below. Major Schilling took his flight down but overshot. A second flight was more successful, and its leader, Captain Walter Cook, fired at 300 yards and saw pieces fly from the wing of an Fw 190 before it went into an uncontrollable spin. The next day would prove to be even more fruitful.

A formation of Fw 190s was seen some 10,000ft below the Thunderbolts, and Zemke led two flights down to intercept. The enemy flight selected for attack apparently did not see the P-47s

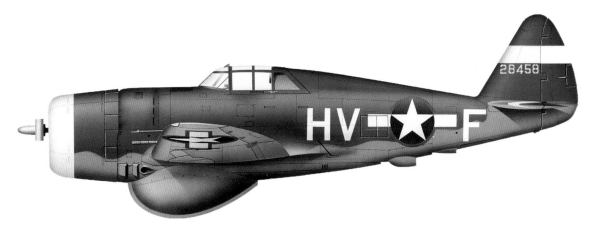

**P-47D-5 42-8458 of Captain Francis Gabreski,
61st Fighter Squadron, September 1943**

This 56th Fighter Group fighter is equipped with the rarely used Republic Aviation
200-US-gallon "paper" ferry tank, fitted flush to the aircraft's underfuselage.
(Artwork by Chris Davey © Osprey Publishing)

approaching for the group CO shot down two and 2nd Lieutenant
Robert Johnson was credited with destroying another. However,
Johnson's success was tempered by his breaking away from his flight
without permission—the second such occasion he had done this
during combat. Much as he admired Johnson's aggressiveness, Zemke
could not condone this breach of air discipline, and the errant pilot
was duly admonished.

This pattern of operations continued through June, the group
flying mostly Rodeos and the occasional close escort for B-17s
attacking targets within the P-47's radius of action. The average
duration of these missions was one-and-a-half hours, of which some
30 minutes was spent over enemy-occupied territory.

Extending the Range

To extend the P-47's range, the large 200-gallon ferry tank was fitted.
These bulbous, bathtub-shaped tanks, fitted closely under the fuselage
of the P-47, were used on August 12. Unfortunately, they were only
suitable for low- and medium-altitude operation, for they lacked a
means of pressurization. Fuel could not be drawn much over 20,000ft,
which meant that the tanks had to be released before reaching the
P-47's usual operational altitude.

Their use on this occasion enabled the group to be airborne for two hours and 12 minutes, giving some 20 minutes of extra cover for B-17s bound for the Ruhr. No successful contact was made on this mission, or on the next two occasions when use was made of the troublesome tanks but, on August 17, the extra duration they provided gave the 56th the opportunity it had been seeking.

This day was famous for the first shuttle raid undertaken by Eighth Air Force bombers, which successfully struck the Regensburg Messerschmitt factory, before flying on to land in Africa. August 17 also marked the first occasion that the Schweinfurt ball-bearing works was struck, a second force of bombers being sent to attack this well-defended target. Finally, this date proved infamous for the loss of 60 B-17s during these operations.

The 56th flew two missions. The first saw P-47s covering the bombers making for Regensburg, and although some interceptions of enemy aircraft took place, there were inconclusive results. The second was to meet the B-17s returning from Schweinfurt. With the extended range provided by the auxiliary tanks, the group formations penetrated some 15 miles beyond Eupen to find the bombers heavily engaged with enemy fighters. Most of the enemy aircraft were at the same level as the bombers, orbiting some miles ahead or behind their quarries to reform before launching another attack. This gave the P-47s the advantage of being able to initiate diving attacks on the enemy aircraft before they reached the bombers.

Many Luftwaffe fighters appeared to be taken off guard, probably not expecting the P-47s to be so far inland. Claims of 17 enemy fighters shot down were made as a result of this action for the loss of three P-47s. Two of the successful pilots—1st Lieutenant Glen Schiltz and Captain Gerald Johnson—were credited with three victories each. Two days later, the group was able to use similar tactics to claim another nine victories, with the single victory credited to Gerald Johnson making him the 56th's first ace.

On October 2, the 56th claimed three enemy aircraft, one of which fell to the guns of "Hub" Zemke, making him the group's second ace, although due to reassessment he was actually the first. Group and squadron leaders always had more opportunity to shoot down the enemy simply because they headed squadron formations.

After D-Day June 1944, more and more aircraft retained their all-metal finish in place of camouflage paint. These two P-47Ds of the 62nd Fighter Squadron, 56th Fighter Group are ready for their next long-range escort mission equipped with two 108-gallon drop tanks. (littlefriends.co.uk)

The 56th Fighter Group endorsed its commanding position among the USAAF fighter groups flying from Britain by claiming its 200th victory on January 30, 1944, which meant its tally was exactly double that of the second most successful group, the 4th Fighter Group.

The Strafing War

General Doolittle, in his capacity as the Eighth's new commander, had, early in the new year, given permission for his fighters to go down and strafe enemy airfields once their escort duties were over. By this time, with some 1,000 fighters available, a relay system had become the main method of support, each fighter group being given a defined area through which to shepherd the bombers until they were relieved by another group.

The first ground strafing by the 56th occurred on February 11, when after engaging in air-to-air combat they returned to find the B-17s they had previously been escorting guarded by other fighters. Colonel Zemke then spotted an airfield near Reims—later identified as Juvincourt—and led his force down to shoot up parked aircraft. A Bf 109, which caught the full force of Zemke's guns, was the first of many enemy aircraft destroyed by the 56th on the ground.

P-47 Thunderbolt vs Bf 109G/K (previous pages)

On March 8, 1944, 623 bombers from ten combat wings were sent to attack Berlin for the third time in a week. The 352nd Fighter Group was one of the fighter groups that provided withdrawal support that afternoon for the "heavies" returning from "Big B." Ten minutes after meeting the bombers, the group's 487th Fighter Squadron spotted three Bf 109G-6s, led by Major Klaus Mietusch of III./JG 26, performing a beam attack out of the sun on the bombers in the rear combat wing. Mietusch claimed a B-17 shot out of formation south of Zwolle-Braunschweig at 1325hrs, but he was in turn engaged by Captain Virgil K. Meroney in P-47D-5 42-8473 *Sweet Louise* and eventually shot down, giving the American his eighth victory. (Artwork by Gareth Hector © Osprey Publishing)

Now an efficient fighting team with good air discipline and aggressive leadership, the 56th was in the forefront of the American fighter counteroffensive. The attitude that pervaded pilot get-togethers at Halesworth was that of the hunter, for the Luftwaffe opponents came increasingly to be considered prey. The group had even dubbed itself the Wolfpack, which the press would quickly embrace as Zemke's Wolfpack.

56th Fighter Group's Final Tally

The end of hostilities in Europe was officially declared as May 8, 1945, following which the 56th Fighter Group expected to be moved to Germany for occupational duties.

After the final round of missions, the 56th's score of enemy aircraft destroyed stood at 1,005½, whilst its great rival the 4th Fighter Group had claimed 1,002. These figures were to be frequently revised during the next few weeks as information was received from Germany and from airmen returned from captivity. Eighth Fighter Command issued its final tallies for its fighter groups in September, the 4th having its score elevated to 1,052½ whilst the 56th's was reduced to 985½. These changes largely resulted from the inspection of airfields strafed in the final weeks of war.

However, when it came to aerial combat victories, the 56th was far and away the leader with 674½, followed by the 357th Fighter Group

Captured examples of the Fw 190A-8 and Bf 109G-10/R2. While production of both types increased in 1944, their quality and reliability was questionable. Lack of fuel left little or no time for bench-testing the engines, and the slave labor used sabotaged hundreds of airframes. (Author's collection)

with 609½. In later years, a further re-assessment boosted the 56th's score to 677 and reduced the 357th's to 575, giving the "Wolfpack" a clear 100-plus lead over any other fighter group in the ETO.

THE OPPOSITION: DEFENDING THE REICH

In any examination of the experiences of the bomber and fighter crews of the Mighty Eighth, some attention must be given to the opposing technologies, and deadly opponents in the air, that they faced. The Defense of the Reich (*Reichsverteidigung*), to use the name given to the strategic campaign fought by Nazi Germany, was one of the longest of the war, and sought to protect Germany's civilians, and its military and civilian industries, from the death and destruction raining down from the Allied bombers.

The Early Phase

In 1942 and early in 1943, central Germany was almost undefended against daylight attack because there was a huge demand for fighters for the Eastern and Mediterranean fronts, as well as daily RAF fighter-bomber raids along the European northwest coast. The German air defenses in the west had only two *Jagdgeschwader*, about 145 fighters, on the northeast French, Dutch, and German coasts. Because they were in constant combat with RAF raids on the coast, even with their small number these wings were considered the most skillful in the Luftwaffe and through 1942 had the situation well in hand.

The small, escorted US heavy bomber raids that began in August 1942 were quickly noticed by German fighter pilots on the coast, who realized that attacking American bombers packed with heavy machine guns was a different game than attacking lightly armed RAF attack aircraft.

At the beginning of 1943, both Galland and Milch warned Göring that the build-up of American bombers was an existential threat, especially with the American mass-production capability, and that the German air defenses had little depth. At first, their warnings were ignored, and German weapon procurement priorities put fighters low on the list. Fortunately for the advocates of Reich defense, events of the war slowly changed the Air Defense of the Reich force structure. Beginning in February 1943, fighter units began to be transferred back from Russia, and in the spring German fighter production began to increase dramatically as priorities were rearranged. When the Mediterranean Front collapsed, more fighters were moved to Germany and, after the massive defeat on the Eastern Front at Kursk, the Luftwaffe high command downgraded close air support and moved more and more fighters back to Germany. By June 1943, when the US Eighth Air Force began to fly serious unescorted missions into northwestern Germany, the Luftwaffe had increased the number of fighters on the Western Front from 350 to almost 600, with more coming in.

Changing Luftwaffe Tactics

Commencing in the summer of 1942, B-17 Flying Fortresses began attacking targets in occupied France and, from January 1943, in Germany too. Luftwaffe tacticians quickly realized that it was no mean feat to bring down just one heavily armed *Viermot* (a contraction of "four-engines"). Breaking through a fighter escort in an Fw 190 so as to get close enough to the bombers to ensure success was a difficult

and draining task. German pilots would usually resort to making a single high-speed diving pass through the ranks of the escorting fighters, firing their weapons at the nearest bomber, and then seeking refuge in cloud, followed by a quick return to base.

As the range of the raids increased and the escort reduced, so the Luftwaffe invariably attacked from the rear of a formation. Such a method resulted in heavy losses incurred from the bombers' intense rearward defensive fire, however. This in turn meant that the *Jagdflieger* were often reluctant to press home an attack to close range, opening fire only at extreme, and thus ineffective, distances of around 1,000m.

From the American point of view, in a revealing report prepared for the British Air Ministry in September 1942, a USAAF liaison officer wrote:

The "Bloody 100th" developed a reputation as the 3rd Bomb Division's unluckiest unit. During the March 6, 1944 mission to Berlin, it lost 15 bombers, with one squadron entirely wiped out. This remarkable photo taken in September 1944 shows a B-17G of the 100th Bomb Group with a German Me 410 heavy fighter closing in on its tail. (Author's collection)

This photograph was taken by crewman Victor Labruno from B-17G 42-97184 *Lady Godiva* of the 562nd Bomb Squadron, 388th Bomb Group as an Me 410 passed close by on its starboard side after engaging the bomber during the raid on Brüx on May 12, 1944. The *Zerstörer* was almost certainly Me 410 Wk-Nr 10241 *Black 13*, flown by Lieutenant Paul Kaschuba and Feldwebel Karl Bredemeier. They crashed to their deaths minutes after the shot was taken, their aircraft's starboard engine having been set on fire by 50-cal. rounds fired by one of the B-17's gunners. (Author's collection)

Our gunners are given sectors to search so that all fields of view are covered. At least three guns may be brought to bear on any point 400 yards from a B-17F. Mutual firepower from ships in formation greatly increases the number of guns that may fire at enemy aircraft attacking the formation.

Enemy fighter attacks from all angles have been experienced. They started with stern attacks, then went to quarter, beam, below, bow and, on the last two missions, head-on attacks. The success of all these attacks has been about the same. The B-17s that have been shot down have been from the usual causes of straggling and gunners getting killed. Damage to airplanes returning has been slight, and there have only been two airplanes at any one time out of commission due to enemy gunfire. Gunners have caused many fighters to decide not to attack by firing a burst just as the fighter begins the turn-in to attack. This has been done on some occasions when the fighter was 1,000 yards away or more.

On November 23, 1942, a force of 36 unescorted B-17s and B-24s attacked the St Nazaire U-boat base. As the B-17s made their bomb run, Fw 190s from Hauptmann Egon Mayer's III./JG 2 swept in to meet them. The attack provided Mayer with the perfect opportunity to test a new tactic that had been the subject of discussion among German fighter commanders for several weeks. Forming into *Ketten* of three aircraft, the Fw 190s went into the attack from dead-ahead, and at speed, before firing a no-deflection burst and breaking away in a climb or half-roll beneath the bombers. Mayer believed that a frontal pass, as opposed to the customary rearward attack, offered the best chance of hitting the bombers' vulnerable cockpit area. Even more importantly, the B-17's frontal arc of defensive fire was the weakest. Four bombers went down following the attack for the loss of only one Fw 190. "From that moment," one historian recorded, "the B-17 was obsolete as a self-defending bomber."

Encouraged by this success, Generalmajor Galland issued a following circular to all Luftwaffe fighter units, stating: "The attack from the rear against a four-engined bomber formation promises little success and almost always brings losses … The attack from the front, front high or front low, all with low speed, is the most effective of all." As the air war over Europe intensified during the first half of 1943, German tactics seemed to sway between attacks from the rear and from head-on. Those pilots persisting in rearward attacks found that the most vulnerable spot on a bomber was the wing area between the fuselage and the in-board engines. The No. 3 engine on a B-17 was considered particularly important because it powered the hydraulic system.

When necessary, in executing the head-on attack, the cockpit and the No. 3 engine became the key targets. However, in August 1943, the *Oberkommando der Luftwaffe* (OKL, Luftwaffe High Command) ordered that all attacks must be made from the rear once again, rather than by a frontal pass, chiefly because a large percentage of the young,

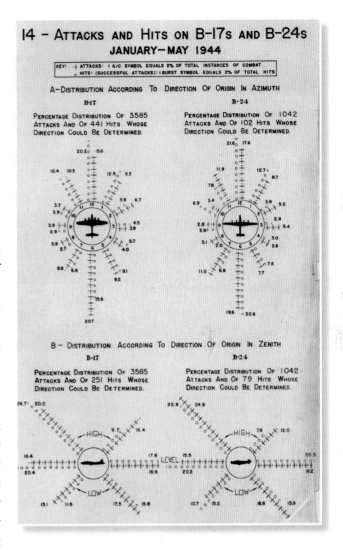

This graphic, produced in 1944, shows that the great majority of fighter attacks on American heavy bombers came from the 12 and six o'clock positions. (Author's collection)

This British Air Intelligence cutaway drawing of the Me 410 would have been found in briefing rooms throughout the Eighth Air Force's fighter and bomber stations. Pilots could pinpoint the weaknesses and strengths of the aircraft. (Author's collection)

inexperienced pilots now equipping the *Jagdgeschwader* encountered difficulty in undertaking the latter type of attack. The frontal pass involved a high combined closing speed which, in turn, demanded great skill in gunnery, range estimation, and flying control. The slightest evasive action on the part of the bombers made this type of attack even more difficult. In contrast, evasive action taken against attacks from the rear was thought ineffective.

The reversion to rear-mounted attacks proved to be timely, for September 1943 saw the appearance of the new B-17G fitted with a Bendix twin-gun chin turret. This provided the Fortress with the vital forward armament it needed to counter frontally mounted attacks.

The autumn of 1943 saw Major Hans-Günter von Kornatzki, a member of Generalmajor Galland's staff, suggest an innovative response to the bomber threat, proposing the formation of a specially equipped *Sturmstaffel*. Kornatzki advocated radical new tactics involving massed rear attacks by tight formations of heavily armed and armored Fw 190s. Kornatzki also suggested that as a last-ditch resort, when pilots were close enough and if ammunition had been expended, a bomber could be rammed in order to bring it down. It seems that Galland needed little convincing. He immediately authorized the establishment of Sturmstaffel 1 and appointed Major Kornatzki its commander.

New Luftwaffe Weapons

Improvements in weapons, firepower, and tactics substantially increased the lethality of German fighters in their encounters with the B-17. The rate of kills per engagement rose from 2.3 kills per hundred attacks in late 1942 to 3.6 kills by mid-1943, 5 kills by late 1943, and to a high of 17.7 kills by the spring of 1944.

It quickly became clear to the German fighter pilots that they needed heavier armament. An operational test unit, Erprobungskommando 25 (Test Unit 25, or ErprKdo 25), was established to develop cannon, air-to-air missiles, and anything else to counter Allied bombers.

One promising weapon was the Wfr. Gr. 21 rocket, used by the German Army's 21cm Nebelwerfer 42 infantry multiple rocket launcher. This was a large, solid-fuel, spin-stabilized rocket with a 90lb warhead, with a lethal blast area of approximately 100ft and a range of over half a mile, well out of reach of the bombers' defensive 50-cal. guns. The rocket was fitted into a rifled, braced "stovepipe" tube carried under a fighter's wing. The Wfr. Gr. 21 was first used in July 1943.

The Mk 108 30mm cannon was a fearsome weapon and one the B-17 and B-24 crews feared the most. The Germans calculated that it would take only three hits to down a heavy bomber. This weapon would equip later variants of the Bf 109, Me 110, Fw 190, the Me 262, and Me 163.

The 55mm R4M appeared as an 814mm-long, unrotated, rail or tube-launched, solid fuel-propelled, multi-fin stabilized rocket, with its 520g warhead contained in an exceptionally thin 1mm sheet-steel case. With the Me 262, R4Ms were launched from wooden underwing racks that could carry a maximum load of 12 rockets under each wing. Its destructive effects were immense.

BELOW Twelve R4M rockets are shown loaded onto the launch rack carried by an Me 262A-1a. (Author's collection)

The Bf 110 *Zerstörer* was a true bomber destroyer. This example was armed with four Wfr. Gr. 21 rocket tubes, extra fuel tanks, two extra 20mm cannon in the belly, and two 30mm cannon in the nose. (Author's collection)

New Weapons, New Fighters

New types of German weapons were also deployed specifically for use against the "heavies." Fw 190s of JGs 1 and 11 carried 21cm Werfergranate mortar tubes (or "stovepipes") under their wings. Originally designed as an infantry weapon, the mortar was to be fired from beyond the defensive range of the bombers. However, the blast effect from a shell exploding within the confines of a formation, or even just near to it, would scatter the *Viermots*, thus weakening their defensive firepower and rendering individual bombers more vulnerable to attack. In a report prepared in late August 1943, the Eighth Air Force warned, "It would appear to be the most dangerous single obstacle in the path of our bomber offensive." The weapon was perhaps used to its greatest effect against the raid on Schweinfurt on October 14, 1943, when 62 bombers were downed, many as a result of being dispersed from their formations by the use of the mortar.

The difficulty of the single-engine fighters in dealing with the bombers led to increased use of twin-engine Zerstörer heavy fighters, starting in the autumn of 1943, primarily the Bf 110G-2 and G-3. The new Me 410 began to be issued in October 1943, eventually becoming the predominant type by the spring of 1944. In mid-1944, the more heavily armed, and armored, Fw 190A-8 *Sturmjäger* entered service.

American Bomber Formations

Historically, the Americans had favored an 18-aircraft "combat box" formation of B-17s, comprised of three six-aircraft squadrons, each broken down into two three-aircraft flights. Succeeding "combat boxes" of a similar composition trailed in one-and-a-half-mile breaks behind the lead box.

By late 1943, however, in a measure intended to stiffen defensive firepower and increase protection, bombing formations were usually made up of a 36-aircraft box. This formation, similarly, composed of squadrons of six aircraft broken into two elements of three aircraft, had developed from attempts to concentrate as many aircraft together to take advantage of the relatively few radar Pathfinders available at that time. All aircraft in an element flew at the same level, but the elements themselves were separated in altitude by a little stagger, forming into high, low, and "low-low" positions.

These combat boxes then formed a bomber column, with groups in trail, each flying at the same altitude and separated by some four miles. Such a formation was more suited to "blind" bombing, and it was also easier for fighters to escort since it was a more "disciplined" structure than had been used before. But, as with all large formations, it was difficult to hold.

By the winter of 1943–44, combat attrition (losses, as well as aircraft grounded with battle damage and in need of repair) caused by German

Airborne Rocket Attack, October 14, 1943 (overleaf)

Four Bf 110Gs from I./ZG 26 attack the low box of B-17s from the 305th Group, 1st Bomb Division on the second Schweinfurt raid on October 14, 1943, around 1300hrs. The 305th Group lost 16 B-17s on this raid. The Bf 110Gs' tactic was to attack from slightly below the B-17 box and then, after firing their 16 Wfr. Gr. 21 rockets—four per aircraft—at a range of about 1,000 yards, break off to keep away from the B-17s' tail gunners.

The Wfr. Gr. 21 was a converted spin-stabilized infantry rocket that had a very low launch velocity and thus had to be "lobbed" into the bomber formation from large upward-slanted tubes. The drag of these tubes severely reduced the Bf 110s' already limited performance. The fuzes on the rockets had to be preset on the ground and, since the launch range had to be estimated, the rockets were inaccurate, but they were only intended to break up the bomber formations. However, the rockets had a blast area of 100ft, and American bomber crews considered them by far the most dangerous German airborne weapon. (Artwork by Jim Laurier © Osprey Publishing)

Jim Laurier

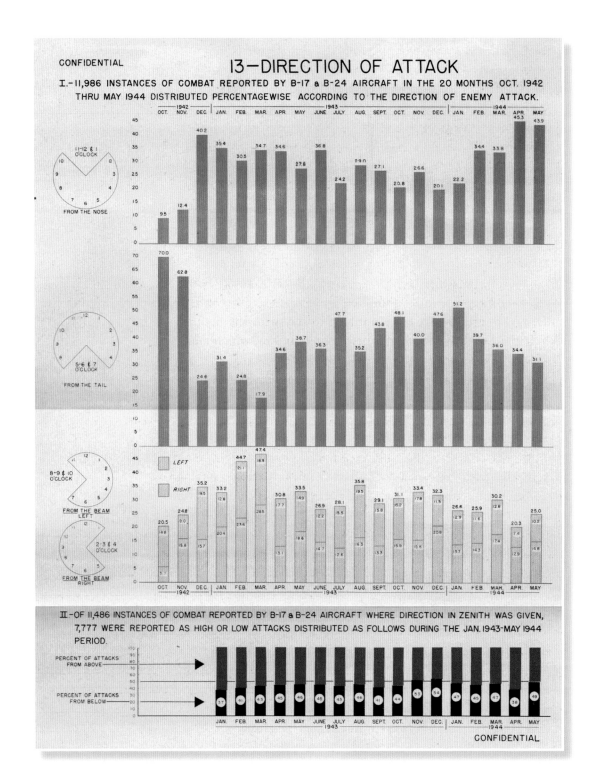

fighters attacking *en masse* often compelled the Eighth Air Force to despatch combat boxes reduced from 36 to just 18 or 21 aircraft.

By March 1944, a typical 21-aircraft box comprised three squadrons, each of two elements: the lead squadron with six aircraft, the low squadron with six, and the high squadron with nine. The high and low squadrons flew on opposite sides of the lead, forming a "V" pointing in the direction of flight and tilted to 45 degrees. The spacing of individual bombers in a box (usually 100–200ft, the equivalent of between one and two wingspans) maximized collective firepower but minimized the risks of unwieldiness, interference with bomb runs, and buffeting and displacement from slipstream.

When fully assembled, a bomber stream could stretch for 90 miles, presenting a problem for the escort fighters, which had to zigzag to compensate for the bombers' lower speeds. Furthermore, individual fighter groups were not able to stay with the bombers for much more than 30 minutes before fuel ran low, which meant that only a small number of escorts covered the bombers at any one time. It was normal that a third of the escort flew "up front" to cover the head of the bomber stream and protect it from a head-on attack.

In a report compiled during the summer of 1944, Eighth Air Force analysts acknowledged: "Even extensive escort cover cannot prevent a relatively small but determined enemy force from avoiding, or swamping, the cover and attacking the bombers at some point in the long formation."

OPPOSITE In November of 1944, the Eighth Air Force Operational Analysis Section produced an in-depth study titled *An Evaluation Taken to Protect Bombers from Loss and Damage*. Part of the report dealt with fighter attacks and their effectiveness. This chart reveals the direction of attack taken by enemy fighters in the period October 1942 to May 1944. (Author's collection)

Eight Air Force Heavy Bomber Losses, August 1942–September 1944		
Period	Total Bombers Lost	Total Bombers Lost as Percentage of Attacking
5 months August–December 1942	31	4.0 percent
4 months January–April 1943	87	5.5 percent
4 months May–August 1943	369	6.4 percent
4 months September–December 1943	516	4.4 percent
2 months January–February 1944	425	3.5 percent
2 months March–Aprril 1944	659	3.5 percent
2 months May–June 1944	540	1.4 percent
2 months July–August 1944	464	1.2 percent
1 month September 1944	248	1.6 percent

> ### Fw 190 Engages a B-17 Flying Fortress (opposite)
>
> The Fw 190A-7, A-8, and A-9 variants were fitted with the Revi 16B reflector gunsight, shown here in this cockpit view. This sight required the pilot to estimate the angle of deflection to the target according to combat conditions. When attacking a Flying Fortress from either the side or behind—which would attract determined fire from its tail, top, and ball turrets, as well as the waist guns—the pilot of a Fw 190 would have to remain equally determined and focused on his gunnery skills. (Artwork by Jim Laurier © Osprey Publishing)

Flak

The term Flak refers to antiaircraft fire from antiaircraft guns, derived from the German *Flugabwehrkanone* (aircraft defense cannon). At the beginning of the war, the Luftwaffe Flak force was the most lavishly equipped in the world. There were 2,628 heavy Flak guns (88mm and 105mm) compared with about 1,300 heavy antiaircraft guns in Britain. Although the Luftwaffe was responsible for both strategic air defense of the Reich and tactical air defense of the army, in 1939 about 80 percent of its resources were devoted to homeland defense.

By February 1944, the Luftwaffe's ground-based defenses of the Reich and occupied territories reached a wartime high of 13,500 heavy guns, 21,000 light guns, 7,000 searchlights, and 2,400 barrage balloons.

The Flak defenses were enormously complex and expensive, requiring not only an extensive array of complex heavy artillery, but also an associated fire-control system based on searchlights and acoustic sensors, and later relying on radar. In 1943, Flak constituted 29 percent of the German weapons budget and 20 percent of the munitions budget, and the Flak force included half of all Luftwaffe personnel.

The most numerous heavy anti-aircraft gun in the *Flakwaffe* was the famous 88mm weapon, which served as the basis for four principal variants. It was also the most mobile. Here, a gun crew and battery prepare to fire their camouflaged FlaK 37 weapon from a standard reinforced 88mm *Flak Gefechtsstand* (G-Stand) 1943-pattern gun pit. (Author's collection)

The Kommandogerät 40 was the brains of the Flak battery, the 1.5-ton director requiring 13 personnel to operate it. Normally attached to a four-gun battery, the KodoG 40 combined an optical range finder with a ballistic computer. This combination produced precise firing solutions for visible targets. (Author's collection)

The different types of heavy Flak guns in service during the war comprised:

- 88mm FlaK 18/36/37
- 88mm FlaK 41
- 105mm FlaK 38/39
- 128mm FlaK 40

By late 1943, the USAAF began to take the science of "Flak analysis" seriously after it had realized, to its cost, that the *Flakwaffe* posed a far greater threat than had originally been estimated. The number of heavy bombers shot down and damaged was increasing month on month, forcing a change in tactics and the use of electronic countermeasures. In October of that year, the USAAF introduced a gun-laying radar jammer codenamed *Carpet I*, and two months later, on December 20, the Eighth Air Force used chaff for the first time. While these methods reduced losses, they were never totally effective.

FlaK 18 Fixed High Explosive (HE) 88mm Shell

The shell weighed 31.69lb and had a length of 36.69in. The 88mm HE round was clearly identified to those handling the shell by its distinctive yellow-colored projectile. (Artwork by Jim Laurier © Osprey Publishing)

Flakzwilling 40/2

Codenamed *Innsbruck*, the twin-barreled 128mm Flakzwilling was one of the best, largest, and most effective heavy Flak weapons of the war. Compared with the standard 88mm Flak gun, the 128mm's powder charge was four times as large, reducing shell flight time by two-thirds. This in turn meant that gunners could engage fast-moving targets more effectively. Crewed by up to 12 men (usually the best gunners in the *Jagdwaffe*), the Flakzwilling 40/2 had a rate of fire of 24 rounds per minute. (Artwork by Jim Laurier © Osprey Publishing)

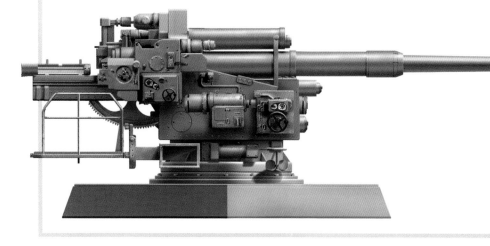

In November 1944, Headquarters, Eighth Air Force Operational Analysis Section produced an in-depth study titled *An Evaluation Taken to Protect Bombers from Loss and Damage*. The results were sobering. New tactics were recommended, but many of the old methods remained. An extract from the report follows:

As formidable as they were, only 33 128mm Flakzwilling 40/2s had been deployed by 1945. Principally sited atop specially built Flak towers in Berlin, Vienna, and Hamburg, these guns were manned by the *Flakwaffe*'s best troops. This example is mounted on the *Gefechtsturm IV* tower in the Heiligengeistfeld district of Hamburg. (Author's collection)

During the past year enemy Flak defenses have been concentrated and our bombers faced many more guns. The percentage of bombers lost to or damaged by enemy fighters has declined sharply, while the percentage lost to Flak has declined only moderately. The percentage damaged by Flak has remained almost constant. As a result, there has been a steady increase in the relative importance of Flak until in June, July and August 1944, Flak accounted for about two-thirds of the 700 bombers lost and 98 per cent of the 13,000 bombers damaged.

In number, the current rate is startling. From 3,360 to 4,453 bombers have returned with Flak damage in each of the six months ending September 1944—a monthly average just about double the total number damaged by Flak in the entire first year of operations. All our efforts to reduce Flak damage have apparently been offset by the fact that we have increasingly flown over targets defended by more and more guns. Further, enemy equipment, gunnery and ammunition have probably improved. The 60-gun target of a year ago is likely to be defended by 300 guns today. This makes it essential that we increase our efforts to decrease Flak risks by re-examining the tactics we have been using and such new tactics as offer real possibilities.

The Eighth lost a total of 1,798 heavy bombers to Flak, with the Fifteenth Air Force losing a further 1,046, between November 1943 and May 1945. In addition to the number of B-17s and B-24s the *Flakwaffe* shot down, and the effect it had on the bombing accuracy of American crews, German gunners damaged an astonishing 54,539 Eighth Air Force Flying Fortresses and Liberators between December 1942 and April 1945.

Taking on the German Jets

Messerschmitt 262

In the early afternoon of October 7, 1944, in one of the largest daylight bombing raids so far mounted, the Eighth Air Force suffered its first-known loss of a heavy bomber to a deadly new form of aircraft when Leutnant Franz Schall, flying a Messerschmitt Me 262 A-1, a jet-powered interceptor, attacked the B-24s. Schall had used the Me 262's formidable armament of four nose-mounted 30mm Mk 108 cannon to literally blast one Liberator from the air in the Osnabrück area, while his fellow jet pilot Feldwebel Heinz Lennartz also accounted for another.

The Allies had scant intelligence on the Me 262, but its very existence was cause for great concern. They knew if the Germans had a jet, it was certain to be faster than any of their piston-engined fighters. The Messerschmitt Me 262 represented a giant leap in fighter technology. Powered by two Jumo 004B turbojet engines, it had a top speed of 525mph at 29,500ft. The P-51D's top speed was 438mph. Armed with four 30mm cannon, it was a formidable weapon.

On August 2, 1944, 82nd Fighter Squadron CO Major Joseph Myers was leading Surtax Blue" flight tasked with strafing rail targets in Charleroi, Belgium. While flying his P-47 at 11,000ft

P-51D-10 44-14164 of 1st Lieutenant Urban "Ben" Drew, 375th Fighter Squadron, 361st Fighter Group, October 1944

On October 7, near Achmer, Drew shot down two Me 262s, becoming the first of only two USAAF pilots to achieve the feat. (Artwork by Jim Laurier © Osprey Publishing)

A *rotte* of III./EJG 2 Me 262A-1as taxi out for training sortie in early November 1944. III./EJG 2 was the official training establishment for all future Me 262 fighter pilots. Despite fuel shortages and prowling Allied fighters, III./EJG 2 operated until overrun by American troops in April 1945. (Author's collection)

near Brussels, Myers caught a glimpse of what he thought was a B-26 Marauder flying at low level and went down to investigate. When Myers got down to around 5,000ft he was indicating 450mph and the unidentified aircraft began evasive action that allowed him to close to within 2,000ft above and astern. Myers later noted in his Encounter Report: "With full power on and the advantage of altitude, I gradually started closing on the enemy aircraft and drew up to within 500 yards astern. I was about to open fire when the enemy pilot cut his throttle and crash-landed in ploughed field."

P-47M-1 44-21160 of Major George Bostwick/Captain John Fahringer, 63rd Fighter Squadron, March 1945

On March 25, 1945, Bostwick shot down an Me 262 jet attempting to land at Parchim airfield. On April 5, a further Me 262 was dispatched by *Devastatin Deb*, this time flown by Fahringer. (Artwork by Jim Laurier © Osprey Publishing)

With all its firepower and speed, however, there were too few Me 262s to make any real difference. In the relatively brief period that Me 262s were operational, air combat tactics and formations were fluid, and varied within the two predominant fighter units, JG 7 and JV 44, as time progressed. It must be stressed that the principal task for Me 262 pilots was to get to the Allied bombers, using the unmatched speed of their aircraft to achieve this—getting into an effective attack position at about 1,000m range on a dead-level approach often proved challenging, however.

Mustang vs Me 262 (overleaf)

The scene shown here is taking place near Quackenbrück on November 8, 1944. Within a few seconds, Leutnant Franz Schall of 2./*Kommando Nowotny* will be forced to bale out of his Me 262A-1a "White 1." He is being pursued by 1st Lieutenant James W. Kenney of the 362nd Fighter Squadron, 357th Fighter Group. Kenney's Mustang has managed to stay on the jet's tail.

Bearing in mind the relatively small number of operationally ready Me 262s at any one time (100 or so across all units at the most), Eighth Fighter Command groups accumulated some impressive scores against the Messerschmitt jet fighter. The 357th Fighter Group claimed 19 Me 262 kills to become the highest-scoring Eighth Air Force group. Five fighter groups (4th, 339th, 78th, 55th, and 357th) scored ten or more kills. In total, USAAF fighter units lodged 166½ air-to-air destroyed, probable, and damaged Me 262 claims. Additionally, there were numerous ground victories claimed in strafing runs. (Artwork by Gareth Hector © Osprey Publishing)

From the perspective of a P-51 pilot, for example, just successfully engaging an Me 262 in combat was a challenge. In order to stand any chance of catching a fully functioning Messerschmitt spotted trying to attack bombers, the pilot had to immediately drop his fighter's external tanks, which then adversely affected the Mustang's key asset—range. This in turn meant a P-51 could no longer escort bombers all the way to a distant target. "This left the bombers unprotected and juicy targets for conventional fighters," recalled Stephen C. Ananian of the 339th Fighter Group. "This tactic was taking a heavy toll. Eighth Air Force ordered the practice of dropping tanks merely to chase jets to be stopped. We were ordered not to chase the jets unless we were directly attacked."

Me 163

The only other advanced fighter the Luftwaffe used against the Eighth Air Force was the rocket-powered Messerschmitt Me 163 Komet. The Me 163 was a failure from the outset. It was more a danger to itself than any Allied aircraft. The Walter rocket engine that powered the Me 163 was a nightmare. The volatile mix of the two different fuels required to

Aided by his mechanic, a pilot climbs up into the cockpit of his Me 163. Although wearing a one-piece protective suit and gloves, they offered little protection in case of fuel leak or rupture. According to German sources, 80 percent of all Me 163 losses resulted from accidents during take-off and landings. (Author's collection)

P-38J-15 42-10442 of Captain Arthur Jeffrey, 434th Fighter Squadron, 479th Fighter Group, July 1944

On July 28, 1944, Jeffrey shot down an Me 163 rocket fighter. That particular Me 163 was the only jet/rocket-powered aircraft to fall to a P-38. (Artwork by Jim Laurier © Osprey Publishing)

power the rocket meant that the slightest leak, or anything but the smoothest of take-offs or landings, could result in a violent explosion. It was also very short of range. The rocket engine had barely four minutes running time. But once airborne the Me 163 had incredible performance: 560mph and a rate of climb of just over 5,000ft per minute. Time to 39,000ft was just three minutes and 45 seconds.

The Eighth Air Force first encountered the Me 163 on July 28, 1944, when the Komets of I./JG 400 tangled with P-38 Lightnings of the 479th Fighter Group, which was providing withdrawal support for a group of B-17s. Leading "Newcross Yellow" flight was future 14-victory ace Captain Arthur F. Jeffrey, who joined the 479th Fighter Group's 434th Fighter Squadron in October 1943. It was a very cloudy day over Holland and Jeffrey noticed a straggler just above the undercast that was steadily falling behind the formation. The aircraft in question was B-17G 42-107997 *She Hasta* from the 100th Bomb Group, which had been severely damaged and had several wounded crewmen on board. Jeffrey, noticing the bomber was heading northwest—a heading that would cause it to miss the UK completely—left "Yellow Three" and "Four" at altitude while he took his wingman down to give *She Hasta* some close support and navigational assistance. Even though their P-38s looked like no other fighter in the world, the gunners of the rookie crew manning the Flying Fortress fired at the Lightnings as they approached. A short while later, Jeffrey found himself engaging an Me 163, as he described in his Encounter Report:

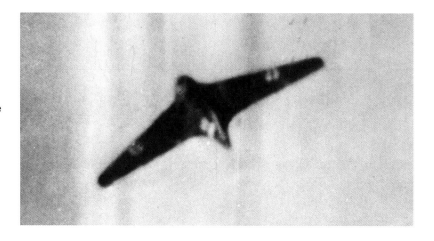

An Me 163 is caught on film by the gun camera fitted to the P-51D of Lieutenant Willard Erkamp during an action fought on October 7, 1944. The Me 163 crash-landed, with the pilot surviving. (Author's collection)

The B-17 plodded along at 11,000ft, dodging holes in the overcast to keep out of the Flak, and at 1145hrs I observed an Me 163 in attack position behind it. The Me 163 made a slight low-side "five o'clock" pass at the B-17, followed through in a slight dive and then levelled off. At about this time the German must have seen me because he made another slight dive. He then started a very steep climb, weaving all the while, as though he was trying to see behind him. During this weaving I closed with him and opened fire, observing strikes on the Me 163.

At 15,000ft the pilot levelled off and started to circle to the left, as though positioning himself to attack me. I could turn tighter than he could, and I got a good deflection shot, with the closest range estimated to be 200 to 300 yards. I thought I was getting hits, but my shots seemed too far away for effect when puffs of smoke started to emanate from the tail of the jet.

Jeffrey seemed to think that the Komet pilot had never been in combat before, for it seemed like he did not know what to do. There are no records to indicate who the aviator was or what kind of combat experience he had, but he did do what most fighter pilots do instinctively—he turned into his attacker. Jeffrey continued:

At about 15,000ft he turned and attacked, with me looking right down his throat. We got into a tight circle and I saw some good deflection shots hitting him. Then he rolled over and went straight down, with me fire-walled behind him. For the first time in my life I found out how—

at more than 500mph—your props can act as brakes. I was shooting at him as I was going straight down, and my tracer path was walking forward of the "bat" [Me 163]. Then I got into an arc of an outside loop, and when I finally pulled out a few hundred feet above the ground, I blacked out.

Jeffrey, flying P-38J-15 42-104425 *Boomerang*, quickly regained his senses, but by then the rocket fighter had vanished. He duly claimed it as a probable. While Jeffrey had been wrestling his Lightning out of the death-grip of compressibility, his wingman, 1st Lieutenant Richard G. Simpson, watched the Me 163 enter the clouds: "I started to pull out at 3,500–4,000ft, indicating a little over 400mph. The Me 163 went into the clouds, which were at around 3,000ft, still in a dive of 80 degrees or better. He must have been indicating 550–600mph, and showed no signs of pulling out. I don't see how the German could have gotten out of that dive."

To this day, no records have been located that indicate the loss of an Me 163 on this day, yet Captain Arthur Jeffrey's probable claim was upgraded to destroyed, thus giving him the distinction of being the first Allied pilot to down a German jet. His Me 163 also proved to be the only jet/rocket-powered aircraft victory credited to the P-38.

This gun-camera image shows a hit by a 30mm cannon shell on B-17 42-97571 of the 457th Bomb Group on August 24, 1944. The aircraft was shot down and claimed by Me 163 pilot Feldwebel Siegfried Schubert of 1./JG 400. (Author's collection)

Eighth Air Force top brass during the April 11, 1944 visit of Allied Supreme Commander Dwight D. Eisenhower to the 4th Fighter Group at Debden. In front of the officers' club are (left to right) Brigadier-General Jesse Auton (65th Fighter Wing commander), Eisenhower, Lieutenant-General Carl "Tooey" Spaatz, Lieutenant-General James H. Doolittle (Eighth Air Force Commander), and Major-General William Kepner (Eighth Fighter Command commander). (NARA)

CHAPTER 7

EIGHTH AIR FORCE PERSONNEL

Leaders and Aces

When war began in September 1939, the US Army had a 190,000-man regular army, an air arm, a 200,000-man National Guard composed of civilian volunteers, and an Organized Reserve with a nucleus of reserve officers. It was quickly apparent that the army was far too small. In particular, it severely lacked professional officers. A rapid and enormous expansion began that saw regular army officers, who had been stuck among the ranks of the junior officers for years, vault into senior command levels.

The outbreak of global war, and the attendant need to cooperate with other nations, revealed the urgent necessity for a stronger civilian-military command structure and army–navy coordination. Consequently, in February 1942, the Joint Chiefs of Staff (JCS) replaced the Joint Board as the highest military authority. Among the four members of the JCS were Army Chief of Staff, George Marshall, and the commanding general of the US Army Air Forces, Lieutenant-General Henry Arnold. The JCS both controlled the nation's armed forces and advised the president on everything from strategy to industrial policy.

As with the ground forces, in September 1939, the Army Air Forces were minuscule in comparison to national needs. There were only 17 air bases in the United States. By 1943, this had grown to 345 main bases, 116 secondary bases, and 322 auxiliary fields. The wartime expansion saw a force of 20,196 with 2,470 mostly obsolete planes grow to almost 1.9 million men and women with 79,908 modern aircraft. Sixteen air forces were raised to carry out combat missions. Larger forces required higher command structures. In January 1944, the Eighth and Fifteenth air forces formed Carl Spaatz's Europe-based US Strategic Air Forces.

SENIOR LEADERSHIP OF EIGHTH AIR FORCE

With America's entry into the war, both President Roosevelt and Prime Minister Churchill agreed that strategic air power would be one of the keys to victory. The Air War Plan that was drawn up in August 1942 and endorsed by Lieutenant-General Arnold made clear that aircraft production would be given top priority.

Eighth Air Force Commanding Officers	
Colonel (later Brigadier-General) Asa M. Duncan	January 28, 1942 to May 4, 1942
General (then Major-General) Carl A. Spaatz	May 5, 1942 to November 30, 1942
Lieutenant-General Ira C. Eaker	December 1, 1942 to January 5, 1944
Lieutenant-General James H. Doolittle	January 6, 1944 to May 9, 1945
Major-General William E. Kepner	May 10, 1945

Those in command of the Eighth Air Force were strong proponents of strategic air power. They were all supremely competent and forward thinking and eager to push their prewar bombing theories to the limits. Command in the Eighth Air Force, like the rest of the US Armed Forces, was based on merit. Those who did not perform, in all ranks, were quickly demoted or reassigned. Friendship and loyalty only went so far. This was a new type of warfare and for the young airmen of the Eighth and those in command, the lessons of modern air combat would be learned the hard way. It was not for the faint of heart.

Henry Harley Arnold

Born in 1886 in Gladwyne, Pennsylvania, Henry "Hap" Arnold graduated from West Point in 1907 and entered the infantry. In 1911, he transferred to the Signal Corps' aeronautical section and received flight training from the Wright brothers themselves. He obtained his pilot's license very quickly, thus becoming one of the first American military aviators. In 1912, he set a world altitude record and won a high aviation honor, the Mackay trophy. Arnold did not see combat in World War I and ended the war as a captain.

After serving in a variety of staff positions, including several involved with public relations, in 1931 Arnold received orders to transform a training base in California into a fully operational military base. This assignment gave Arnold an opportunity to display his full range of skills. He experimented

General Henry H. "Hap" Arnold. (Public Domain)

with tactics, intensified pilot training, and worked closely with scientists from the California Institute of Technology to develop new materials. Three years later, he won his second Mackay trophy for commanding a flight of ten bombers that completed a round trip flight from Washington, DC, to Alaska.

In 1936, Arnold became assistant chief of the US Army Air Corps. Two years later, he rose to major-general and became chief of the corps, which was redesignated the US Army Air Force in 1941. Although he held a variety of titles thereafter, in essence, from this date until 1946, Arnold was in charge of the American Air Force. His management and public relations experience served Arnold well during the furious bureaucratic struggles in Washington, DC. He was a strong advocate of more funding to increase the air corps' size and combat readiness. He persuaded industrialists to modernize manufacturing processes in order to build more planes. Arnold also accelerated pilot training and pushed hard to create more private flying schools. With war drawing nearer, in 1941 Arnold managed to convince Congress to spend 2.1 billion dollars on aircraft production.

In August 1941, Arnold accompanied President Roosevelt to the Atlantic Conference. Here, he met British air leaders and began a close relationship that continued throughout the war. For the war's duration, Arnold would attend virtually every important strategic conference. In the autumn of 1941, Arnold joined the British-US Combined Chiefs of Staff as well as the US JCS. With these prestigious assignments came promotion to lieutenant-general. Within the army chain of command, Arnold served as deputy to General George Marshall. However, he sat as an equal on the JCS. Consequently, he was able to develop a large, efficient staff to support his positions during his frequent disagreements with JCS members. Throughout the war, inter-service rivalry and Arnold's ambition to create an independent air service often rose to the surface during debates over strategic planning.

Arnold believed in the dominance of strategic bombing as articulated by theorists such as Giulio Douhet, "Billy" Mitchell, and Hugh Trenchard. A war plan he prepared in September 1941 provided the foundation for the air war logistics and strategy used in the great bombing campaigns against Germany and Japan. Arnold steadfastly focused his efforts on strategic air power, sometimes to the detriment of the overall American war effort. For example, at a time when the forces on Guadalcanal were badly in need of all possible support, Arnold resisted navy appeals for help. He suspected that it was a navy ruse to claim more resources for the Pacific. Instead, Arnold wanted all attention focused on building up forces in England to begin the massive aerial bombardment of Germany.

After the capture of Guadalcanal, planners debated how best to continue the offensive. Again, the army and MacArthur quarreled with the navy. Both wanted the support of heavy bombers. Arnold wanted most of these still-scarce planes sent to Europe. He also observed that the bombers in the Pacific were not being wisely used. As early as September 1942, he cogently commented, "It becomes more and more apparent that until there is one command, one plan, one thinking head, we will continue to misuse and hold idle our air force and our army."

In April 1944, Arnold finally obtained the combat position he desired. He became commander of the 20th Air Force in the Pacific.

Although he retained his other duties and spent most of his time in Washington, DC, he personally directed the 20th's strategic bombing of Japan. Because he believed that conventional aerial bombardment alone could defeat Japan, and because this victory would enhance air force prestige enormously, Arnold opposed the use of the atomic bomb. He and Admiral Leahy were the only high-ranking officers to do so.

Arnold became general of the army, a five-star rank, in December 1944. Plagued by a heart condition throughout the war, Arnold retired in early 1946 and died in 1950. Although Arnold badly wanted an independent air service, he patriotically deferred fully promoting this goal until the war was over. Still, the effort to position the air service so that it could achieve independence colored Arnold's actions. In view of the fact that Arnold led a force that began the war with only a handful of modern aircraft and ended the war with the greatest air force in the world, he is remembered as the "Father of the US Air Force."

General Carl "Tooey" Spaatz, a portrait painted by Louis Behan. (NARA)

Carl Andrew Spaatz

Born in Boyertown, Pennsylvania, in 1891, Carl A. Spaatz graduated from the US Military Academy in 1914. During his days at West Point he acquired the nickname "Tooey" on account of his resemblance to another red-headed cadet named F.J. Toohey. He became one of the army's first pilots and was a member of the 1st Aero Squadron, which flew in support of the Pershing Punitive Expedition to Mexico in 1916. This involved exceptional risk by flying "canvas-and-bamboo contraptions" through mountain thermals and shifting winds. Promoted to captain, he commanded the 31st Aero Squadron in France in 1917. Because he was one of a handful of experienced American pilots, he was given the duty of organizing and commanding a flying school in England. He successfully clamored for a combat opportunity and flew combat missions for three weeks. He shot down three German airplanes and once narrowly avoided death when two Fokkers got on his tail. After the war, he remained in the military. In 1927, as part of a publicity campaign to draw attention to military aviation, he was a member of a team, which included Captain Ira Eaker and Lieutenant Elwood Quesada, that achieved a flight endurance world record.

He admired General "Billy" Mitchell, the most vocal advocate for air power in the United States, and testified in Mitchell's defense during his court-martial for criticizing existing aviation policies. This unpopular act kept Spaatz stuck at the rank of major for 15 years. Finally, in 1935, he received another promotion and graduated the next year from the prestigious Command and General Staff College at Fort Leavenworth. His big opportunity came in July 1941, when he received appointment as chief of staff to General "Hap" Arnold. Henceforth, Spaatz became one of the prime movers behind the American air campaign in Europe.

In May 1942, Spaatz became commander of the US Eighth Air Force. As a disciple of "Billy" Mitchell, he strongly believed in the American doctrine of daylight, precision bombing attacks. A well-publicized, successful first raid by 12 B-17 bombers against Rouen, France seemed to vindicate the doctrine. It soon became apparent, however, that daylight bombers required fighter escorts. In their absence, Spaatz considered taking a colossal gamble: an unescorted raid deep into Germany to bomb fighter factories. Fortunately, before such a raid could be planned, strategic attention switched to North Africa. As head of Air Force Combat Command, Spaatz assumed command of the Allied air forces involved in Operation *Torch*, the invasion of North Africa. His ability to cooperate with British leaders led to his return to Europe in 1944 as a lieutenant-general in command of US Strategic Air Forces. He quickly fell foul of the head of the Royal Air Force Bomber Command, Arthur Harris. Spaatz believed in the American approach of "pinpoint" bombing of selected targets, based on careful study of the enemy's economy. In particular, Spaatz wanted to concentrate on the German transportation system and oil production sites. Harris, in contrast, favored area bombing of German cities. The only point of agreement between Spaatz and

Harris was the belief that air power alone could obviate the need for major ground campaigns. Spaatz's desire to leap beyond traditional army and navy objectives to destroy key elements of the enemy's economy constantly came into conflict with Allied leaders. His strategic forces were repeatedly diverted for ancillary efforts, such as bombing the U-boat pens to reduce the German submarine menace. On March 5, 1944, Spaatz presented General Eisenhower with an "Oil Plan" to cripple the German war effort but more direct support for the Normandy invasion received top priority. The summer of 1944 finally witnessed the intense bombing of oil targets. These raids dramatically reduced the German ability to wage war.

Following Germany's surrender, Spaatz went to the Pacific, where he directed the strategic air bombardment of Japan. After the war, he followed "Hap" Arnold as chief of the US Army Air Force. Spaatz lived an unremarkable retirement, beginning in 1948, until his death in 1974.

To the war's end, Spaatz remained a true believer in the war-winning potential of strategic air power. He was also one of the few senior leaders who thought in classic strategic terms. As befitting his Pennsylvania Dutch upbringing, he was patient and persistent rather than bold and brilliant.

General James H. Doolittle. (Public Domain)

James Harold Doolittle

Born in Alameda, California in 1896, James "Jimmy" Doolittle did not attend military schools. Instead, he received his education at California public schools and graduated from the University of California School of Mines in 1917. He enlisted in the army during World War I and became an expert aviator and flight instructor. He remained in the Army Air Corps after the war. The army sent him to the Massachusetts Institute of Technology for advanced studies. Doolittle earned an engineering doctorate in 1925. For the next five years, he worked as a designer and test pilot. He resigned in 1930 to take charge of the Shell Oil Company's aviation department. Two years later, he set a world speed record. During the interwar years, he also served as an aviation consultant to the government and the military. The outbreak of World War II brought this distinguished flyer and aeronautical engineer back into active service.

President Roosevelt wanted a bombing raid on the Japanese homeland. Short-range naval aircraft could not do the job at this time so 16 army bombers, modified B-25B Mitchells, were used. General "Hap" Arnold selected Lieutenant-Colonel Doolittle, who was on his staff at this time, to serve as the army coordinator for this operation. In spite of his age, 45, Doolittle secured permission to lead the raid. On April 18, 1942, Doolittle flew the first B-25 from the deck of the carrier *Hornet* to attack Japan. The bombers inflicted minor damage and continued to China, where the air crews baled out or crash-landed. A postwar US Naval War College study determined that there was "no serious strategical reason" for this raid. Yet, it had an enormous impact on Japanese planners. It served as the catalyst for the Japanese to accelerate plans to attack Midway Island. Because he knew that the bombers had inflicted minimal damage, Doolittle expected to be court-martialed for failure. Instead, he returned a hero, was promoted two ranks to brigadier-general, and received the Congressional Medal of Honor for leading this morale-boosting raid.

Promoted again to major-general, Doolittle assumed command of the Twelfth Air Force in support of Operation *Torch*, the invasion of North Africa. Doolittle's leadership then, and thereafter, while supporting the invasions of Sicily and Salerno, impressed General Eisenhower. When Eisenhower took charge of Operation *Overlord*, he requested that Doolittle join him in the UK. Accordingly, Doolittle took command of the Eighth Air Force. In March 1944, he became a lieutenant-general and received an honorary Knight Commander, Order of the Bath from King George VI. The Eighth's role was to help prepare the way for the cross-channel attack. When, in early March, Doolittle visited the Eighth Fighter Command, a unit assigned to bomber escort, he saw the unit's motto on a sign: "Our Mission is to Bring the Bombers Back." Doolittle ordered the sign taken down. "From now on that no longer holds," he explained. "Your mission is to destroy the German Air Force." The ensuing air war over Germany became a grim battle of attrition. Doolittle deliberately chose targets that he knew would compel the German planes to take to the air to defend them. Fierce aerial battles raged but Doolittle knew that his forces could afford the losses and that the Germans could not.

Doolittle retired from the Air Force in 1946. He returned to the Shell Oil Company, while continuing to fill many advisory slots in both the public and private sectors. He retired from business in 1959 and died in 1993. He was one of America's great aviators.

Eight Air Force Awards and Decorations, August 17, 1942–May 15, 1945	
Medal of Honor	14
Distinguished Service Cross	220
Distinguished Service Medal	11
Legion of Merit	207
Silver Star	817
Distinguished Flying Cross	41,497
Soldier's Medal	478
Purple Heart	6,845
Air Medal	122,705
Unit Citation	27

Lieutenant-General Ira C. Eaker. (US Air Force)

Ira Clarence Eaker

The Eighth Air Force was commanded by Lieutenant-General Ira C. Eaker from December 1942. He served in Army aviation units in the 1920s and was involved in a number of the early record-breaking flights. Eaker was a close associate of Hap Arnold, and in the late 1930s they jointly authored several books promoting the Army Air Corps. In 1941, he was assigned to special duty with the RAF to observe British tactics and doctrine, and in January 1942 he was appointed commanding general for the bomber command of United States Army Forces in the British Isles (USAFBI), the initial version of what would emerge at the end of the year as the Eighth Air Force. Arnold was not entirely satisfied with Eaker's performance in the autumn of 1943, being particularly distressed by the low readiness rates of the bombers.

Brigadier-General Haywood S. Hansell (left, commander of 1st Bomb Wing, Eighth Air Force) and Colonel Curtis E. Lemay (right) pose beside the Boeing B-17 *Dry Martini 4th, The Cocktail Kid*s of 305th Bomb Group on May 13, 1943. (US Air Force)

At the end of 1943, Arnold decided to shift Eaker to take control of the Mediterranean Allied Air Forces in Italy.

Curtis Emerson LeMay

Born in Columbus, Ohio, in 1906, LeMay left college to enlist in the National Guard as a flight cadet. He received his pilot's wings in 1929 and joined a fighter squadron. After completing a civil engineering degree, he transferred to bombers because he believed that bombers were more likely than fighters to have a decisive impact in any future war. He quickly became known as the best navigator in the air force. In 1937 and 1938, he was the lead navigator on two mass B-17 demonstration flights. LeMay was a major on December 7, 1941. The following May, he took command of a bomb group that was slotted to be the first unit to enter the European war. He proved a driven and demanding leader, earning the nickname "Iron Ass."

LeMay brought the 305th Bomb Group to Britain in the autumn of 1942. At this time, bombers typically flew evasive patterns while trying to drop their bombs. He brought mathematical modeling to bear to challenge the prevailing wisdom that stated that any bomber in a combat zone that flew straight for more than ten seconds would be shot down. To prove his point, he led an attack, during which he flew a straight course for seven minutes until he released his bombs. His new technique soon became standard practice. LeMay also designed a formation that massed 18 bombers in such a way that defensive fire could cover all angles.

In June 1943, LeMay assumed command of the Eighth Air Force's 3rd Bombardment Division. On August 17, 1943, LeMay led one of the war's most famous missions, the "shuttle mission" that took off from Britain, raided Regensburg, and landed in North Africa. For his personal heroism, leadership, and innovative tactics, LeMay received promotion to brigadier-general in September 1943 and major-general in March 1944. He was just 37 years old. In August of that year, he transferred to the China-Burma-India Theater.

Earle Everard Partridge

Earle E. Partridge was born in 1900 in Wichendon, MA, and enlisted in the US Army in 1918. He served in France that August and took part in the St Mihiel and Meuse-Argonne offensives.

He re-enlisted in the Army in 1920, and four years later graduated from the US Military Academy as a 2nd Lieutenant in the Air Service. After undergoing flight training in Texas, he served with the 3rd Attack Group, became a flying instructor, and taught mathematics at West Point. He then served as commanding officer of the 94th Pursuit Squadron, before becoming a test pilot at Wright Field, flying many of the planes which were later used in World War II.

From October 1941, Partridge was a member of the Air War Plan's Division at Headquarters Army Air Forces, and subsequently a member of the Joint Strategy Committee, Strategy and Policy Group of the War Department General Staff in 1942. He was posted overseas and became chief of staff of Twelfth Bomber Command and Fifteenth Air Force. He moved to the UK in January 1944 as deputy commander of Eighth Air Force and was promoted to major-general that May. He then became commanding general of the 3rd Bomb Division. Partridge once again became deputy commander general of the Eighth Air Force in August 1945, assisting in its reorganization and movement to Okinawa.

Brigadier-General Earle E. Partridge. (US Air Force)

HEROES AT THE SHARP END

Kermit Douglas Stevens

One of the Eighth Air Force's most experienced staff operations officers and group commanders, Kermit D. Stevens was born in Roseburg, Oregon, on December 16, 1908. He embarked upon his first military service as a Reserve Officers' Training Corps (ROTC) student at the University of Oregon, from where he graduated with a Bomb Squadron degree. Stevens entered the Army Air Corps as a

Kermit D. Stevens.
(Public Domain)

flying cadet in 1935, and was commissioned the following year at Kelly Field, in Texas. For four years thereafter, he served with the 3rd Attack Group, which was eventually equipped with A-20 Havocs. Rising to the rank of squadron commander, Stevens eventually joined the Eighth Air Force upon its formation at Savannah Army Base, in Georgia, in late January 1942.

Soon after, Stevens journeyed to England as a member of one of the first command staffs to arrive at the fledgling Eighth Air Force's new headquarters at Daws Hill Lodge, a country house in High Wycombe, Buckinghamshire.

He served with the Eighth Air Force as an operations officer until transferring to the 303rd Bomb Group (H), based at Molesworth in Huntingdonshire, as group Commanding Officer until July 19, 1943, taking over from Colonel Charles E. Mario. Stevens then began an illustrious career with the "Hell's Angels," leading the group on many successful missions to Germany, amongst them Huls, Schweinfurt, Frankfurt, Bremen, Cologne, Berlin-Erkner, and Hamburg.

On August 16, 1943, just under a month after having assumed command, Stevens led 20 of the 303rd Bomb Group's B-17s to Le Bourget airfield in France, during which he piloted B-17F 42-5431 *Vicious Virgin* of the 427th Bomb Squadron. Ball turret gunner Sergeant Frank Garret participated in this mission in B-17F 41-24606 *Knockout Dropper*, and he later commented, "Followed those bombs all the way down and they really smacked the place. Shot at plenty of fighters." Stevens, on the other hand, commented somewhat laconically, "Left a lot of smoke down there. We blew a few people's hats off anyway," and was duly awarded the Silver Star for Gallantry for his conduct during this highly successful raid.

Stevens relinquished command of the 303rd Bomb Group on September 1, 1944. It subsequently became the first Eighth Air Force bomb group to complete 300 missions from the UK, and ultimately flew more missions than any other B-17 outfit, and was beaten by just one other unit in dropping more bomb tonnage. In November that year, while on leave in the United States, Stevens was appointed

CO of a B-29 training field that was operating as part of the Second Air Force.

Colonel Stevens retired from the US Air Force on January 31, 1964 and lived in California. He died on November 21, 2004.

Hubert "Hub" Zemke

Hubert "Hub" Zemke. (www.littlefriends.co.uk)

Born on March 14, 1914 in Missoula, Montana, Hubert Zemke was of German ancestry. Going on to attend Montana State University, he left his studies six months short of graduation to join the Army Reserves as a flying cadet in February 1936, and was rated an AP on February 17, 1937 at Kelly Field, in Texas. He was assigned to the 36th Pursuit Squadron /8th Pursuit Group, and was rated as a pilot on August 15, 1939. Becoming a 1st Lieutenant on September 9, 1940, Zemke's next assignment was the 56th Pursuit Group's Headquarters Squadron on May 22, 1941. With the start of the war, promotions were rapid, and he became a captain on February 1, 1942 and a major on March 1 of the same year. When hostilities commenced in Europe, Zemke was sent to Britain to act as an observer and then to Russia as a military air attaché, where he taught Russian pilots how to fly their new P-40s. By September 1942, Zemke had become commanding officer of the 56th Fighter Group, and he duly led the group to Britain in December of the same year. He scored his first confirmed victory on May 14, 1943 when he damaged a Fw 190 near Antwerp, in Belgium, and achieved ace status on October 2 that same year.

By August 1944, Zemke had been credited with 15¼ victories (out of a total of 665 kills achieved by the 56th, which had become known as "Zemke's Wolfpack"). He was then transferred to take command of the 479th Fighter Group, forsaking the P-47 for the P-51. Whilst leading his new group, he ran into a violent storm over Germany on October 30, 1944 that forced him to bale out of his fighter. Zemke was quickly captured by the Germans and transferred to Stalag Luft I, where he remained until war's end.

P-47D-11 42-75510 of Lieutenant-Colonel Francis S. Gabreski, 61st Fighter Squadron, January 1944

"Gabby" Gabreski's P-47D-11 42-75510 was a remarkably plain fighter, being adorned with standard Eighth Fighter Command white recognition bands. (Artwork by Tom Tullis © Osprey Publishing)

Following repatriation, he stayed in the USAF and served in a variety of commands before retiring as a colonel on July 31, 1966. "Hub" Zemke died in California on August 30, 1994 after contracting pneumonia. His final tally was 17¾ confirmed, two probables, and nine damaged.

Francis S. Gabreski. (www.littlefriends.co.uk)

Francis Stanley Gabreski

Born to Polish parents in Oil City, Pennsylvania, on January 28, 1919, Francis Stanley "Gabby" Gabreski was studying medicine at the University of Notre Dame when he decided to join the Army Reserve in July 1940. Enrolling in the USAAC, he graduated from flying training at Maxwell Field, Alabama, on March 14, 1941. Initially assigned to the 15th Pursuit Group's 45th Pursuit Squadron at Wheeler Field, Hawaii, Gabreski witnessed the Pearl Harbor raid on December 7, 1941. Having seen no combat flying P-40s in defense of the Hawaiian islands, he volunteered to be sent to the UK to gain combat experience with a Polish squadron—he was a fluent Polish speaker.

After spending two months in the ETO ferrying USAAF aircraft to various bases in the UK, a chance meeting with Polish Spitfire pilots in London's

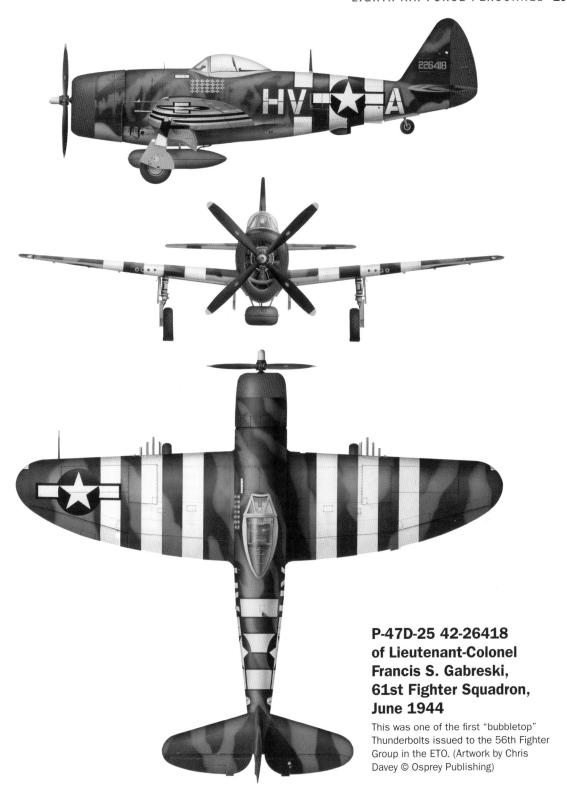

**P-47D-25 42-26418
of Lieutenant-Colonel
Francis S. Gabreski,
61st Fighter Squadron,
June 1944**

This was one of the first "bubbletop"
Thunderbolts issued to the 56th Fighter
Group in the ETO. (Artwork by Chris
Davey © Osprey Publishing)

Embassy Club saw Gabreski temporarily assigned to No. 315 Sqn. He fitted in well at RAF Northholt and flew 11 combat and two rescue missions in Spitfire IXCs in January–February 1943.

With combat experience under his belt, Gabreski was transferred to the Thunderbolt-equipped 61st Fighter Squadron, 56th Fighter Group at Boxted in late February. Made CO of the latter unit on June 9, 1943, "Gabby" claimed his first kill (an Fw 190) on August 24. Further claims were made in the autumn, and on November 26 he downed two Bf 110s over Germany to attain ace status. The first of an eventual 11 Bf 109s destroyed by Gabreski followed three days later.

Promoted to lieutenant-colonel in January 1944, Gabby continued to add to his score. Until mid-July, he was the ETO's leading ace with 28 victories (in 153 missions). Volunteering to lead his unit on one final mission on July 20, prior to heading home tour-expired, he was in the process of strafing a number of He 111 bombers at an airfield at Bassenheim when he flew too low in his Thunderbolt and struck the ground with its propeller. Managing to clear the airfield, Gabreski bellied the aircraft into a nearby field. He spent the rest of the war in Stalag Luft I.

Robert S. Johnson.
(www.littlefriends.co.uk)

Robert Samuel Johnson

Born on February 21, 1920, in Lawton, Oklahoma, Johnson graduated from Cameron Junior College and went to enter the aviation cadet program in Call 42-F on November 11, 1941. Commissioned as a pilot on July 3, 1942 at Kelly Field, he was then transferred to the 56th Fighter Group's 61st Fighter Squadron, which was equipped with Thunderbolts at Stratford, Connecticut, on July 20, 1942. He sailed for England with the group on January 13, 1943.

Flying from Boxted, Johnson completed his first operational mission during April 1943 and scored his first victory, over an Fw 190, on June 13. From that point on, he began to rapidly compile an impressive victory list, becoming an ace on October 10 and a double ace on December 31. He soon became the first ETO pilot to better the score of American World War I ace Eddie Rickenbacker.

However, Bob Johnson's career in the front line was about to come to an abrupt end. Deemed too valuable to lose in combat by senior USAAF officers, Johnson was transferred out of the 56th Fighter Group after scoring his 27th and 28th kills on May 8, 1944. He was transferred back to America, where he teamed up with Pacific P-38 ace Richard Bong on a bond tour. He then took command of a Thunderbolt operational training unit at Abilene, Texas, for the rest of the war. Joining Republic Aviation after the end of the war, Johnson remained in the reserves and rose to the rank of lieutenant-colonel. He passed away in 1999. With a final tally of 27 confirmed and three damaged (in just 91 missions), Johnson was the second-highest-scoring American ace in the ETO.

Johnson collaborated with aviation author Martin Caidin to pen his autobiographical story of the 56th Fighter Group, *Thunderbolt!*

George Earl "Ratsy" Preddy, Jr.

George E. Preddy.
(www.littlefriends.co.uk)

George Preddy, who would become the top-scoring Mustang ace of World War II, was born on February 5, 1919, in Greensboro, North Carolina. He obtained a civilian pilot's license during 1939 and barnstormed for a year before attempting to join the Navy as a pilot. After being rejected three times, he joined the Air Corps in 1940 and received his wings on December 12, 1941.

Preddy was assigned to the 49th Fighter Group and sent by ship to the southwest Pacific on January 12, 1942. Flying the Curtiss P-40E in combat for seven months, he was involved in a mid-air collision on July 12, 1942. Baling out, Preddy was injured and spent three months in hospital before being transferred back to the USA after being released for training in the P-47.

On December 28, 1942, he was assigned to the 352nd Fighter Group and soon shipped out with the group to Britain. Becoming a captain with the 487th Fighter Squadron, Preddy scored three victories in December 1943/January 1944 with the P-47 prior to the unit transitioning onto the Mustang.

Once he mastered the P-51, Preddy rapidly built his score, claiming 19 and three shared kills in just five months—including six Bf 109s on August 6, 1944. The ace was sent back to the USA soon after this spectacular haul, but returned to combat with the 352nd Fighter Group in October, taking command of the 328th Fighter Squadron on October 28. On Christmas Day 1944, Preddy destroyed two Bf 109s near Koblenz and then attacked a low-flying Fw 190, but was in turn shot down and killed by American antiaircraft fire. His final tally was 26¾ confirmed, three probables, and four damaged.

John Charles Meyer

John C. Meyer was born on April 3, 1919, in Brooklyn, New York, and he subsequently attended Dartmouth College. He joined the Army Reserves and became a flying cadet, being commissioned a pilot and 2nd Lieutenant on July 26, 1940, at Kelly Field. His first assignment was as a flight instructor and he remained in this posting for a year. Meyer was then transferred to the 33rd PS in Iceland to fly convoy patrols before returning to join the 352nd Fighter Group in Massachusetts. He was made commanding officer of the group's 487th Fighter Squadron on December 28.

John C. Meyer.
(www.littlefriends.co.uk)

Meyer became a captain on January 21, 1943, and took the P-47-equipped 487th Fighter Squadron to Britain that June. The unit commenced combat operations in September, flying a series of bomber escort missions. On November 26, the now Major Meyer scored his first victory when he downed a Bf 109. During April 1944, the unit began converting to the Mustang, and Meyer enjoyed his first success in the North American fighter on April 10. On May 8, he celebrated his promotion to the rank of lieutenant-colonel with a triple-kill haul that gave him ace status.

Meyer and the Mustang were a formidable duo, and he rapidly pushed his score past the 20-kill mark—this tally included two "triples" and a "double" haul. In February 1945, he was sent back to the USA, tour expired.

P-51D-44-15041 of Lieutenant-Colonel John C. Meyer, 487th Fighter Squadron, December 1944

On December 31, 1944, 352nd Fighter Group deputy CO Meyer downed the first Ar 234 jet bomber to fall to the USAAF. (Artwork by Tom Tullis © Osprey Publishing)

Staying in the air force postwar, Meyer assumed command of the 4th Fighter Interceptor Group in August 1950, and led the Sabre-equipped unit to Korea, where he destroyed two MiG-15s. Meyer eventually rose to the rank of general, and Commander of Strategic Air Command. Retiring on August 1, 1974, he died of a heart attack while jogging on a Los Angeles beach on December 2, 1975. His final tally was 26 confirmed (24 with the Eighth Air Force), one probable, and three damaged.

Top Aces of the Eighth Air Force	
Francis "Gabby" Gabreski 56th Fighter Group	28 victories
Robert Johnson 56th Fighter Group	27 victories
George Preddy 352nd Fighter Group	26.8 victories
John C. Meyer 352nd Fighter Group	24 victories
Rat Wetmore 359th Fighter Group	22.6 victories
David C. Schilling 56th Fighter Group	22.5 victories
Donald Gentile 4th Fighter Group	21.8 victories
Fred J. Christensen 56th Fighter Group	21.5 victories
Walker M. "Bud" Mahurin 56th Fighter Group	20.8 victories
Glenn E. Duncan 353rd Fighter Group	19.5 victories
Duane W. Beeson 4th Fighter Group	19.3 victories
Leonard "Kit" Carson 357th Fighter Group	18.5 victories
Glenn T. Eagleston 354th Fighter Group	18.5 victories
Walter C. Beckham 353rd Fighter Group	18 victories
John Godfrey 4th Fighter Group	18 victories
Hubert "Hub" Zemke 56th Fighter Group	17.8 victories

CHRONOLOGY

1942

January 28   Eighth Air Force activated at Savannah, Georgia.

August 17   First mission: 12 B-17s bomb Rouen.

October 9   B-24s join the air assault. First mission of over 100 bombers attacks airfields in France.

1943

January 3   First use of "formation" (instead of individual) precision bombing.

January 27   First mission to Germany. Ninety-one bombers are dispatched to Wilhelmshaven and Emden.

May 13   3rd Division becomes operational. Air Force now has 12 heavy bomb groups.

May 14   First mission of over 200 bombers. P-47s begin regular escort up to 200-mile range.

July 28   P-47s, equipped with auxiliary fuel tanks, escort bombers across the German border for the first time.

August 17   First shuttle mission to North Africa bases after attack on Schweinfurt and Regensburg. Sixty bombers are lost on attack.

September 27   First use of radar instruments to bomb through cloud—used over Emden.

P-47 range increased to 325 miles. Air Force drops over 5,000 tons in one month.

October   214 bombers are lost—9.2 percent of aircraft entering enemy territory.

November 3   First mission of over 500 bombers—574 are dispatched to Wilhelmshaven.

December 5   First P-51B squadrons become operational in escort role.

December 13   P-51s fitted with two 75-gallon external tanks fly their first long-range escort mission—490 miles to Kiel and back.

1944

February 11	The first P-51s are assigned to Eighth Fighter Command.
February 20–25	Four devastating attacks on German aircraft plants and assembly factories.
March 6	First major attack on Berlin. Sixty-nine bombers missing in action—largest total in one day.
March	First month over 20,000 tons of bombs dropped. P-47s and P-38s escort up to 500 miles range.
May 7	First mission of over 1,000 bombers.
June 6	D-Day. 40½ heavy bomb groups are operational. 2,698 bombers drop 4,778 tons of bombs on two missions. 1,966 fighters provide escort and cover.
July 28	First GAF jet/rocket enemy aircraft being used operationally encountered by US fighters.
August 16	First jet aircraft destroyed by fighters.
November 27	Fighters encountered 747 enemy aircraft—greatest number sighted in one day—102 enemy aircraft destroyed.
December 24	Largest bomber mission to date—2,055 in the air at one time to attack targets in the "Ardennes Bulge" sector. 4,302 tons of bombs dropped on operation.

1945

January 14	Fighters destroy 161 enemy aircraft in the air—largest fighter claims in one day.
January	An average of 2,799 bombers and 1,484 fighters are assigned—greatest aircraft strength of the US Air Force.
March 28	Last mission to Berlin—the most heavily bombed US target (27,985 tons on greater Berlin). Greatest bomber effort for any month. 31,297 bombers are sortied. 73,878 tons of bombs are dropped, 74,009,324 gallons of gasoline consumed in 395,829 flying hours. 92.3 percent of bombers sortied are effective. Jet enemy aircraft shoot down 24 bombers.
April 16	752 enemy aircraft destroyed in one operation by fighters—34 fighters missing in action on strafing attacks.
April 25	Last Eighth Air Force bombing operation carried out.

FURTHER READING AND RESEARCH

PRIMARY SOURCES

The Strategic Air War Against Germany 1939–45: British Bombing Survey (undated)

An Evaluation of Defense Measures Taken to Protect Heavy Bombers from Loss and Damage, Headquarters, Eighth Air Force Operational Analysis Section, November 1944

US Strategic Bombing Survey Reports

The Effects of Strategic Bombing on the German War Economy (No. 3, Office of the Chairman)

Aircraft Division Industry Report (No. 4, Aircraft Division)

The Defeat of the German Air Force (No. 59, Military Analysis Division)

US Air Force Historical Studies

Boylan, Bernard, *Development of the Long-Range Escort Fighter* (No. 136, 1955)

Ferguson, Arthur, *The Early Operations of the Eighth Air Force and the Origins of the Combined Bomber Offensive, 17 August 1942 to 10 June 1943* (No. 118, 1946)

Grabmann, Walter, *German Air Force Air Defense Operations* (No. 164, 1956)

Heinrichs, Waldo, *A History of the Eighth USAAF Fighter Command* (n.d.)

Kammhuber, Josef, *Problems in the Conduct of a Day and Night Defensive Air War* (No. 179, 1953)

Nielsen, Andreas L. and Grabmann, Walter, *Anglo-American Techniques of Strategic Warfare in the Air* (No. 183, 1957)

Norris, Joe, *The Combined Bomber Offensive: 1 January to 6 June 1944* (No. 122, 1947)

Ramsey, John, *The War Against the Luftwaffe: USAAF Counter-Air Operations April 1943–June 1944* (No. 110, 1945)

Renz, Otto von, *The Development of German Antiaircraft Weapons and Equipment of All Types up to 1945* (No. 194, 1958)

Schmid, Josef, *The German Air Force versus the Allies in the West: German Air Defense* (No. 159, 1954)

Schmid, Josef and Grabmann, Walter, *The German Air Force versus the Allies in the West: The Air War in the West* (No. 158, 1954)

Stormont, John, *The Combined Bomber Offensive, April through December 1943* (No. 119, 1946)

SECONDARY SOURCES

Bishop, Stan D. and John A. Hey, *Losses of the US 8th and 9th Air Forces* (Bishop Books, 2004)

Boiten, Theo and Martin W. Bowman, *Raiders of the Reich. Air Battle Western Europe: 1942–1945* (Airlife, 1996)

Boiten, Theo and Martin W. Bowman, *Battles With the Luftwaffe* (Janes, 2001)

Bowman, Martin W., *Castles in the Air: The Story of the B-17 Flying Fortress Crews of the US Eighth Air Force* (Patrick Stephens, Wellingborough, 1984)

Bowman, Martin W., *Great American Air Battles of World War 2* (Airlife, 1994)

Bowman, Martin W., *USAAF Handbook 1939–1945* (Stackpole Books, Mechanicsburg, 1997)

Bowman, Martin W., *Osprey Combat Aircraft 18—B-17 Flying Fortress Units of the Eighth Air Force (Part 1)* (Osprey Publishing, Oxford, 2000)

Craven, W. F. and J. L. Cate, *The Army Air Forces in World War II, Volume I: Plans and Early Operations (January 1939 to August 1942)* (The University of Chicago Press, Chicago, 1948)

Fairfield, Terry A., *The 479th Fighter Group in WW2 in Action over Europe with the P-38 & P-51* (Schiffer, 2004)

Freeman, Roger, *American Bombers of World War Two, Volume One* (Hylton Lacy Publishers, Windsor, 1973)

Freeman, Roger, *The U.S. Strategic Bomber* (Macdonald and Jane's, London, 1975)

Freeman, Roger, *B-17 Flying Fortress* (Janes, London, 1983)

Freeman, Roger, *Mighty Eighth War Manual* (Janes, London, 1984)

Gobrecht, Lt Col (USAF Ret), Harry D., *Might in Flight: Daily Diary of the Eighth Air Force's Hell's Angels—303rd Bombardment Group (H)* (The 303rd Bombardment Group (H) Association, Inc., San Clemente, 1993)

Gotts, Steve, *Little Friends: A Pictorial History of the 361st FG in World War 2* (Taylor Publishing, 1993)

Green, William, *Warplanes of the Third Reich* (Doubleday, 1972)

Gruenhagen, Robert W., *Mustang: The Story of the P-51 Fighter* (Arco, 1976)

Hammel, Eric, *Air War Europa: America's Air War Against Germany in Europe and North Africa: Chronology 1942–1945* (Pacifica Press, 1994)

Jablonski, Edward, *Flying Fortress: The Illustrated Biography of the B-17s and the Men Who Flew Them* (Purnell Book Services, London, 1965)

Johnson, Robert S., *Thunderbolt!* (Honoribus Press, 1973)

Kaplan, Philip and Currie, Jack, *Round the Clock* (Random House Inc., New York, 1993)

Ludwig, Paul, *Development of the P-51 Mustang Long-Range Escort Fighter* (Classic, 2003)

McFarland, Stephen and Newton, Wesley, *To Command the Sky: The Battle for Air Superiority Over Germany 1942–44* (Smithsonian, 1991)

McLachlan, Ian, *USAAF Fighter Stories* (Haynes Publishing, 1997)

Murray, Williamson, *Strategy for Defeat: The Luftwaffe 1933–45* (Air University Press, 1983)

Nijboer, Donald, *Cockpit: An Illustrated History* (Airlife, 1998)

Nijboer, Donald, *Graphic War: The Secret Aviation Drawings and Illustrations of World War II* (Boston Mills Press, Erin, 2005)

O'Leary, Michael, *Osprey Production Line to Frontline 1: North American Aviation P-51 Mustang* (Osprey, 1998)

O'Leary, Michael (comp.), *Osprey Aircraft of the Aces 31: Eighth Fighter Command at War "Long Reach"* (Osprey Publishing, 2000)

Price, Alfred, *Battle Over the Reich* (Ian Allen: 1973)

Price, Alfred, *Battle Over the Reich: The Strategic Bomber Offensive Over Germany, Volume Two 1943–45* (Ian Allen, 2005)

Speer, Frank E., *The Debden Warbirds: The 4th FG in World War II* (Schiffer Military History, 1999)

Svejgaard, M., *Der Luftnachrichten Dienst in Denmark* (Gyges, 2003)

Westermann, Edward, *Flak: German Anti-Aircraft Defenses 1914–45* (University Press of Kansas, 2001)

Wolf, William, *US Aerial Armament in World War II: Volume 1: Guns, Ammunition, and Turrets* (Schiffer, Pennsylvania, 2010)

Wolf, William, *US Aerial Armament in World War II: Volume 2: Bombs, Bombsights, and Bombing* (Schiffer, Pennsylvania, 2010)

Wolf, William, *US Aerial Armament in World War II: Volume 3: Air-Dropped, Air-Launched, and Secret Weapons* (Schiffer, Pennsylvania, 2010)

Zemke, "Hub," as told to Roger A. Freeman, *Zemke's Wolfpack* (Orion, 1998)

COLLECTIONS AND MUSEUMS

Readers may wish to know that over 40 official websites are maintained by the Eighth Air Force Bombardment Group and the Eighth Air Force Historical Society, relating to the wartime activities of American bombers operating out of Britain during World War II. In addition, numerous museums in the United States and Britain maintain original bomber and fighter aircraft, as well as collections of, and exhibits relating to, the equipment, uniforms, and lives of bomber and fighter crewmen. Among these are the following:

United Kingdom
Bassingbourn Tower Museum, Bassingbourn
Imperial War Museum, Duxford

United States
Air Museum Planes of Fame (Chino, CA and Valle, AZ)
EAA Air Adventure Museum (Oshkosh, WI)
Mighty Eighth Air Force Museum (Savannah, GA)
Museum of Aviation (Warner-Robins, GA)
National Museum of the United States Air Force (Wright-Patterson AFB, OH)
Smithsonian National Air and Space Museum (Washington, DC)
Strategic Air and Space Museum (Ashland, Nebraska)

WEBSITES

www.303rdbg.com
www.8thafhs.org
www.100thbg.com
www.mightyeighth.org
www.aircrewremembered.com
www.littlefriends.co.uk

LIST OF ACRONYMS AND ABBREVIATIONS

AAA	antiaircraft artillery
AAF	Army Air Forces
ACTS	Air Corps Tactical School
AEAF	Allied Expeditionary Air Force
AFN	Armed Forces Network
CBO	Combined Bomber Offensive
CCS	Combined Chiefs of Staff
CO	Commanding Officer
ECCM	Electronic counter-countermeasures
ETO	European Theater of Operations
IP	initial point
MPI	Mean point of impact
OKL	Oberkommando der Luftwaffe
RAF	Royal Air Force
RLV	Reichsluftverteidigung
SAD	Strategic Air Depot
SHAEF	Supreme Headquarters Allied Expeditionary Force
USAAC	United States Army Air Corps
USAAF	United States Army Air Force
USSTAF	United States Strategic Air Forces
XO	Executive Officer

P-51D-25-NA 44-73156 WR-B *Wolverine* of the 355th Fighter Group, 354th Fighter Squadron seen here at Schweinfurt, Germany, during summer 1945. The red-yellow-red fuselage band was applied to all aircraft attached to the occupational forces in Germany as recognition markings. (littlefriends.co.uk)

ACKNOWLEDGMENTS

This book is a compilation of the following Osprey books:

Aircraft of the Aces 001: *Mustang Aces of the Eighth Air Force*

Aircraft of the Aces 019: *P-38 Lightning Aces of the ETO/MTO*

Aircraft of the Aces 024: *P-47 Thunderbolt Aces of the Eighth Air Force*

Aircraft of the Aces 031: *Eighth Fighter Command at War*

Aircraft of the Aces 051: *"Down to Earth" Strafing Aces of the Eighth Air Force*

Aircraft of the Aces 084: *American Nightfighter Aces of World War 2*

Aircraft of the Aces 096: *Mustang Aces of the 357th Fighter Group*

Aircraft of the Aces 115: *Aces of the 78th Fighter Group*

Aircraft of the Aces 136: *Allied Jet Killers of World War 2*

Air Campaign 005: *Operation Crossbow 1944*

Air Campaign 014: *Schweinfurt–Regensburg 1943*

Aviation Elite Units 002: *56th Fighter Group*

Aviation Elite Units 007: *354th Fighter Group*

Aviation Elite Units 008: *352nd Fighter Group*

Aviation Elite Units 010: *359th Fighter Group*

Aviation Elite Units 011: *303rd Bombardment Group*

Aviation Elite Units 030: *4th Fighter Group*

Aviation Elite Units 032: *479th Fighter Group*

Air Vanguard 004: *Martin B-26 Marauder*

Campaign 236: *Operation Pointblank 1944*

Combat Aircraft 002: *B-26 Marauder Units of the Eighth and Ninth Air Forces*

Combat Aircraft 008: *P-61 Black Widow Units of World War 2*

Combat Aircraft 015: *B-24 Liberator Units of the Eighth Air Force*

Combat Aircraft 018: *B-17 Flying Fortress Units of the Eighth Air Force (part 1)*

Combat Aircraft 036: *B-17 Flying Fortress Units of the Eighth Air Force (part 2)*

Duel 001: *P-51 Mustang vs Fw 190*

Duel 011: *P-47 Thunderbolt vs Bf 109G/K*

Duel 024: *Fw 190 Sturmböcke vs B-17 Flying Fortress*

Duel 098: *German Flak Defences vs Allied Heavy Bombers*

Duel 100: *Me 262 vs P-51 Mustang*

Elite 046: *US Army Air Force (1)*

Elite 051: *US Army Air Force (2)*

Elite 085: *US Commanders of World War II (1)*

Warrior 119: *American Bomber Crewman 1941–45*

X-Planes 014: *World War II US Gunships*

INDEX

Figures in **bold** refer to illustrations.